GUIDE TO ICELAND;

A USEFUL HANDBOOK

FOR

TRAVELLERS AND SPORTSMEN.

BY

WM. GEO. LOCK, F.R.G.S.,

AUTHOR OF 'PISCATORIAL RAMBLES IN ICELAND,' PUBLISHED IN 'THE FIELD'; 'ASKJA, ICELAND'S LARGEST VOLCANO'; 'JOTTINGS ON SPORT IN NORWAY'; TRANSLATOR OF 'SPORTING LIFE ON THE NORWEGIAN FJELDS,' ETC.

'If he who long hath dwelt at ease
Surrounded by ancestral trees
In some fair English home,
Resolve at last from pride or taste,
To visit classic land and waste
A traveller to roam . . . .
O! many a path will woo his feet
To scorn luxurious ease . . . .
And many a scene his vision meet
Of wild, and wonderful, and sweet
Among the *Icelandese.*'

1882.

WORKS BY THE AUTHOR.

NORWAY.
THE SPORTSMAN'S HANDBOOK.

Crown 8vo., 376 *Pages, cloth, bevelled boards,* 10s. 6d. ; *by post* 11s.

'SPORTING LIFE ON THE NORWEGIAN FJELDS'
('TILFJELDS').

By Prof. FRIIS, with a MAP printed in colours, showing where ELK, REDDEER, and REINDEER are to be found. An ENGLISH TRANSLATION of the above by W. G. LOCK, with a SYNOPSIS of the NORWEGIAN GAME LAWS, and chapters on the RENTAL of SHOOTINGS, SALMON FISHING, ETC., forming the most perfect SPORTSMAN'S GUIDE TO NORWAY yet published.

'THE FIELD,' in its Review of 'TILFJELDS,' as a Norwegian work, stated : —

'Regarded by his countrymen as one of the most accomplished and successful of the newer school of Norwegian sportsmen, Herr Friis volunteers to act as guide to districts, where his wanderings, extended over more than twenty summers, have rendered him familiar with every streamlet, tarn or waste every haunt of fish or game. He would appear, at some time or other, to have extended his search for game over all the principal fjelds in the south of Norway and to be nearly as much at home on Dovre, or on the Lessje Fjelds, in Jotunheim, or on the Hardanger-vidde. The traveller . . . will find Herr Friis's book . . . well worthy of a place among his baggage . . . as a guide book, or also as a pleasant resource in times of unavoidable idleness.'

'THE FIELD,' thus Reviewed the ENGLISH VERSION :—

'We congratulate the numerous class of Anglo-Scandinavian sportsmen who have not mastered Norsk on the very readable addition to their literature afforded by the above translation, for which we have to thank Mr. Lock. A review of Professor Friis's original work appeared in our number of 24th of March, 1877 (p. 347), and to the favourable opinion therein expressed we can only add that the English version is faithful and fluent. Professor Friis is such a master of his subject, and so enthusiastic and yet simple in his treatment of it, that Mr. Lock, who is also a sportsman and lover of the rifle, must indeed have found it a labour of love to Anglicise the book for the benefit of his fellow islanders. Indeed, the work can be safely recommended for perusal by the non-sporting public, as the purely shooting and fishing episodes are so pleasingly interwoven with descriptions of scenery, natural history, and botanical notes, and happy illustrations of the inner life of peasants, milkmaids, and other minor *dramatis personæ*, that there can be no lack of interest. There is, moreover, a vein of quiet humour in the author, which at times is quaintly comical. . . .

'Mr. Lock, besides some useful explanatory notes, adds hints to English sportsmen visiting Norway, accounts of rental of shootings, instructions for salmon fishing, and a synopsis of the Norwegian game laws, so often of late discussed in our columns.

'The map referred to in the title shows by coloured patches where reindeer, elk, and red-deer are found in Southern Norway—somewhat on the same scheme as the excellent maps of

WORKS BY THE AUTHOR (continued).

Schubeler and Collett, which respectively illustrate botanical and zoological distribution in the Scandinavian peninsula.'

'THE LIVE STOCK JOURNAL'S' critique was as follows:—

'Now that every one goes to Norway at some time or other, all books—and they are growing—on the sport and adventure to be had on its fjelds and fjords are eagerly sought after. The one before us now is a translation of Professor Friis's "Tilfjelds," a work of the highest authority, and one which every sportsman visiting Norway ought to have. In its English dress it will be available to a large number to whom in the original it has hitherto been a sealed book. Mr. Lock won the copy from which he made his translation as a prize in a sort of Arctic Wimbledon in which he took part against Norwegian riflemen at Harstad. Save for the honesty which confesses it, no one would guess this was a translation, it reads so fluently and easily.'

PUBLISHED BY THE TRANSLATOR, at 16, Kingston Terrace, Charlton, S.E. Only a few copies now Remaining on Hand.

ICELAND.

Crown 8vo., 110 pages, cloth, bevelled boards, 3s. 6d. Net, post free.

ASKJA, ICELAND'S LARGEST VOLCANO.

A MONOGRAPH, descriptive of the above VOLCANO and its ERUPTIONS in 1875; with a Chapter on the GENESIS AND GEOLOGY OF ICELAND, and a LARGE MAP of the island specially compiled for this work and 'The Guide to Iceland,' by W. G. LOCK, F.R.G.S., who has twice visited the Volcano.

ASKJA is a vast Crater over 17 miles in circumference, lying nearly 4,000 feet above sea level. The eruptions in 1875 continued for several months, and the pumice and ashes erupted covered an area of 3,000 square miles. A lava-flood at the same time forced an outlet from a rift commencing at a spot 30 miles distant from Askja, presumably above a subterraneous channel connected with that volcano. The lava now covers a tract about twenty miles in length, by from one to five in breadth. At the commencement of the eruption an explosion took place which disrupted a mass of the lava-deposits in the crater five miles in circumference, and of unknown but immense thickness, which sunk in the bowels of the mountain to a depth of over 700 feet! So violent was the concussion that it caused an earthquake felt over the whole island, but most severely in the N.E., where rifts of immense depth, and over twenty miles in length, were torn in the rocky strata forming that part of the island.

PUBLISHED BY THE AUTHOR, at 16, Kingston Terrace, Charlton, S.E., who will forward Copies on receipt of Crossed Cheque, or P.O.O., payable at Lower Charlton Post Office.

CONTENTS.

CHAPTER I.—INTRODUCTION.
	PAGE
SECTION I.—GENERAL INFORMATION	1
,, II.—OUTFIT, GUIDES AND PONIES	22

CHAPTER II.—SUCCINCT ACCOUNT OF ICELAND.
SECTION I.—BRIEF TOPOGRAPHICAL AND GEOLOGICAL NOTICE .	37
,, II.—THE PEOPLE AND THE CLIMATE . . .	49
,, III.—HISTORICAL NOTICE, AND OUTLINE OF 'THE NJÁL SAGA'	53

CHAPTER III.—NOTES ON SPORT.
SECTION I.—SHOOTING	75
,, II.—ANGLING, AND LIST OF ICELANDIC SALMON RIVERS AND CHIEF TROUT STREAMS . .	80

CHAPTER IV.—THE CAPITAL AND VICINITY.
SECTION I.—THE CAPITAL	87
,, II.—EXCURSIONS IN ITS VICINITY	90

ROUTES.
ROUTE I.—TO ÞINGVELLIR, GEYSIR AND HEKLA. . .	93
,, II.—THROUGH 'THE NJÁL COUNTRY' . . .	116
,, III.—A SUMMER'S TOUR	124
,, IV.—UP THE WEST COAST	162
,, V.—SEYÐISFJÖRÐR TO AKUREYRI . . .	172
,, VI.—AKUREYRI TO REYKJAVÍK	173
CONCLUSION.—DESERT ROUTES	174

HANDBOOK
FOR
TRAVELLERS AND SPORTSMEN
IN
ICELAND.

CHAPTER I.
INTRODUCTION.
SECTION I.—GENERAL INFORMATION.

THREE AND A HALF DAYS' steam from Granton will land the tourist on the shores of Iceland; that strange volcanic isle on the verge of the Arctic sea, 'where *Geysir* spouts its steaming waters high and *Hekla's* craters are embosomed amid eternal snows.' An impression, however, prevails, begot in many cases by the perusal of Lord Dufferin's charming work, 'Letters from High Latitudes,' that a trip to Iceland is a most expensive affair; that the tourist will have to purchase a large number of ponies, as his lordship did; hire several men; take at least two tents, unless he be willing to sleep side by side with the Icelanders it will be necessary to employ; moreover that no steamers run regularly to and from the island, and that when once there there is no absolute certainty when he will be able to get away again; so that many a one with but a limited sum at his disposal, and an allotted time for his summer outing, is year after year deterred by these, in the main, erroneous ideas from making a tour in 'Ultima Thule.' The author has made three lengthy summer tours in Iceland, and his experience has been that two persons travelling in company do not find it a whit more expensive than travel in Norway and Sweden, there being no absolute necessity to travel *en grand seignior* with a number of followers, tents and ponies: and the end and aim of this present work is to place before the reader reliable information upon every point connected with a tour in Iceland.

First, and most important, are the means of communication. Messrs. R. and D. Slimon, of Leith, now run during the summer and autumn months the S.S. Camoens, at regular intervals of about a fortnight, to and from Granton and *Reykjavík* (Reek-wick),[1] the capital of Iceland, with occasional calls at other ports. See Sailing Bill of this steamer for the present year attached to this work. The Camoens is a very comfortable, fast, high-class steamer, designed originally for the Brazilian mail service. There are also two Danish mail steamers running between Copenhagen and Iceland, but as these on the outward voyage do not go direct to *Reykjavík*, or return direct therefrom, but call at the Faroes and steam round the island, making calls at various trading posts, the voyage to or from Leith occupies between a fortnight and three weeks, and consequently is of too long duration for those whose summer vacation is limited to a month or six weeks. The average 'run' of the Camoens direct to or from *Reykjavík* is but three and a half days, and even when calls are made at one or more of the northern or eastern ports the voyage is never of longer duration than six or seven days. The interval between the arrival of this steamer at the capital on one voyage and her departure therefrom homeward-bound the next, is from fourteen to eighteen days; and those whose absence from England is limited to a month can, in that short time, make a very pleasant tour to the three most famous of the 'lions' of Iceland,' viz. (1) *Þingvellir* (Thing-fields), a wild romantic spot rich in historical interest, for here in the lawless days of the tenth century an insulated mass of lava, in the midst of a deeply-fissured lava-covered plain, was selected as the meeting-place of the Alþíng, or House of Representatives; (2) the world-renowned *Geysir* (Gusher), and (3) the equally famous volcano *Hekla* (Mantle). Also on this tour two very fine waterfalls will be seen, the *Gullfoss* (Gold-fall) on the *Hvítá* (White-river), and the fall formed by the *Oxará* (Axe-river), where it leaps into the largest of the rifts at *Þingvellir*; and by returning *via* the south coast, the solfatarar at *Krísuvík* (Cross-wick), with their boiling

---

[1] When the name of a place first occurs, its English equivalent, when known to the author, is given. Many names have very doubtful roots, while others are utterly untranslatable. In pronouncing Icelandic words: Þ has the sound *th*, as in think. Ð, ð=*th* soft, as in father; a=a, in far; á=*ou*, as in loud, pound; é=*ye*, in yellow; *f*, when it precedes *l* or *n*, is sounded *b*, i.e. *Krafla*=Krabla, *Hrafn*=Hrabn; *h*=*k*, before *vi* and *rau*; í=*ee*, in meek; j=*y*; o=*oa*, in road; ú=*o*, in move; ý=*ee*, in meet; æ=*i*, in prize; ö=*u*, in murmur; au=*oi*, in coin; and *ey* and *ei*=*ay*, in hay.

mud-cauldrons, hot springs, live sulphur-pits, *i.e.* spots where the sublimation of this mineral is taking place, and other interesting volcanic phenomena, will likewise be seen. The tourist, if an angler, may obtain in addition a day or two's very fair trout fishing. Route 1 will give all particulars.

The cost of this highly interesting tour, including the hire of ponies, guide, etc., also first cabin passage and provisions to and from Scotland, will not exceed £30, if the tour is made by two persons travelling in company; and it may even be done for £20 if a dozen or more persons arrange to travel together. A number of the passengers by the Camoens invariably form such a party to visit *Þingvellir*, and the *Geysir*, and of course by joining it tourists travelling alone, who would be satisfied with this short excursion, effect a considerable saving, as such a party only needs two or three men and a large tent, and each one has to bear but a proportionate part of the expense incurred. These parties, however, seldom go on as far as *Hekla*; but in the future they should do so, and return *viâ* the south coast as recommended; for the tour would, as above said, just fill up the interval between the arrival of the Camoens on one voyage and her departure on the next.

It is utterly impossible for tourists unacquainted with Icelandic or Danish to travel in Iceland unaccompanied by a native speaking English, to act in the double capacity of interpreter and guide; and it is customary when travelling quickly, or any great distance, to have two ponies for each load, animate or inanimate, the ridden or laden pony being relieved every two hours or so, by transferring its rider or burthen to one of the comparatively fresh spare ones, which are driven by the guide on ahead—a long way ahead too, if the travellers are wise, that they may not be incommoded by the dust. Geir Zœga (pron. Geer Surgha), the only person from whom ponies are obtainable with certainty at *Reykjavik*, declines to furnish animals for long journeys unless two are hired for each person's riding, and for every one and a half cwt. of baggage taken.

The *Geysir* is very uncertain in its displays, and the nearest farm where decent quarters are obtainable is some distance off, therefore a tent is quite indispensable if tourists would be on the spot when it

'Erupts its steaming columns high.'

What is somewhat annoying, the expense of hiring and transporting a tent about on this tour has to be incurred by two or more persons travelling together, or even by a tourist travelling alone with his guide, merely for use on the night or two that they remain encamped at the *Geysir;* comfortable quarters for several travellers being obtainable at Þingvellir and in the vicinity of *Hekla.* There is no need to take a tent for the guide or guides, as he or they will sleep at *Haukadalr* (Hawk-dale), a farm in the vicinity. A large party making the tour recommended would keep their tents with them the whole tour; but a party of two or three should arrange with Zœga for the loan of a tent and its transport to and from the *Geysir*, and use it only while encamped there awaiting a display. He sometimes has a tent at *Haukadalr*, and when this is the case its loan can be obtained on payment of a small sum. Zœga bears a good name for fair dealing.

Enough has been said to show those contemplating a tour to the sights *de rigeur* that the demands upon their purse and time will be considerably lessened by the selection of Messrs. Slimons' steamer as the one by which to visit Iceland, and making one of a party formed on board; and the author will only add that he sincerely hopes every such party will in the future include several ladies, as their presence conduces greatly to the pleasure of these picnic parties in the wilds of Iceland. A tent will be provided by Zœga for the special accommodation of the fair sex.

To those who are in the habit of spending their summers abroad, the author ventures to recommend Iceland as a comparatively fresh field for a summer outing, for he knows of no country within easy reach of England where it can be spent more pleasantly than it can be there, that is by those who are not unwilling to 'rough it' occasionally. The scenery in many parts of the island is magnificent, while the volcanic phenomena are on a grander scale and show greater activity than elsewhere in Europe. The author passed nearly five months in Iceland in 1878, over three months in 1880, and a like period last year; and his experience is that two persons travelling together may make any of the tours recommended in this work and dispense with tents entirely after visiting the *Geysir*, fair quarters being obtainable nearly every night at a farm-house or a parsonage. The inhabitants of the country districts, with very few exceptions, are extremely hospitable and obliging to travellers, especially English tourists and sportsmen, and a night's lodging is obtainable everywhere at the higher class farms, where the best room in the house is invariably reserved for the use of visitors. There being no hotels in the interior, the author would observe here that two persons are as many as should ever travel together in Iceland, save to Þingvellir and the *Geysir*, as at many isolated farms it would be difficult to find accommodation for more than that number and their guide. The truism that two are company while three are not, holds good in Iceland as elsewhere, and three persons would probably require two guides, but one will suffice for two, as they would invariably go out together when making short tours, shooting or fishing.

Some may perhaps think it would be better to make up a party of half a dozen or so, and take a tent, and be independent of the farm-houses altogether; however, the author's opinion is that prolonged tent-life in Iceland is a mistake, and likely to sour the temper of the most enthusiastic and genial of tourists. It's all very well for a few days when reindeer-stalking, or fishing and shooting among the 'Fish-lakes,' as described in Route 3, or while awaiting an eruption of the *Geysir*. The pleasure of a tour in Iceland—and every other country, it may be said—is in a precisely inverse ratio to the amount of baggage taken; and the daily packing up and unpacking of a couple of tents, and their accessories, causes great delays, and soon becomes to be considered an abominable nuisance. Two tents would have to be taken, one for the men, otherwise excursions in thinly-peopled districts would be impracticable, as the party would be compelled to encamp every night in the vicinity of a farm, that their employés might seek the shelter of its roof. Moreover, it must be borne in mind that each tent—with cooking apparatus, oil to burn in it, etc.—would need two pack-ponies, if a tour of any length is made, or rapid travelling desired; and a supply of provisions for a large party would entail the hire or purchase of a large number of ponies, for, as previously stated, two will be required for the transport of every one and a half cwt. of baggage taken, and a large number of ponies would necessitate the engagement of several men to drive and look after them. An extended tour in Iceland is only to be economically made with any degree of comfort by travelling two in company, and in as light marching order as possible—say one and a half cwt. of baggage between the two, depending wholly on the farms for quarters, and mainly for provisions.

The author fancies he hears some one say, Yes, it's very fine telling us all this, but 'we have heard with our ears and seen in books with our eyes' the Icelandic farm-houses described as wretched hovels, and have also heard that no food fit for a civilized palate is obtainable; while, moreover, is it not on record in the book of 'Umbra,' that a tourist hight Digwell, the author of the plaintive lament which bears his name, perished of starvation during a tour in this *ultima Thule*, and was buried at *Mosfell?*

True, O Doubter, but Iceland has improved in many things since the days of Digwell, and to show that this is so with respect to the Icelanders' dwellings, and that they are not invariably the hovels it is commonly but fallaciously believed they are, it is only necessary to mention that an English lady, accompanied by her brother, a Colonel in the Army, journeyed about the country for over three months in 1878, unfurnished with a tent; and she expressed herself perfectly satisfied with the farm-house accommodation obtained during her lengthy tour, save upon two occasions. The author can assure the reader that he by no means fared badly during his three summer tours, though he did not have the advantage of a guide-book in which the farms where the best quarters were obtainable were pointed out, and had to trust entirely to his guide, who was frequently, when far distant from his home, as much at sea as the author himself as to which farm to select for quarters for the night. It must be confessed that occasionally, in out-of-the-way places, one has to put up with rather rough accommodation; but at most of the farms and parsonages mentioned in the Routes laid down in this work, at least one decent match-boarded room will be placed wholly at the service of the travellers, and good eider-down beds with snow-white sheets will be provided. The taking of a 'Garnet Wolseley,' or the travelling sleeping arrangement described in the Section devoted to Outfit, will enable the tourist to tide over a night's rough quarters occasionally without much inconvenience. It may happen once or twice in the course of a lengthy tour that earlier arrivals will be found in possession of the 'guest-room' upon the arrival of a party at the best farm in the neighbourhood; and in that case if there is another decent farm within half an hour's ride the later arrivals should proceed there for quarters, but should there not be, the 'Garnets' will come into requisition, and the later arrivals will extemporize beds on tables and chairs, or even on the floor. Formerly travellers were allowed to utilize the churches for night quarters; but thanks to the sacrilegious way in which a party conducted themselves at Þingvellir church—among other things throwing boots at the lighted candles standing on the altar, to extinguish them,—the Bishop has very properly commanded that travellers be no longer permitted to sleep in the sacred edifices.

At all the well-to-do farms, an abundance of excellent coffee, milk, pancakes, butter, brown rye-bread (usually somewhat stale), and smoked, salted, or fresh mutton and fish, are procurable, and with these and the produce of the rod and gun, if sportsmen, and about a half cwt. of preserved provisions and biscuits, travellers will not fare badly. Of course if the expense of two additional pack-ponies is no object, another cwt. of tinned luxuries, and two or three dozen of wine, may be taken. In Section 2, under the heading Outfit, what should and—equally important, what—should not be taken will be fully entered into.

Having shown that Iceland is easily accessible by steamer, and mentioned that farm-house accommodation is obtainable when travelling in the interior; also that a tour may be made to Þingvellir, the *Geysir*, and *Hekla* for £30, the author will next enter somewhat fully into the expenses that will be incurred by two persons travelling together, in making a more extended tour. Before doing so it will be well to mention, as it will save a number of interpolatory explanations, the money current in Iceland. It is Danish, and a decimal coinage, *öre* and *kroner*; 100 öre=1 krone. A *krone* is about 1s. 1½d., the exchange being 18 kroner=£1 sterling. The coins in use are 5-öre, 2-öre, and 1-öre pieces in bronze; 50-öre, 25-öre, 10-öre, 1-krone and 2-kroner pieces in silver; and 10-kroner and 20-kroner pieces in gold. The Danish paper-money will not be taken by the farmers.

In all tours of over a week's duration, it will be evident from what has been already stated, each tourist and the guide will require two ponies, and two also will be required for the transport of every one and a half cwt. of baggage taken, otherwise but very short day's journeys will be accomplished. The hire of a pony and saddle (either pack or riding) in the capital and at the trading posts is invariably two *kroner* per diem. In the country districts a pony may be hired for ten *kroner* a week, or for a month for three times that amount. The guide's wage will be from five to six *kroner* per diem, to board himself, which is the best plan. The usual charge for a night's lodging at a farm-house, with supper and breakfast, varies from two to three *kroner*, and for the night's pasturage for the ponies, from ten to fifteen *öre* per head. It will be seen from the foregoing that the daily expenses of two persons travelling together with one guide, and one and a half cwt. of baggage each, would be about £1 17s.=18s. 6d. each, thus:—

Ten ponies,	@	Kr. 2 =	Kr. 20.
Guide	,,	,, 6 =	,, 6.
Pasture, say	,,		1.
Lodging, etc., for two persons, say	,,		6.

Kr. 33 = £1 16s. 8d.

Two additional *kroner*, however, must be allowed, as occasionally it will be necessary to employ a ferryman, and, when a mountain is ascended or difficult ground traversed, a local guide. The above includes everything save the midday meal, which should be carried by the travellers and eaten *al fresco*—a few biscuits and a tin of tongue and chicken, or some other portable provision that may be eaten cold. In round figures, a pound each will be ample to cover the expenses of two persons travelling in company in Iceland; save on the *Geysir* trip, when, if it should not happen that Zœga has a tent at the farm near, or the tourists join a large party from the steamer, an additional expense of about £5 will have to be incurred to transport a hired tent to and from the *Geysir*. If the author and a companion were about to visit the *Geysir*, and Zœga had not got a tent at the farm near (he generally has throughout the summer), the author would not incur the trouble and expense of transporting one to and from *Reykjavik*, but would trust to be able to borrow at *Haukadalr*, or some other farm in the vicinity, one of the small tents of home manufacture, which most large farmers possess for the use of their servants when haymaking at a distance from home. The number of tourists visiting Iceland showing a large annual increase, no doubt in the course of a year or so it will pay the farmer owning the site of the *Geysir*, or some enterprising individual, to run up a substantial wooden building in its immediate vicinity as a summer hotel. This would be a great boon to tourists, as to see this great natural wonder in a state of activity an individual travelling alone has frequently to incur an expense of several pounds to bring a tent for use here for a night or two, which is not required elsewhere on the tour.

Reykjavik is the best starting-point for tourists and anglers, Þingvellir being distant therefrom but one day's easy ride, *Geysir* two, and *Hekla* three, if one proceeds by the most direct route; while there are several rivers where fishing is obtainable within from two to three days' ride. Guides and ponies are more readily obtainable in the capital than at any of the trading posts round the coast, Zœga being generally in a position to furnish from fifty to a hundred ponies at a day's, or at the most two days' notice. It is a good plan, however, even if it is intended to make a tour only as far as *Hekla*, to write to Zœga by the mail preceding, by at least a month, the departure of the steamer by which it is proposed to sail, and request him to have the number of ponies required, and a guide, ready against the arrival of the steamer with the tourists on board; or when they arrive it may chance that both

Danish and French men-of-war will be in the harbour, and the officers away on an excursion with most of Zœga's ponies. It is cheaper and better to buy ponies for a tour which is to extend much over a month, fair riding ponies being obtainable for about £7 each, and pack-ponies for from £4 to £5, and to hire them for one of less duration. Tourists cannot do better than buy from Zœga, writing of course beforehand asking him to have the number required ready to leave *Reykjavik* the day after that appointed for the arrival of the Camoens. Zœga supplied a party last year (1881) with very fair riding and baggage ponies indeed at the prices just mentioned.

With reference to guides, Zœga has always several qualified men in readiness to travel with those hiring or buying ponies from him. His nephew is, without exception, the best guide on the island, having been in almost every part of it: he crossed the interior *viâ* the *Sprengisandr* (Bursting-sand) last summer with the party above alluded to as having purchased ponies from his uncle. At the various trading posts round the coast there is seldom any difficulty in picking up one or two men speaking English, generally young students home for their summer vacation, and from half a dozen to a dozen ponies. There are also several men—one a schoolmaster named Gudmunsen, living at *Akranes*, who is a very good man—who make a business in the summer of conducting parties of tourists about, and who, when disengaged, board the Camoens directly she arrives at *Reykjavik*. Further information on the subject of guides and ponies will be found in the Section devoted to Outfit.

The two hotels which the capital boasts are not expensive, if somewhat primitive; four *kroner* per diem being the charge for bed, morning-coffee and rusks, and three meals. Smith's hotel—formerly a club-house—ranks first, being the largest, but Japhetsson's is very comfortable, though smaller; and the author, when he stayed there in 1878, found the proprietor exceptionally obliging in every way.

Apart from the fact that the long-felt desire to visit this wonderful volcanic isle will be gratified, the three and a half to four days' voyage direct to *Reykjavik*, and the tour to Þingvellir, *Geysir*, and *Hekla*, have much to recommend them to those who have but a month or so's summer vacation. In the months of July and August, gales are of rare occurrence in the North Sea and North Atlantic between Scotland and Iceland, consequently a smooth water passage is the rule rather than the exception, while the air is bracing and exhilarating in the extreme; and during the month first named there is virtually no night north of the Shetland Isles. When the tourist lands, all is new and strange and interesting; and once away from *Reykjavik* all conventionality is left behind, and a fortnight's glorious Arab-life is before him: and what an indescribable charm there is in the nomad-existence one leads in Iceland! Mounted upon a sure-footed and good-tempered pony, that a child might ride without fear of mishap, one passes almost daily through scenery wild and weird in the extreme; one hour skirting a tranquil lake or a fjord engirdled with lofty snow-capped mountains, and the next wending one's way slowly through a bristling, awe-inspiring lava-flood of vast extent, with enormous rugged masses piled up in the wildest confusion on either hand. Tremendous rifts extending for miles, the work of quite recent earthquakes, are a common feature of an Icelandic landscape; as also is the *laug* (pron. lurg) or hot spring, where boiling water bubbles forth like cold in an ordinary spring in less wonderful lands, and a cloud of steam ascends like the misty spray that marks where a mighty river leaps into space. Often, also, will this be seen beckoning the tourist to direct his footsteps to waterfalls unsurpassed in Europe for height, or the gloomy grandeur of the chasms into which the impetuous waters leap; for Iceland is indeed rich in magnificent cascades and picturesque rapids, three of its principal rivers coursing downward over a thousand feet in a distance of a few miles. It is hardly to be wondered at, therefore, that even Captain Burton, with his world-wide experience, wrote thus enthusiastically of travel in Iceland. Premising that 'nowhere, even in the fairest portions, can we expect the dense forest on the Alp, "up to the summit clothed with green"; the warbling of birds, the murmur of innumerable bees, the susurrus of the morning breeze, or the melodious whispering of the "velvet forest";' the veteran traveller continues, 'their places are taken by the black rock and glittering ice, by the wild roar of the foss, and by the mist cloud hung to the rugged hill-side. We may not look for that prodigality of colour with which sun and air paint the scenery of the happier south. . . . But during the delightfully mild and pleasant weather of July and August, seen through a medium of matchless purity, there is much to admire in the rich meads and leas stretching to meet the light-blue waves; in the fretted and angular outlines of the caverned hills, the abodes of giant and dwarf; in the towering walls of huge horizontal steps which define the Fjörðs; and in the immense vista of silvery cupolas, "cravatted" cones, and snow-capped mulls, which blend and melt with ravishing reflections of etherial pink, blue, azure, and lilac, into the grey and neutral tints of the horizon.'

The tour to *Þingvellir*, the *Geysir*, and *Hekla* is the one usually made by tourists visiting the island for the first time, as it embraces the sight *de rigeur*, which *must* be seen, otherwise upon one's return he will be told by his friends he hasn't seen the chief sights; but these by no means exhaust the 'lions' of Iceland; nor is *Hekla* the only volcano on the island, as is generally believed; for upwards of twenty volcanic vents have been witnessed in active eruption during historical times, and no less than eighty-nine eruptions are recorded!

The most important and interesting volcano in the island is *Askja* (Basket), a vast, almost circular crater between seventeen and eighteen miles in circumference, lying amidst the great central lava-desert, the *O'ddðahraun* (Misdeed-lava), which covers an area of 1,200 square miles. This volcano erupted as recently as 1875, when an explosion took place that disrupted a mass of the lava deposits in the crater five miles in circumference, and of unknown but immense thickness, which sunk into the bowels of the mountain to a depth of over 700 feet! The concussion was so great that it caused an earthquake felt over the whole island, but most severely in the north-east, where rifts of immense depth, and over twenty miles in length, were torn in the rocky strata forming that part of the island. The greatest disturbance, at a distance from the volcano, occurred in a desert region known as the *Mývatns Öræfi* (Midge-lake Desert), and here from a vast fissure molten lava welled forth nearly continuously for over four months after the earthquake. The fissure commences at a spot distant thirty miles from the subsidence in *Askja*, and extends in a north-north-easterly direction for over twenty miles. It is evident from the nature of the eruption at the two places that this flood of molten rock came through a subterraneous channel from *Askja*, for here prodigious quantities of pumice and volcanic-ash were ejected, but it is believed no lava. According to Professor Johnstrup, over 3,000 square miles of country east of the volcano were buried to a depth varying from several feet in the vicinity of the crater to two inches near the coast. Ash during the eruption was wafted across the North Sea and scattered over the Scandinavian peninsula as far inland as the central districts of Sweden; and the column of fire from *Askja*, after the explosion, was so high and brilliant that it was visible at *Reykjavík*—over a hundred miles distant—for four days, and was thought the first night to be a farm on fire near the capital.

A map of the *Askja* crater by Lieut. Caroc, of the Danish Navy, with additions by the author, to a scale of $\frac{1}{100000}$ will be found in the lower right-hand corner of the map attached to this work. Route 3 will show how *Askja*, the largest of the Icelandic volcanoes, may be visited. The author has crossed the *O'dáðahraun* to this volcano twice,[1] and he found that the difficulties in the way of doing so were far from being insuperable, provided the latter part of the month of July was chosen for the excursion.

Bordering the *O'dáðahraun* on the north is a wonderful volcanic region which no one, who can spare the time, should fail to visit. See Route 3 for particulars. Professor Johnstrup says, 'it deserves the appellation classic, it is "The Fire Focus of the North," where hundreds of volcanoes stand silent witnesses of convulsions respecting which history hath penned not a word.' A glance at the map will show in the north-east part of the island a large lake, *Mývatn* (Midge-lake), with a mountain range to the east of it, stretching north and south. These mountains are all volcanic, and have erupted time after time since the settlement of Iceland, and to this day show signs of active volcanicity in the form of extensive solfatarar. The most famous of this range of volcanoes are *Krafla* (pron. *Krabla*) and *Leirhnúkr* (Clay-peak). From a crater called *Víti* (Hell) on the western side of the former a terrible eruption of pumice and ashes took place in the year A.D. 1724, when the eastern shores of *Mývatn* were covered with ashes to a depth of over three feet. *Leirhnúkr* was active at the same time, and remained so until 1729; immense floods of lava streaming from its craters. In 1728 lava burst from the range in two other places, *Hrossadalr* and *Bjarnarflag;* and the following year also from other newly formed craters on the western slopes of the mountains, and coursed down to the lake, destroying three farms. What was somewhat extraordinary, *Reykjahlíð* church, standing upon a knoll, escaped undamaged, though surrounded on all sides with molten rock, while the parsonage and two adjacent farms were destroyed. Close by *Krafla* is a very remarkable mountain, the *Hrafntinnuhryggr* (the *f* here is also sounded *b*), which is

---

[1] An account of the journey in 1880, with a detailed description of the volcano and the *O'dáðahraun*, will be found in a monograph entitled 'Askja, Iceland's Largest Volcano,' by the author. Published at 16, Kingston Terrace, Charlton, S.E. Nett price, post free, 3s. 6d.

largely composed of obsidian—a black glass-like volcanic product. *Mývatn* is surrounded on all sides with lava and crater-cones, and is studded with innumerable crater-islets; and when seen under a wild sunset sky, with

> 'Clouds in grandeur breaking
> In the richly crimsoned west,'

to harmonize with its weird surroundings, forms a magnificent landscape, one which will not be easily effaced from the memory of the beholder. The recollection of such a scene, it has been rightly said, 'will seem rather the fantastic image of a dream than a reminiscence of one's actual life.'

In the south part of the country, not far distant from the coast, is a famous volcano, the *Kötlugjá* (Cauldron-rift), a terrible crater-fissure amidst the glaciers of the *Mýrdals Jökull* (Muir-dale Glacier), which has laid waste a larger tract of country since the island was inhabited than any other volcano. Thirteen eruptions are recorded. It is said that this volcanic outlet has never been visited; although it is believed there are no difficulties in the way of making an ascent but what would be readily overcome by an experienced mountaineer, the altitude of the *Mýrdals Jökull* being less than 6,000 feet. Here is an opportunity for any member of the Alpine Club desirous of placing his foot in an unexplored crater surrounded with virgin ice! Route 2 will conduct him to the farm which should be made a base for the ascent. The monarch of the Icelandic mountains, the *Öræfa Jökull* (6,455 feet, Gunnlaugsson; 5,927 feet, Watts), is also, as far as is known, a virgin peak. It is a volcano, and eruptions in A.D. 1341, 1362, 1598, and 1727 are recorded.

About midway between the *Mýrdals* and *Öræfa Jöklar* is also another volcanic region well worthy of a visit. In A.D. 1783 prodigious floods of lava burst forth from rifts in and adjacent to the river valleys at the base of the *Skaptár Jökull* (? Shaft-river Glacier), the westernmost of the ice-clad group of mountains known as the *Vatna Jökull* (Water Glacier). 'These eruptions,' it is said, 'were of a magnitude unparalleled on the earth in historic times;' and the calculations of Professor Bischoff show that the cubic contents of the lava-floods which then issued exceed those of Mont Blanc. Rushing seaward down the river-valleys the glowing lava formed fiery cascades where the ousted rivers had recently leaped over precipices, and now that these are solid rock they present the appearance of petrified cataracts. These lava-filled valleys with a background of ice-clad mountains, present another weirdly grand landscape for which it would be difficult to find a compeer out of Iceland. Route 2 will conduct the tourist hither, and also to the farms at the base of the *Öræfa Jökull*. A list of all the Icelandic volcanoes mentioned in the Icelandic annals, and the number of eruptions with which each is credited, will be found in the right-hand upper corner of the map attached to this work; and as each will be briefly described in the Route through that part of the country in which it is situated, there is no occasion, the chief ones having been alluded to, to notice more of them here.

Besides those already mentioned, the most famous 'sights' of Iceland are (1) *Asbyrgi* (the Gods' retreat or inclosure), a remarkable ⊃-shaped valley insulating a vast mass of rock. This, in the author's opinion, must be classed among the most wonderful of the Icelandic phenomena; the valley being such as would be formed were it possible to remove a gigantic ⊃-shaped mass of unchangeable rock, with arms 300 feet in thickness, 500 yards in width, and a mile apart at their extremities, that had stood in the midst of a number of molten lava flows while they were being deposited, leaving a triangular impression with vertical declivities on either hand. (2) The *Hljóðaklettar* (Sounding or Speaking-cliffs), a group of fantastically-shaped, insulated masses of igneous rock and curiously-formed craters in the wild valley of the northern *Jökulsá* (one of the chief rivers), which present the appearance of a vast ruinous castle, and, so perfectly do they echo back sounds, one can fancy that it was here in the valley of the northern *Jökulsá*, and not on the bank of the Cephīsus, that Echo, the Oreade, pined away upon being slighted by Narcissus; or that Scott's enchanted castle in the vale of St. John had been transported to Iceland. Route 3 will conduct the tourist to these places, also to (3) the Northern Geysir, the *Uxahver* (Ox-spring), which 'spouts' with great regularity at intervals varying from six to ten minutes; to (4) the Boiling-mud Cauldrons and other phenomena in the solfatarar round *Mývatn*; to Iceland's most famous fall, (5) the *Dettifoss*; likewise to (6) the *Goðafoss* (Gods-fall) and (7) *Eldeyjafoss* (Fire-island-fall). These falls no admirer of cataracts should neglect to visit; the terribly Plutonic nature of the chasm into which the waters of the one first named leap, far exceeds in gloom and weirdness the chasm of the Vöringfoss, the most famous fall in Norway. The tour laid down in Route 3 is unquestionably one of the most interesting that can be made in any part of the world, one, of which the author thinks it can safely be said, that cannot be equalled anywhere, save in the Yellowstone region of North America or among the Hawaiian islands. Starting from *Reykjavík*, *Þingvellir*, the *Geysir*, *Hekla* and the *Gullfoss*, being the sights *de rigueur*, are first visited ; then striking across country from the *Geysir* by a fine mountain pass, with the grand glacial scenery of the *Geitlands* (Goatland's), *Skjaldbreiðar* (Broad-shield) and *Láng* (Long) *Jöklar* on the right, the traveller will descend into the wonderful valley of *Reykholt* (Reek-holt), where hot springs issue from a rocky islet in the midst of the icy-cold river. A day or so later, if an excursion is not made to the *Snæfells* peninsula, a descent will be made into the *Surtshellir* (Surtr's cave), an immense lava-cavern, with an ice 'gallery of fairy-like magnificence, everywhere hung with the purest crystal, which the light of our torches reflected in a thousand ways.'[1] Thence to the north coast over a wild uninhabited moorland waste, studded with innumerable lakelets abounding in fish and fowl. *Hólar* cathedral, where a printing-press was established in about A.D. 1530, and many Icelandic bishops are interred, will be visited *en route* to *Akureyri*, the chief town in the north. The tour culminates in a visit to *Askja*, taking the 1875 lava-flood in the *Mývatns Öræfi* on the way, the path thereto lying up the weirdly wild valley of the northern *Jökulsá*, which forms fall after fall, rapid after rapid, as it courses downward to the sea from the elevated plateau of the interior. This tour, returning to Scotland from one of the northern or eastern ports, would occupy six to eight weeks from the time of landing at *Reykjavík*, and £80 to £90 would cover the expenses of two persons for that period, if ponies were bought (ten would be needed) and sold when done with—say for a pound a piece, which is about as much as would be obtained for them in the latter part of the summer.

Even this, the most comprehensive tour practicable with pleasure and safety within the limits of an Icelandic summer, will not exhaust the wonders of Iceland, but leave much to see on a future visit. There are (8) the celebrated Basaltic Caverns at *Stapi*, near *Snæfells Jökull* on the west coast (the *Jökull* chosen by Jules Verne as the volcanic outlet through which to descend to the centre of the earth). Route 4 will give full particulars ; and also direct the tourist who may wish to explore the north-west peninsula, and invade the icy precincts of the *Dránga* (? Lonely-peak) and *Glámu* (? Noisy) *Jöklar*, how to do so. This is a very grand but some-

[1] '*Voyage de la Recherche.*'

what difficult tour; the scenery on the *Breiðifjörðr* (Broad-fjörd) with its countless isles—many of which are ruinous craters of submarine volcanoes—is enchanting; as also is that of the *Isafirðir* (Ice-fjords), and several other fjords in the west and north-west. On this tour, moreover, will be seen the first volcano mentioned in the Icelandic annals, *Eldborg* (Fire-burgh), which erupted towards the close of the ninth century.

The tourist who has read Dasent's English version of the most interesting of all the Icelandic sagas, The Njál Saga, would prefer, probably, to turn his footsteps in another direction, southward to the 'Njál country,' and thence farther afield to the vast lava-floods in the vicinity of the *Skaptár Jökull*, and the grand glacial scenery of the icy region lying beyond. Not the least remarkable of the sights that will be seen on this tour is a birch 'forest' just west of the *Öræfa Jökull*, environed on three sides by the glaciers, which flourishes amidst its chilly surroundings in a most extraordinary manner. Route 2 will embrace this part of the country, and the tourist who selects this tour will, after seeing the sights *de rigeur*, be led to

'. . . many spots of beauty lone
The haunts of old romance.'

To the *Arnarstakksheiði* (Eagle-stacks-heath), where the sorcerer, Hedinn of *Kerlingardalr* (Carline-dale), made a great sacrifice to the pagan gods as Thangbrand, the first Christian apostle, was riding westward : ' Then the earth burst asunder under his (Thangbrand's) horse, but he sprang off his horse and saved himself on the brink of the gulf, but the earth swallowed up the horse and all his harness, and they never saw him more. Then Thangbrand praised God.' (Dasent's Story of Burnt Njál, vol. ii. p. 67): to *Bergþórshvoll* (Bergthora's-knoll), where Njál was burnt; to *Hlíðarendi* (Lithe-end), where Njál's true-fast friend, the brave Gunnar, dwelt, and many other spots interesting to those who have read the old-world story told in the Saga. An outline of the Njál Saga is appended to the Historical Notice, Chapter 2.

Moreover, several fine waterfalls will be seen, the *Gullfoss*, *Seljalandsfoss* (? Shealing-land's-fall), and *Skógarfoss* (Grove-fall), being the chief; and an attempt may be made to scale the icy fastnesses of the *Mýrdals Jökull* and invade the virgin precincts of the *Kötlugjá*. Owing, however, to the number of glacial-fed streams which have to be forded or ferried, this tour is somewhat difficult of accomplishment, and exceptionally good ponies are necessary. It would take from five to six weeks, as after several of the day's journeys the ponies would be greatly fatigued by the fording of the broad, rapid rivers, and need a day's rest. To two persons travelling together the cost of this tour would not exceed a pound a head daily for each person, unless a strong party of guides were hired for the exploration of the *Köllugjá*.

Having mentioned the outlines of the four chief tours in Iceland, the author will next say a few words to that numerous class who aim in their vacation tours to combine sport with sight-seeing. To those who would be satisfied with a bag of a couple of hundred brace or so of feathered game, which would include swans, curlew, plover, snipe, duck, and grouse—chiefly, the author believes, a hybrid between the willow grouse (*Lagopus subalpina*, Nilss.) and the ptarmigan (*Lagopus Alpina*, Linn.), and a creel of about the same number of trout, running from one to four lbs. in weight, and the *chance* of a shot at a reindeer, the author can safely say, Go to Iceland; for he knows of no country in Europe, now Norway is virtually closed to alien sportsmen by the order prohibiting the disembarkation of dogs from foreign countries, where such good sport with the gun is obtainable *free* as in this island. Upon each of the author's three visits, the time slipt away there like a pleasant dream, and the hour of departure came all too soon: the month of July was passed riding from one river to another, waging war against the Salmonidæ,[1] with an occasional excursion to a volcano or some other point of interest; the early part of August scouring the wilds east of *Mývatn* in search of reindeer, and the latter part of that month and the first week or so in September were spent grouse and duck shooting.

The author regrets to be compelled to say, he cannot hold out much chance of salmon fishing, unless the nets are bought off a river, or one is rented on lease. Either of these modes of procedure would be very expensive, as all the riparian owners net their waters unmercifully, and, as some years salmon attempt—they rarely succeed, thanks to the nets—to ascend the Icelandic rivers in vast numbers, make a considerable sum of money by selling the fish to English fish-dealers and the Danish merchants, therefore the nets are not to be bought off lightly. Last year (1881) as much as 7*d.* per lb. was being paid for salmon at the trading posts.

[1] Under the heading 'Piscatorial Rambles in Iceland,' an account of these angling excursions in 1878 and 1880 will be found in 'The Field,' Nos. 1483 to 1488. Doubtless a few copies are still obtainable at 'The Field' office.

Nor is it by any means easy to get a shot at a reindeer, the three herds known to exist in the island having each chosen as an habitat a wild mountainous region abounding in lava-beds, to which the deer flee for safety when alarmed, and where it is next to impossible to follow them. The author, however, in 1880, was fortunate enough to fall in with a small herd twice on favourable stalking ground, and upon each occasion two fell to his rifle, the first of these animals, it is believed, that had ever fallen to an Englishman's rifle in Iceland. Lord Binning, later on in the year, also succeeded in shooting one, a patriarchal buck, with magnificent antlers having close upon forty tines. Last year (1881) — Campbell, R.E., and a French Baron each succeeded in shooting a fine deer.

A word or two here to the sporting tourist with but a limited time at his disposal will not be out of place, as members of this class by shooting game in the month of July have brought their countrymen into disrepute with the educated classes in Iceland, and compelled the Alþing last year to pass a law enforcing a close time from April till the 1st of August. He can have fishing *or* shooting in abundance if he will only visit Iceland at the right season, viz. July for the fishing, August for the shooting. For both he must either make a lengthy stay, or visit the island late in July or early in August, when he could have a fortnight's fishing before taking to the gun. The early part of July, however, is the best time for the angler. Any one who visits Iceland for the shooting alone should do so not later than the end of the first week in August, as in this hyperborean isle the season during which it is possible to shoot over dogs is usually of but brief duration ; the young birds, even in favourable years, are not strong on the wing before the time mentioned, and about the middle of September bad weather frequently sets in ; the grouse pack among the lava-beds or along the border of the snow-line on the precipitous fjeld slopes, where it is next to impossible to follow them, and the ducks, curlew and plover take flight to more temperate climes; but between those dates, especially in the North, a month's excellent sport is to be had.

Many a sportsman has hurried home to shoot grouse on a Scotch moor, or to keep 'The Feast of St. Partridge,' when had he but remained in Iceland he might have shot over some of the best-stocked unpreserved moors in the world, moors where the hybrid grouse mentioned are that plentiful twenty to thirty brace can be easily bagged by a fair shot in the course of a few hours. At the present time an occasional sporting visitor is allowed to shoot at will over the moorland wastes; but without doubt an influx of sportsmen will cause payment to be demanded, these wastes being private property or glebe lands. There are no fjeld wastes in Iceland, abounding in game, the property of the State, as in Norway. However, as the farmers and peasants sell the grouse they shoot and snare to the Danish merchants (who pack them in salt for exportation to Copenhagen) for a sum equivalent to three halfpence each, permission to shoot will doubtless for many years to come be readily granted upon payment of that amount for every bird killed.

Prior to last year when, as just observed, a law was passed protecting not only the feathered game but also the reindeer to the 1st August, all game was unprotected, save the seals and eiderduck; and would have been still, had not certain English tourists and the French and Danish naval officers shot the birds down during the breeding season in a shameful manner. No such law was needed for the Icelanders themselves, for, to their credit be it said, they never shoot the grouse before the middle of August. Both seals and eider-duck are the property of the owner of the shore, and he may give permission to shoot the former, but not the latter. The seals are mostly caught in nets, and, save at the mouths of salmon-rivers, the owners of the shore which seals affect are averse to a gun being discharged in the vicinity.

The lover of the trigger will find further on, in the Chapter devoted to Fishing and Shooting, and in the several Routes, full information as to the best localities to visit in search of sport. The angler will find a list of the Icelandic salmon rivers and the chief trout streams at the end of the same chapter, and in the Routes, mention will be made of the lakes and rivers abounding in fish in that part of the country to which they respectively appertain.

The sporting tourist, who has not visited Iceland before, should make the greater part of the tour described in Route 3, or make an excursion to the sights *de rigeur*, return to *Reykjavik* and proceed thence round the coast by steamer to *Akureyri*, in the north, or to *Seyðisfjörðr*, in the east, as the best grouse moors on the island and the habitats of two out of the three herds of reindeer are distant but from three to four days' journey from those ports; where shot, gunpowder, not very good, and numerous other small stores, save cartridge cases and good tea are procurable. Ponies and guides may be obtained at *Akureyri* by writing by a prior mail to Herra Havsteen, the manager of the Icelandic trading company's store at *Oddeyri*, near *Akureyri* ; and at *Seyðisfjörðr*, by writing to the enterprising proprietor of the very comfortable hotel recently erected there.[1] The hire of ponies at either place will be about the same as at *Reykjavík*, *viz.* two *kroner* each per diem, including the loan of a saddle; but they cannot, as a rule, be bought so cheaply. Some further hints as to the selection of localities for fishing and shooting will be found under the heading Outfit, and in the Chapter devoted to those subjects.

The Camoens makes a voyage to *Borðeyri*, *Seyðisfjörðr* and *Akureyri* in September, therefore sportsmen experience no difficulty now in returning to England if they stay on into the autumn for the grouse shooting.

Húsavík, in the north-east, and *Sauðárkrókr*,[2] in the north-west, called at by the Danish steamers, are also good ports at which to land, shooting and fishing being obtainable within easy distance of each place; but there would be some difficulty in obtaining guides speaking English were a number of sportsmen to flock there at one time. A letter by a prior mail to Herra Guðjohnsson, the hospitable merchant at *Húsavík*, requesting him to mention to the farmers trading at his store, that a couple of Englishmen would arrive by a certain steamer and need ten ponies and a guide, and doubtless he would do so; and both guide and ponies would be at *Húsavík* when the steamer arrived, so that there would be no delay in making a start. At *Sauðárkrókr*, a similar letter to the innkeeper there would doubtless also result in the providing of ponies and guide.

Reykjavík being the nearest port to *Þingvellir*, the *Geysir* and *Hekla*, the author has selected it as the starting-point for four out of the five tours which he recommends tourists to make in Iceland. *Akureyri* should be selected as the port of debarkation by any one who has seen, or who does not care to see, the sights *de rigeur*, but who wishes to visit *Askja*, the *Mývatn* region, the wild valley of the northern *Jökulsá*, and other places of interest in the north and east. He will find the tour from *Akureyri* eastward described in Route 3, and should he wish to cross the island to *Reykjavík*, he should return to *Akureyri*, and thence Routes 3 and 6 will guide him westward and southward to the capital by the road usually travelled. Should he desire to cross

---

[1] The author does not know the hotel-keeper's name, but a letter addressed Herra Gæstgiver, *Seyðisfjörðr*, Iceland, will find him.
[2] Substitute *Sauðárkrókr* for *Seyðisfjörðr*.

the island by the *Sprengisandr* or *Stórisandr* (Great-sand), he will find a few words upon the matter in the concluding chapter. *Seyðisfjörðr* is a good starting-point for the reindeer ground in the eastern part of the country, also for a tour through the *Mývatn* district to *Askja*, thence down the valley of the *Jökulsá* to *Húsavík*, and on to *Akureyri*. Route 5 will conduct the tourist on this journey. From *Seyðisfjörðr* an excursion may be made round the S.E. coast, skirting the *Vatna Jökull*, to the 'Njál country' and the various places of interest mentioned in Route 2, but there are such a number of bad glacier-fed rivers to cross that the tour is not recommended. No route can be laid down, it being impossible to say what will be the distance accomplished in each day's journey, as this depends entirely on the state of the rivers. Eight to ten days would probably bring the tourist to *Sandfell*, the easternmost point mentioned in Route 2, and thence westward information as to the country passed through will be found in that route. The Route that would probably be travelled is shown on the map by a dotted red line.

The following are the outlines of the routes given:—

ROUTE 1. REYKJAVÍK TO ÞÍNGVELLIR; *Gullfoss* and *Hekla*; returning *viâ Krísuvík*; *Hafnarfjörðr* and *Bessastaðir*. A Twelve days' Excursion, which may be Extended to Eighteen; Suitable for those who only contemplate remaining in Iceland during the Interval between the Arrival of the Camoens on one Voyage and her Departure on the next.

ROUTE 2. A MONTH'S EXCURSION FROM REYKJAVÍK; Returning to the Capital. An Extension of Route 1, through the 'Njál Country' to the *Myrdals Jökull*, in which is situated the *Kötlugjá* Volcano; and to Þórsmörk, one of the most Enchanting pieces of Scenery in Iceland; thence to the Vast Lava-flood in the vicinity of the *Skaptár Jökull*; to the Grand Glacial Scenery of the *Vatna Jökull*; and to the Monarch of the Icelandic mountains, the *Öræfa Jökull*; Returning *viâ* the South coast and *Krísuvík*.

ROUTE 3. A SUMMER'S TOUR IN ICELAND. The most Comprehensive Tour practicable with Pleasure in the course of an Icelandic summer; Setting out from *Reykjavík* and quitting the island at *Akureyri*, in the North, or *Seyðisfjörðr*, in the East. The chief Places of interest visited on this Tour will be (1) Þíngvellir; (2) *Geysir*; (3) *Gullfoss*; (4) *Hekla*; (5) the *Reykholtsdalr*, with its Hot Springs on an Island in an icily cold River; (6) *Eldborg*; (7) the *Snæfell* Peninsula; (8) *Helgafell*; (9) the Volcanic-islets of the *Breiðifjörðr*; (10) *Surtshellir* caves; (11)

the *Fiskivötn*; (12) *Hólar* Cathedral; (13) *Akureyri*; (14) *Goðafoss*; (15) 'The Fire Focus of the North;' (16) the 1875 Lava-flood, and (17) *Askja*.

ROUTE 4. A SIX WEEKS' EXCURSION. Starting from *Reykjavik* and Returning thereto, or proceeding on to *Akureyri*. Visiting the *Reykholtsdalr*; *Eldborg*; the North-west Peninsula and the *Glámu* and *Drúnga Jöklar*; and *Isafjörðr* and the Lignite beds in its vicinity.

ROUTE 5. SEYÐISFJÖRÐR TO AKUREYRI. A fortnight's Excursion visiting 'The Fire Focus of the North;' the 1875 Lava-flood and *Askja*; the *Eldeyjafoss*, and the *Goðafoss*.

ROUTE 6. AKUREYRI TO REYKJAVÍK. By the Direct Post Route, Seven to Eight Days' Journey.

SECTION II.—OUTFIT.

THE TOURIST making one of a party on a tour to the sights *de rigeur* only, does not need any special outfit for the fortnight or so he will be on the island. He should take with him merely a change of underclothing, a coloured flannel shirt or two, a stout Macintosh, and a few other indispensable articles, and a couple of thick rugs for use during the night or so's tent-life at the *Geysir*. If an angler, such a rod as is hereafter described. Zœga will provide boxes for the articles taken, and also for the provisions; likewise a ground sheet. The tourist or sportsman making a lengthy tour, however, will need to pay some attention to the matter of outfit, and must provide himself with a pair of travelling boxes specially constructed for Icelandic travel, or he will find his impedimenta a constant source of annoyance. Owing to the only means of transport being by pack-ponies, travelling boxes must be limited in length to about two feet, and adapted to the pack-saddle in use in Iceland. The author will therefore give a description of the boxes suitable, so that the tourist may get a carpenter to make a pair for him. It should be premised that it is absolutely necessary that they be made waterproof by some means, and lining with thin sheet zinc is unquestionably the best plan; it is far preferable to caulking and pitching the seams or to the use of tin, as the former is sure sooner or later to jar out, and the latter is liable to rust, while zinc is not. Any tinsmith will line the boxes for a few shillings each; and they should be carefully tested to see that they do not leak anywhere, by filling them with water ere they leave the tinsmith's shop. A stumble over a boulder on the part of a pack-pony is always a possibility, nay, a certainty sooner or later in the driving of loose ponies through the rivers one is compelled to ford daily when travelling in many parts of Iceland. Waller, in his charming little work 'Six Weeks in the Saddle,' says: 'To see your pack-horse calmly seat himself in four feet of water and hear the sea (he was fording at this time a shallow inlet) pouring in gallons into your travelling boxes, is not calculated to enliven even a good-tempered man.' Prevention is better than cure, and a most effectual preventative is the zinc lining, for even if a pack-pony should have to swim a yard or two there is but little fear of the boxes being submerged so deeply that the water will get in beneath the lid.

The boxes should be of the following inside dimensions, and made as light and strong as possible: 2ft. long, 18in. deep, and 1ft. wide. The wood should be well-seasoned pine, ¾in. thick. The sides, bottom and ends, and likewise the lid, should each be of one piece of board, not two pieces joined together, and the sides and ends should be dovetailed together at the corners, not simply nailed. The lid should be arched to throw off the rain, which will be done by affixing a piece of wood, with the upper edge rounded, to each end of the lid in such a manner that it overlaps the end of the body of the box. Nail two one-inch battens along the bottom, to keep the box off the ground when set down; and paint or, better still, varnish it, and the box will be complete save the lining and fittings. First, the hinges for the lid; these should have flaps about six inches long, bent over the lid, and be well secured with screws. Next will be the lock; a stout brass hasp-and-eye and a padlock will be found more serviceable than any ordinary box-lock, as the latter kind are seldom made sufficiently strong to stand the strain that it is necessary to put upon the lock of a box when it is crammed so full that one is compelled to sit or stand upon the lid to close it, and it is only by thus packing a box that one can prevent its contents being damaged by the attrition caused by the jolting to which they will be subjected in pony transport. A pair of irons, somewhat similar to a sailing boat's shroud-irons, will have to be made for each box, but these should not be screwed on until the pack-saddle is seen to which the boxes are to be attached, as it is impossible to know until then the exact distance these should be apart. These irons are to be 1ft. long, 1¼in. wide, and ½in. thick, with an eye at the upper end having an inside diameter of an inch, and holes for half a dozen screws are to be drilled in each, and countersunk for the heads of the screws. In the centre of the front of the box must be affixed by a rivet and a washer inside a small eye-bolt, in the eye of which are to be inserted two triangles or rings, through which a girth and strap may be rove as hereafter described. Of course the eye-bolt in the front of each box must be affixed before the zinc lining is put in, as the washer and rivet must not project, but be let into the wood. A girth will be taken from the lowermost ring or triangle in the front of one box under the pony to that in the other, and from the uppermost a strap will be passed over the pack-saddle and anything that may be packed thereon, and these will be found to effectually secure the boxes and packages to the saddle.

If the person for whom the boxes are made purposes to shoot in Iceland, he can, and should, dispense with his gun and rifle-cases by having another box made, somewhat similar to a gun-case, and each of the boxes described fitted up with two trays, one 2in. deep, and the other 3in. In one box in the uppermost tray he will carry the stock of his gun, and in that in the other the stock of his rifle; each of which must be secured in its compartment by two straps screwed to the bottom of the tray. The 3in. trays are to be partitioned off by thin strips of board for the conveyance of cartridges. These will be the lower tray in each box, and should rest, when the box is empty, upon two wooden ledges screwed firmly one at each end of the box at a depth of five inches from the top, but when the lower part of the box is packed as full as possible the lower tray is to have no bearing upon the ledges but rest upon the contents of the box below and press the uppermost tray against the lid, so that some pressure will be necessary to close it, and thus jam the whole contents of the box so compactly together that they would not be disturbed were the box to be rolled down a flight of stairs. Gun and rifle stocks, and cartridges, will thus be handy; much more so than they would be in a couple of ordinary gun-cases bound together with a number of miscellaneous articles to make a load for one side of the pack-saddle. The barrels will be carried in the third box, which will now be described. If the barrels are of the usual length, 2ft. 6in., its inside dimensions will be 2ft. 7in. long, 2½in. deep, and 6½in. wide; which will allow of a fishing rod, of the pattern recommended, being carried in addition. It will be as well to observe here that if one takes a long jointed rod to Iceland it invariably comes to grief sooner or later. One soon tires of carrying it slung behind his back, and affixes it in some manner to the saddle of a pack-pony; a collision occurs between that animal and another, or it brushes against a rock or the corner of a building, and the finny tribes have nothing more to fear from that implement of piscine warfare, for it will assuredly be damaged beyond repair. This has happened twice to fishermen in Iceland to the author's knowledge. To obviate this he has had made a seven joint rod of the stoutness of a light salmon-rod, with 2ft. 6in. joints = to about 16ft. in length; and every angler thinking of visiting Iceland, who purposes to travel about in the interior, would do well to have one made, as it will meet all his requirements, and in all probability return to England but little the worse for its journeys in Iceland.

The box in which the rod and gun and rifle barrels are carried must be partitioned off lengthwise, that one article may not come in contact with another, and each pair of barrels and the rod will need two straps screwed to the bottom of its compartment that it may be firmly secured by them. A young sportsman, whom the author met in Iceland in 1878, showed him his rifle-barrels, which in a journey across country had been allowed in its case to come in contact with the iron base of a re-capper, and a hole was worn nearly through one barrel. Had he been fitted out as here recommended, at a cost of a few pounds, a forty-guinea rifle would not have been irreparably damaged.

The lid of the box should have a pair of stout hinges, three would perhaps be better, and be secured by a hasp and padlock, like the lids of the other boxes; and if the same key fits all three, it will be preferable to having separate ones. Carry a duplicate key in a safe place. Each of the three boxes should have nailed round the edges of its lid a flap of leather about three inches wide, which should be nailed down to the body of the box at the back over the hinges. This precaution will prevent rain driving in. There is no need to have this third box lined with zinc, as it will be carried on top of the pack-saddle, where it is very unlikely it will ever be immersed; and if on a pack-saddle designed by the author, hereafter mentioned, will be come-at-able without a minute's delay.

This outfit of three boxes will do away with the necessity for carrying a gun or rod slung behind one's back. It looks very sportsman-like, no doubt, in the eyes of young sportsmen to ride thus armed, but the most enthusiastic would vote a gun or rod a nuisance were he to be compelled to bear it, swinging against his back during a ride of several hundred miles. A stout waterproof gun-cover and sling should be taken, notwithstanding, as it will be found of use when riding to and from one's quarters and his shooting ground. Attention to these *minutiæ* before setting out from England will insure everything going smoothly—especially one's temper—while away, and non-attention will assuredly bring its punishment in the constant round of annoyances to which the traveller will be subjected, by one article after another of his 'properties' coming to grief.

The tourist will do well if he purchase a pack-saddle in England before starting, as when many travellers arrive by the same steamer, all are desirous to set out at once, and there is frequently a difficulty in purchasing or obtaining the loan of a really good pack-saddle, and some wretched substitute with turf flaps has to be taken. It is impossible for an English saddle-maker to make one suitable for Icelandic travel from a written description. The tourist by referring to the advertisements attached to this work will see where an improved pack-saddle, designed by the author from the Icelandic model, is obtainable. Its price should not exceed £3; and more than once, when pack-saddles were at a premium, half that sum has been paid for the loan of one and boxes for a lengthy tour in Iceland.

The next important matter is bedding, that tourists and sportsmen may be prepared against the emergencies alluded to in the introductory remarks. A 'Sir Garnet Wolseley' (obtainable at any outfitters) is a really practical, waterproof, portable 'take up thy bed and walk' sleeping sack for travellers. Its price, blankets, etc., complete, is about 35*s*. It can be laid upon a bench, a couple of tables, or the floor; and in fine weather it is no hardship to sleep in it on an open moor.

A preferable, and capital travelling bedstead may be cheaply constructed by affixing a short pipe-like metal socket to each end of the pack-saddle boxes, as close up under the lid as possible, and procuring four 3 ft. 3 in. ash poles, 1¼ in. in diameter. To two of these it will be necessary to attach a stout brass ferrule, about a foot in length, so that the four poles may be joined together into two, like the joints of a fishing rod, when in use. The only other requirement will be a piece of light, strong canvas 2 yds. 4 in. long and 3 ft 3 in. wide. Both sides of this must be turned over for five inches, and sewn strongly the whole length so as to leave space for the poles to pass through, one on each side. The ends of the canvas must also be turned over for about an inch and sewn, bolt-rope fashion, to a piece of rope, ⅜ in. in diameter, each end of which is 'turned' into an eye, through which the end of the pole on each side may be passed, and support what will be the head and foot of the canvas. Place the two boxes six feet apart, insert the ends of the poles into the sockets close under the lids, and the bedstead is complete. No mattrass will be needed, as one can lie soft enough without, owing to the absence of cross bars. The only bedding that will be required is a pair of thick grey or red Canadian blankets, or two or three good serviceable rugs. This form of camp bedstead has one great advantage over all others that the author ever heard of, it adds next to nothing to the weight of one's baggage; and with it or a 'Garnet Wolseley' the tourist and sportsman can pass the night in a fairly comfortable manner wherever he gets a roof to shelter him.

A waterproof bag or wrapper will be necessary in which to carry the blankets or rugs; and this should be protected from the chafing of ropes and straps by being placed in a coarse sack, otherwise holes will be soon worn in it.

TENTS.—With reference to these but little will be said, for, as observed in the introductory remarks, Iceland is no country for tent-life, owing to the difficulty and expense of transporting any great quantity of provisions, fuel and baggage about. The reindeer-stalker and those who intend crossing the island *viâ* the *Sprengisandr*, or any other desert-route, are the only persons who will need one; and to them it may be said, let the tents taken—two will be necessary if three or four persons travel in company, one for themselves and one for their men—be as light and strong as possible, and the fewer poles (which must be jointed with ferrules for pony transport) they need the better. The camping out party will require a spirit or paraffine lamp cooking apparatus, as even enough brushwood to boil a kettle of water is rarely obtainable in the desert interior. The paraffine lamp is to be preferred, paraffine being obtainable at every store in Iceland; as also are very practical little cooking apparatuses with kettles.

As before observed, most of the large farmers own a rude tent of home manufacture, which is used by their farm-servants when haymaking at a distance from home, and the sportsman who purposes merely to spend a few days after reindeer on the moorland wastes in the east, would do far better to borrow a tent from a farmer in the vicinity than incur the trouble and expense of transporting one about the country.

WHAT TO TAKE.—The author is afraid that he will be thought very ungallant in not having alluded to the ladies' outfit first, but never having travelled with a lady in or out of Iceland he is forced to confess that he does not know what they are likely to need. Therefore he will invoke the aid of the well-known lady-artist, Mrs. Blackburn, who quite recently made a tour to *Þingvellir* and the *Geysir*. She says, 'Except a Shetland shawl and cloak sent with the luggage, I carried all I wanted with me on my pony in a pair of coarse woollen saddle-bags, I had bought two years ago in Barcelona, a change of raiment on one side, a pair of strong boots and sketching material on the other, carefully balanced as to weight, and well fastened to the saddle. I took a light Macintosh with me in case of wet, but never had occasion to use it. As to dress, a short serge riding habit with "cleeks" to fasten up the skirt for walking, and a felt hat with brim enough to shade the eyes, but not wide enough to catch the wind, answered the purpose very well.'

As two pack-ponies, one as a relay, will be needed on long journeys for every one and a half cwt. of baggage (really about two cwt. with the boxes, saddle, etc.), it becomes important to consider 'what to take.' The male, like the female, tourist will have no difficulty in limiting his necessaries within the limits of one cwt., so as to have abundant space for the half cwt. of biscuits, preserved provisions, etc., it is advisable to take with one. Therefore it is to the sportsman alone that the author will give a few hints as to what should be taken. At the outset it must be stated that it is impossible for the sportsman who intends making a lengthy tour to do with two pack-ponies, unless he is willing to be content mainly with the native fare, supplemented by the produce of his rod and gun, and at the most half a cwt. of preserved provisions, biscuits, etc. His rifle, gun and rod will weigh about 20 lbs., and 300 cartridges (exclusive of 50 rounds for the rifle)= 35 lbs., while his blankets and poles, or Garnet Wolseley, will weigh, say, another 20 lbs.,=to 75 lbs. ; a spare suit of clothes; a pair of light shooting boots ; a 'relay' of flannel underclothing (no one should travel in Iceland, where occasionally sudden and great changes of temperature take place, without wearing flannel next the buff), two of each article will suffice, as they can be washed at a farm when necessary ; two or three coloured woollen shirts, each with half a dozen collars of the same material; three pairs of socks (excellent hand-knitted socks and stockings are to be bought almost anywhere in the country) ; handkerchiefs, etc., will, with a few tins of soup and meat, a few lbs. of biscuits or a loaf or two of bread, make up one and a half cwt. of baggage. The provisions should be stowed in the lower part of the boxes, as articles of clothing can be carried very conveniently in the pocket of the 'Garnet Wolseley,' or rolled up in one's blankets. The articles mentioned, with the suit he stands up in, a stout Macintosh, a thick woollen scarf, his field-glass, fishing-tackle book, a bottle of brandy or whisky, and a little aperient medicine, is all the sportsman absolutely needs. If he is luxuriously minded, and wishes to take a large supply of wines, preserved soups, meats and vegetables with him, he will have to hire or buy additional pack-ponies to carry them. Preserved provisions are readily obtainable at Leith, therefore there is no necessity to incur the expense of carriage from London. Libby, McLean & Libby's preserved soups and meats are cheaper than those of most other firms, and in the author's opinion the soups are superior even to those of Crosse & Blackwell's, which are one-third dearer.

Sportsmen can shoot and fish very comfortably by sending on a supply of provisions, etc., to the farm or farms at which they purpose to seek quarters; and if they have not been in Iceland before and wish to see the sights *de rigeur*, there are three plans open to them. (1) To select the capital sporting district lying between Þingvallavatn and the Þjórsá (Bull-river), see Route 1; or the valley of the western *Hvitá*—Routes 3 and 4. At *Reykjavik*, a man and ponies can be hired from Zœga to convey the extra baggage, cartridges and provisions to a parsonage or farm in either district. Any parson or farmer, even if he is unwilling to accommodate sportsmen, will readily take charge of any articles left at his house. These districts are respectively two and three days' journey from the capital. A visit can be made to *Krisuvik* later on in search of reindeer. Or (2) select one of the valleys in the N. or N.E.—See List of Salmon Rivers, and Routes 3 and 5—and forward the guns and rifles (it is not allowed to shoot now before August 1st), and other heavy baggage round by the Danish steamer to the trading post nearest the locality selected, and the sportsmen can send for them upon their arrival. They will then be at liberty to start from *Reykjavik* and make a comprehensive tour in the south, and enjoy some fishing, and subsequently cross the island to the north by the very interesting route laid down in Route 3. The third plan is to land at *Reykjavik* from the Camoens, make the tour laid down in Route 1, and return so as to catch the Danish steamer round to one of the northern posts; hire ponies there, and select a locality a day or two's journey distant as a sporting ground. The farmer with whom the sportsmen obtain quarters will bring up their baggage.

CLOTHING.—All clothing should be strong and new, that it may the better stand rough usage. Two suits should be taken, it being advisable to have a change. The material should be a stout tweed of a darkish hue, that it may not soil too readily; but the reindeer stalker will need one suit of lightish grey. Have the coats made with stout woollen linings, and the vests to button up close round the neck when required. Let the coats be doublebreasted, and in shape like a reefing jacket—an excellent style of coat for either shooting, riding, or boating. The shoulders should be protected by a strip of cloth (of the same kind as the coat looks neater than strips of another material or leather), sewn on, four inches wide, reaching from the collar to the sleeve seam, to take the chafe and wear of the gun. The pockets should be made of some strong waterproof material to adapt them for carrying cartridges.

BOOTS.—A pair of good stout sea-boots, reaching well up the thighs, for riding; and a light pair of porpoise hide shooting-boots for ordinary wear. A pair of slippers should be taken, as 'slippered ease' is ease indeed after riding all day in long boots. Mem. Have your sea-boots well greased every morning before setting out: and if they are made on the 'Field-boot' principle to lace over the instep, they will come on and off more easily than the ordinary kind.

WATERPROOFS.—A good stout Macintosh is indispensable. One of the new kind made of *waterproofed* tweed, with a cloth lining and a layer of rubber between, is to be preferred to all other kinds, or to the unpleasantly olfactory and sticky oilskins that have been recommended for use in Iceland. A 'sou-wester' is equally indispensable. These two articles should be strapped behind the traveller's saddle; and in the neighbourhood of the ice-clad *Jöklar*, especially in the south, he should never set out to ride a mile without them, heavy showers frequently coming on very suddenly in the vicinity of the extensive ice-fields.

MAP.—There is an excellent map of Iceland, by Gunnlaugsson, in four sheets, each 22 in. by 17 in. Its price in *Reykjavik*, unmounted, is 12 *kroner*, mounted and in a case, 22 *kroner*. It may be obtained in London at Messrs. Stanford's, Charing Cross; its price, however, mounted and in a case, is £2 16s. 6d. The map with this work will be found, it is believed, sufficiently complete for all the wants of the tourist.

OUTFIT, GUIDES AND PONIES. 31

FISHING TACKLE.—The rod recommended for general use has already been briefly described. The salmon-fisher who purposes to buy the nets off a portion, or the whole of a river, and proceed direct to it, is the only person who should take a long jointed salmon-rod to Iceland. If several rods are taken, let them be packed in a stout wooden case for pony transport.

FLIES.—Any salmon flies answer; the butcher and Jock Scott are perhaps favourites. Have the salmon flies tied on double hooks, it doubles one's chance of landing fish. The trout in Iceland run large, therefore a good stock of lake-trout and small grilse flies should be taken. The author found that gaudy flies were preferred, those with tinsel, or red woollen bodies, bound with gold or silver twist, golden pheasant tails and brownish wings being the most killing. In 1878 and 1880, in the waters of the *Laxá* from *Mývatn*, a river greatly choked with weeds in its shallows, the fish would not look at flies with any green or blue in their composition; while last summer (1881), which was unusually unsettled with spells of cold weather, during which there were no natural flies about, the trout would take anything in the shape of a fly that was thrown to them; and the author disposed of several with green and blue bodies—the only flies he had left, that he had got to look upon as quite useless on that river. Have a hundred yards of line, not too coarse, on your winch, and see that your gut casts are new and sound. Clear out all doubtful flies and casts from your tackle-book, and take a good stock of flies with you, for the lava boulders on the banks of, and in, most of the Icelandic rivers will dispose of as many of your flies as would a dense belt of timber on the banks. The angler will find a mosquito veil very useful; let it be very fine meshed, as it is not needed to keep off that delectable insect after which it is named, but a remarkably minute and persistent species of midge.

BATTERY.—A 450 or 500 gauge double Express-rifle, and a double twelve bore central-fire breechloader, one barrel choked (for swans and ducks), are weapons that most sportsmen possess, and will do very well. A twenty gauge, choked, double shot gun, however, like those spoken so highly of recently in 'The Field,' with a pair of 450 Express-rifle barrels fitted to the same stock, would be the 'tool' for Icelandic sport in the hands of a good shot, as in both weapon and ammunition space and weight would be greatly economized. Take a plentiful supply of tow, or better still lamp cotton, and oil for cleaning.

Dogs.—No great bag of grouse is to be made, unless a good staunch pointer or setter is taken. The author recommends a staunch, wide-ranging setter, that will retrieve well from water.

Guides.—In the introductory remarks the matter of guides was pretty fully entered into, therefore the author has but little to add here. The authors of two of the more recent of the works on Iceland condemn Icelandic guides as being stupid beings, while on the contrary Watts and Shepherd, who both made a hazardous journey under most adverse circumstances, speak very highly of their guides. The author, speaking personally, found the men that he had occasion to hire all that he could wish for; civil, obliging and painstaking. Upon three occasions he pushed into the midst of the deserts without a tent, and upon each occasion passed two nights in the open air, and his men never complained of having to do so, and cheerfully consented to go, knowing what was before them. Once, the ponies ran away when the party were in *Askja*, eleven hours' ride out in the *O'dáðahraun*, and unsolicited one of the men, although he had been out of bed two nights, set out alone to cross the desert on foot in search of the runaways, which he expected to find (and which were found) in a river valley which it would take him ten hours' sharp walking to reach. Whether one's guides are willing or the reverse, depends in a great measure upon the way in which they are treated. An Icelander is very independent minded, and is prone to become sullen if addressed in a high-handed manner, whereas if he is treated with courtesy by his employers he will do anything in reason for them. Should it happen that a young man is engaged who has never travelled with an Englishman before, and whose knowledge of English is limited, it will be well to bear in mind that a little patient explanation is more calculated to make matters go smoothly than the exhibition of ill-temper towards a man who, in all probability, would be only too pleased to give satisfaction if he knew how. It is of course quite impossible to obtain a man as guide so well acquainted with the whole island but that in a long journey it will be occasionally necessary to engage a local one to guide the party on difficult ground, such as across a bog or over a range of hills, or to point out the ford on a river. The author's guides have never incurred this additional expense, save when absolutely necessary; and there is little doubt but that future travellers will be equally fortunate; for Icelanders, as a rule, are remarkably truthful and honest—save when selling ponies.

At *Reykjavik*, as previously stated, Zœga has several good men

OUTFIT, GUIDES AND PONIES.

always in readiness to accompany tourists, and his nephew has been favourably mentioned. Another capital guide is Pál Pálsson, Mr. Watts' chief guide when he crossed the *Vatna Jökull*; but his present address is not known to the author. A letter to him sent three months beforehand inclosed in one to the postmaster at *Reykjavik*, with a request that it might be forwarded, would be sure to find him, and the time allowed would be ample to admit of a reply. He would be an excellent man to take for an assault upon the *Kötlugjá* volcano.

At *Akureyri*, the best guide obtainable is the son of the farmer at *Möðruvellir* agricultural college, distant two to three hours' ride from the town. Any one purposing to start from *Akureyri* should address a letter to the learned and hospitable Herra Jón A. Hjaltalín, the head master at *Möðruvellir*, and should the farmer's son be engaged he will doubtless recommend one of his pupils. It has been before mentioned that guides and ponies may be obtained at *Akureyri* by writing to Herra Havsteen at *Oddeyri*.

At the other ports, save *Húsavik*, two, or perhaps even three, couples of tourists would not find any great difficulty in obtaining ponies and a guide speaking English, the student sons of the farmers all being home for the summer vacation from June till October; but if a number were to arrive at one time, there would doubtless be some delay in obtaining sufficient mounts.

PONIES.—The Icelandic pony is a stoutly made, hardy, sure-footed and sagacious little animal, about thirteen hands high, without a particle of vice in its composition. They vary greatly in colour, chestnut, piebald, white and cream-coloured being the most common. They go very willingly in company, but some have an almost insurmountable disinclination to going alone. The best riding ponies are known as *Vakurhestar*, that is, they amble, or move both legs on each side alternately, and consequently are very easy to ride. However, the author's opinion is that they are not so sure-footed on bad ground as a trotting pony, and when they do stumble, fortunately it is but rarely, they fall sideways in a most dangerous manner. It is seldom that an Icelandic pony stumbles unless it is completely tired out, and even then it recovers itself with remarkable agility. The best ponies rarely fall to the traveller's use, being worth about £20 on the island. With a rider not exceeding twelve stone, or a load of one and a half cwt., a pony will go at a moderate pace for eight hours daily for several days together, if allowed to graze for about an hour after being ridden for four. On a long journey a pony should not be ridden or driven loaded for more than four hours daily in the peopled districts, so as to reserve its strength for unavoidable lengthy journeys when farms are far apart. Relay ponies will be taken, as mentioned in the introductory remarks, so that the party can travel eight hours daily on an average, each pony being used alternately for two hours. The only provender the hardy little brutes require is grass, and upon the arrival of the party at a farm for the night they are hobbled and turned out to forage for themselves. A middle-aged pony, say ten to twelve years old, is to be preferred to a young one, and ponies up to eighteen years of age are very serviceable, and being experienced, they are prudent and very sure-footed. They are very hard-mouthed as a rule, and the rider may tug at the head of an old pony for an hour, but he will not induce it to take a step on doubtful ground. In fording rivers one should let his steed just feel the bit, so as to be prepared to lift its head in case of a stumble, allowing it to pick its way across at its own pace.

Hire ponies for a short tour, buy them for a long one, as previously recommended. In either case have nothing to do, if it can possibly be avoided, with ponies that have sores on their backs, at the roots of their tails, damaged legs or hoofs. See that all the ponies are well shod before starting, and take a half dozen spare shoes and a good supply of nails. Every man on the island is able to shoe a pony. However, if it is intended to make the capital, *Akureyri, Sauðákrókr, Seyðisfjörðr*, or some farm in a valley head-quarters, and from thence make ten to twelve days' excursions into the interior, it is the better plan to hire ponies for each excursion, as fresh ones in good condition will then be obtained each time the sportsmen or tourists set out; and their expenses will be considerably reduced during their stay at head-quarters. It will be as well to buy a pony each for their own riding, and it is absolutely necessary that the guide be kept on with one pony to act as interpreter, and to accompany the tourists on short tours, or the sportsmen when angling or shooting. Timely notice should be given to the guide as to when fresh ponies will be required. This is the plan now adopted by the author, but speaking Danish he only needs a man when making lengthy excursions.

HOBBLES.—These are very important items, as the ponies must be hobbled at night or they will assuredly stray, and half the next day will be lost in hunting them up. Very good hobbles are made in Iceland of plaited woollen rope, but it is seldom that enough new ones for half a score of ponies are obtainable, either before starting or at the first farm. Old ones are useless, as they are invariably rotten. The best plan, perhaps, would be to take a supply of pony-hobbles from England, or a strong sail needle and twine, and get one's guide to buy a half dozen fathoms of the plaited woollen rope, obtainable almost anywhere, and then cut it into lengths and sew it oneself into 'grummets' about a foot in diameter. These make excellent hobbles, as the rope is soft and does not chafe the legs of the ponies. The grummet is simply placed round the legs and secured between them with a rope-yarn. A hank of about a dozen of the latter should be purchased at one of the stores before setting out. The average cost of ponies, either to hire or buy, having already been mentioned, nothing now remains but to say a few words with reference to the saddle, bridle, etc.

SADDLES.—When ponies are hired saddles—sometimes considerably the worse for wear—are usually lent with them. The best plan, however, is to take a well-stuffed cob-saddle with one from England, or an ordinary saddle that has been restuffed to adapt it for a pony. Very good saddles indeed of native manufacture are occasionally to be bought for about £2 each, but it is seldom that there are more than one or two in stock at the stores. Whether you bring, buy, or borrow a saddle, see that its crupper, girth, and stirrup-leathers are in a good serviceable condition. Any number of these articles are to be bought either in the capital or at the trading posts. See that there are two iron loops, one on each side of the one by which the crupper is attached to the saddle, to receive leather straps for the conveyance of waterproofs. Let the stirrups be of good size if a saddle is taken from England. A light snaffle bit and bridle will completely equip the riding pony. Spurs can be taken or not at the will of the tourist; they are seldom used in Iceland. A whip should be taken, and the sportsman's should have a snap-swivel at the end of its stock, with which it may be attached to the saddle without the trouble of binding it fast, whenever he dismounts for a shot.

In concluding these remarks on outfit, the author would impress upon the tourist and sportsman the necessity of seeing *oneself*, every morning before setting out, that the pack-saddle boxes are each packed as nearly as possible of the same weight, otherwise the heavier one will cause the saddle to shift, and a halt will be necessary to readjust. Also to see that everything is jammed fast and secured, especially cigars, biscuits, etc., in separate cases, or the frailer articles will be ground to powder; and, above all, that nothing is allowed to lie loose in the trays in which the gun and rifle stocks are, or they will be assuredly damaged. If these matters are attended to, the traveller will experience no trouble whatever with his baggage; and if not attended to, he will find that the end of each day's journey will disclose one article after another damaged beyond repair, and he will be kept in a constant state of anxiety and suspense while on the move from place to place, as to what will befall his possessions during the day.

CHAPTER II.

SUCCINCT ACCOUNT OF ICELAND.

SECTION I.—BRIEF TOPOGRAPHICAL AND GEOLOGICAL NOTICE.

ICELAND is an island a trifle larger than Ireland, lying in the North Atlantic, about 650 geographical miles distant from the west coast of Norway between the 65th and 66th parallels of latitude, 440 from the east coast of Greenland, on the 65th parallel, and about 500 north-west of Duncansby Head. It is situated just south of the Arctic Circle; north of which one headland, *Rifstángi* (? Rifstongue), projects a little over a mile. West of this headland is a small island, *Grímsey* (Grímr's-isle), the northern half of which is within the Circle. This island can boast of a church, *Miðgarðar* (Mid-house), lying about half a mile north of the Circle, and a resident pastor. Some twenty or thirty people live in the northern half of the island. The southernmost point of Iceland is a cape usually called *Portland*, in N. lat. 63° 24'; off which there is a remarkable islet, *Dyrhólaey* (? Deer-hole-isle), a perforated rocky buttress, through which, it is said, a ship might sail. Its easternmost point is a rounded headland, *Gerpir*, in W. long. 13° 32' from Greenwich; and its westernmost, *Bjargtángar* (Boulder-tongues), an elevated headland in W. long. 24° 33'. Upon some maps and in most books the headland terminating in *Snæfells Jökull* is wrongly shown or said to extend further westward than any other part of the island; this, however, is not the case. The west coast is deeply indented with two large bays, separated by this headland; the northernmost is named *Breiðifjörðr* (Broad-fjord), and the southernmost *Faxafjörðr* (Mane-fjord). Several narrow fjords penetrate inland for several miles beyond the large bays. The eastern, northern and north-western coasts are deeply indented with a number of narrow fjords, while the south coast is very dissimilar, being unbroken by a bay or a fjord capable of affording shelter even to small vessels. There is but one group of islands off the south coast, the *Vestmannaeyjar* (Westmen's or

Irishmen's-isles); the largest of which, *Heimaey* (Home-isle), is inhabited, and possesses a trading post and church.

In the bays on the west coast are innumerable small islands, some inhabited; many of the largest of which are the craters of submarine volcanoes. The encircling wall of a number of these crater-islets is broken down on one side, admitting the sea; and they in consequence present more the appearance of crescent-shaped coral-reefs than of volcanic isles. Several good examples may be seen by taking a boat and rowing to the islands north of *Stykkishólmr* (Stick-holm), a small town on the *Breiðifjörðr*. Space cannot be spared to enter more fully into the configuration of the coasts: a glance at the map will give a good idea of their peculiarities.

According to the Icelandic cartographer, Björn Gunnlaugsson, the area of the island is 38,000 English square miles—Ireland, 32,511. Broadly speaking, only the fertile tracts and valleys of the coastal regions are inhabited, the interior being mainly a barren elevated plateau, studded with ice-clad mountains and slumbering volcanoes; and it is believed there are not half a dozen houses in the whole island distant in a beeline forty miles from salt water. The area of the lava deserts, and sandy, stony wastes of the interior may be set down at about 7,500 square miles; 5,000 of which must be placed to the credit of the latter, which are slowly but surely increasing in extent, as will be hereafter seen. The two largest are the *Sprengisandr* and *Stórisandr* (Great-sand), and these cover the surface of the elevated inland plateau on the west of the *Oddðahraun*, from which the one first named is separated by the *Skjalfandafljót*. The boundaries of the two deserts where they join are the rivers draining the *Láng* (Long) and *Hofs Jöklar*, whose rocky foundations rise through the plateau south of the deserts—in each of which, by-the-bye, is a tract about thirty square miles in extent, covered with lava that has welled forth from rifts. The author must not omit to state that south of the *Vatna Jökull* there is a tract of sand quite 200 square miles in extent, lying but little above sea-level; it is named the *Skeiðarársandr* (Swift-river-sand), and is the detritus of the glaciers.

The area of the lava deserts, that is to say, tracts covered with lava that has welled forth from rifts, or flowed from volcanic mountains in quite recent times (hundreds of miles have been so covered since the settlement of Iceland), is computed at 2,400 square miles, of which the *Oddðahraun* is credited with half, while the lava-covered tract round *Hekla* is said to be but 240 square miles in extent. In the south-western portion of the island, between the capital and the south coast, there are over 500 square miles of country covered with lava; and between the *Myrdal's Jökull* and *Skaptár Jökull* there are the tracts covered with the lava-floods that there streamed forth in 1783; two entire river-valleys and over 200 square miles of low-lying land!

Nearly one-seventh of the whole area of the island consists of *Jöklar*, or glacier-covered heights; the *Vatna Jökull* is credited, as before stated, with an area of 3,000 square miles, the *Hofs Jökull* with 500, *Láng Jökull* with 440, the group of *Jöklar* in the south, of which the *Myrdal's Jökull* is the chief, with about 350, and the *Dránga* and *Glámu Jöklar*, lying on the north-west peninsula, with 400.

With reference to the moorlands and pastures (there is no arable land), Professor Johnstrup says: 'It is exceedingly difficult to give, even approximately, an estimate of the area of the pasture lands of Iceland, as these imperceptibly run into extensive heaths with a most meagre grass growth. The area of the pasture land is usually estimated at 746 (Danish=15,000 English) square miles, but this includes all that can by any means be brought under this heading.' This is, unquestionably, an over-estimate, notwithstanding that a large extent—possibly 3,000 to 4,000 square miles—of the eastern part of the island is elevated moorland, for year after year the area of the pasture land is decreasing, while that of the sand deserts is increasing—every gale of wind sweeping over the latter, when uncovered by snow, spreading over the former a thin covering of wind-borne sand; and it is impossible to travel far, especially in the vicinity of the larger deserts, without coming across extensive tracts of moorland buried to a depth of several inches, which but a few years since nourished a growth of stunted birch and willows, whose stems project through the black sand bleached and dead. With reference to the thousand square miles or so of moorland in the east, buried under pumice by the 1875 eruptions, it is believed they will only remain useless as pasture land for a few years, the expansive action of the frost upon the rain and snow water within the porous pumice will soon degrade it into fertilizing soil, and the grass growth here will be richer than ever. There is no great depth of soil upon the elevated moorlands; a depth of five feet is about the average.

The glaciers, lava and sand deserts, moorlands, and pastures thus cover about 28,000 square miles, and the remaining 10,000 consist chiefly of mountain masses varying in altitude from 2,000 to 3,500 feet, snow-covered for nine months out of the twelve.

The island boasts of four large lakes—the monarch is Þingvallavatn, area about forty square miles—innumerable lakelets, and a number of rivers, the largest of which drain the more extensive of the glaciers. None of the rivers are navigable, but for a mile or so at the mouth; although 'their magnitude, as well as the dimensions of their basins, are out of all normal proportion to the area of the island.' The quantity of water in the rivers 'varies as rain falls or snow and ice melts.' Those flowing southward from the *Jöklar* on the south coast, although of no great length, are the worst to ford or ferry, being liable in summer to the sudden downpour of vast floods of water from the glaciers. A glance at the map herewith will show the position and relative size of both lakes and rivers, equally as well as a written description here.

VOLCANOES.—In the right-hand upper corner of the map will be found a list of those of which mention is made in the Icelandic annals as having been witnessed in a state of activity in historical times, with the dates of the eruptions recorded. A glance over the body of the map will also show their sites; and as the chief ones will not only be noticed further on in this section, when treating of the geology of the island, but also briefly described in the route through that part of the country in which they are respectively located, there is no occasion to allude to them further here.

To the foregoing very cursory topographical description of Iceland, the author will only add that there are innumerable hot springs scattered over every part of the island; and six solfatarar of considerable extent; the largest of which exist in the vicinity of *Mývatn*, in the N.E., and at *Krisuvik*, in the S.W.

A few pages must now be devoted to what may be termed the island's foundation. A great deal was written about the geology of Iceland by several early travellers who did not penetrate the interior, whose dread deserts guarded the key to the formation of this interesting volcanic isle; and one ingenious but fallacious theory after another to account for its genesis was built up upon these very superficial geological examinations as a basis, by geologists who had never even set foot on the island.

It was for a long time assumed that a fissure filled in with trachytic-lava bisected the island from S.W. to N.E., and that all the volcanic vents lay upon this fissure; but as the interior became better known to modern travellers, this theory was exploded, it being impossible to travel any distance without falling in with beds of lava that had welled forth through rifts in the more superficial rocky strata, presumably above channels in the substrata; while, moreover, in every part of the island volcanic mountains were met with that had erupted in comparatively recent times, and, as we shall presently see, there is a chain of volcanoes stretching across the island from south to north. Still, no great central vent was suspected in the interior, although in the last few years a vague belief has prevailed that the various volcanic mountains that had been active since the settlement of the island were connected in some manner. That a central vent with radiating channels does exist is, however, now quite certain; and it is moreover equally so that vast sheets of molten rock welled forth from the outlet before it was narrowed down to its present, comparatively speaking, insignificant dimensions, and built up the greater part of the interior, and likewise a considerable extent of the less elevated portions of the coastal regions.

English scientists of late years have greatly neglected Iceland; and notwithstanding that one of the most violent volcanic eruptions of modern times took place in 1875 from a vast volcano in the desert interior, whose existence till then was unsuspected, the scene of the eruption, prior to the author making his way to it in 1878, was visited by but one of our countrymen, the intrepid law-student, Mr. William Lord Watts. *Askja* is here alluded to, whose dimensions were given in the introduction, *viz.*, an almost circular crater between seventeen and eighteen miles in circumference. (See Map.) The author was convinced by the magnitude of this volcano and the peculiar nature of the eruption in 1875 (briefly described in Introduction, p. 11), that it had played no unimportant part in the construction of the island; in fact that it was the key to its formation; and he determined to pay it a second visit, and likewise to closely examine the volcanic region to the northward. In 1880 and last year (1881) he carried out these determinations—in the meanwhile devoting considerable time to the study of the volcanic history of the island, and early this year published a monograph, 'Askja, Iceland's Largest Volcano;' in which, besides describing the volcano fully, he ventured to give a chapter on the genesis and geology of the island. A résumé of this he will beg leave to append.

The foundation strata of the island are two distinct formations, one that was in existence anterior to the glacial epoch, and another of subsequent creation. The interior, as before mentioned, is an elevated barren plateau, having an altitude varying from 1,000 to 1,500 feet, studded with detached mountain masses, varying greatly in height up to nearly 6,000 feet. Many of these mountains are ice-clad, and evidently a very old formation, while others are of volcanic origin at a quite recent date. The coastal regions of the south-east, east, north and north-west, are far more elevated than the plateau of the interior, and consist mainly of semi-detached mountain masses varying but little in altitude, about 2,000 feet, with here and there tracts far more mountainous and much broken up, where similar masses have been tilted aside, the upheaved portions raised to a greater altitude than the summits of their fellows, as also is the case where other masses have been bodily uplifted, while in some places masses lie lower, having apparently subsided. There are also low-lying tracts between these mountain regions composed of glacial detritus and alluvial deposits resting upon sheets of igneous rock that have coursed down from a volcanic outlet, or outlets, in the interior in post-tertiary times. The major part of the mountain masses on the coast, and the larger ice-clad *Jöklar* in the interior, are built up of vast horizontal sheets of igneous rock—basaltic and other lavas, tuffs and conglomerates; and, in the author's opinion, are an older formation than the existing inland plateau and other less elevated parts of the island; portions, in all probability, of one of the basaltic plateaux of north-western Europe, which prior to the disturbances of the glacial epoch, there is reason to believe, extended far into the Arctic Sea. Professor Geikie is of opinion that the Faroes and part of Iceland are surviving fragments of this formation; and from the author's examinations of the rock formations of these islands, he is convinced there is almost irrefragable proof of the fact. The Faroes correspond so closely, as to stratification and altitude, with the mountainous masses of the older formation in Iceland, that there can be no doubt as to their being coeval.

There is no dearth of evidence that the mountainous portions of the north and east coasts are of far older formation than the inland plateau, nor that the low-lying portions of the coast and many of the higher volcanic mountains, and several of the ice-clad heights, are coeval in formation with the interior. The author has in various places, from *Seyðisfjörðr* on the east to the south of the north-west peninsula, examined the *upper* strata of the flat-topped mountain masses on the north coast, and *they do not correspond* with those of the existing inland plateau, the former having conglomerate and tuff strata alternating with basaltic and other lavas (in places three or four lava-strata will be found resting one upon the other with a stratum of tuff or conglomerate below and another above), whereas the uppermost strata of the latter, bared by earthquake rifts in many places to a depth of quite two hundred feet, are exclusively of lava that has been deposited unchanged, save by congelation, with thin layers of clinker-like fragments that have never been abraded by ice or waterworn, marking the divisions between; therefore it is evident these mountain-masses, even if they were formerly a continuation of the substrata underlying the existing inland plateau, must have been upheaved prior to the deposition of the later lava-flows bared by the rifts, or the interior now covered by them must have subsided. Moreover, while the coastal valleys and fjord inlets show signs of glacial action, the surface of the superficial sheet of lava on the plateau has never been abraded by ice, otherwise the rounded summits of the dome-shaped bubbles that are to be seen in the *Ódáðahraun* and other parts of the desert interior, would have been ground away; therefore it is certain the later ones must have issued subsequently to the glacial epoch: that they issued subaerially and did not course down an inclined plane, but spread out in an immense basin inclosed—or more strictly, as many gaps doubtless existed, partly inclosed—by the fragments of the older plateau is likewise certain, or they would not have been deposited so horizontally and evenly.

Further proof is to be found in the facts that deep narrow fjords exist only on the east, north, and north-west coasts, where this older formation prevails, and not on the south and south-west, where the island is built up to a great extent by the igneous rock which has coursed between the masses of the older formation—the ice-clad *Jöklar* lying inland to the south and west of the elevated plateau of the *Sprengisandr* and *Ódáðahraun*. The way in which the fjord inlets radiate is convincing proof that they have been mostly hollowed out by glacial action; and in the north-west peninsula the glaciers are still doing their work, though perhaps not so vigorously as of yore, the glaciers being of less extent. Save on the north coast—where we find four, whose beds and continuous valleys lie between detached masses of this older formation—the fjords nowhere have *deep* continuous valleys that penetrate inland beyond the more elevated coastal region; and the river valleys, even those of the *Skjalfandafljót* and *Jökulsá*, rivers which intersect the island northward from the very base of the *Vatna Jökull*, are of no great depth upon the plateau, but abruptly deepen as the coast is approached, the two rivers named each falling nearly a thousand feet in a few miles.

Geologists assign many changes of the earth's surface, a number of rock formations, and a long duration to what they term the tertiary period, and bring it to a close with the glacial epoch. This epoch was one of great disturbance of the earth's crust from other causes than the action of the ice, subsidences and upheavals to the extent of 1,800 to 2,000 feet taking place over the whole of the northern hemisphere from the fortieth or forty-second parallel northward.

The basaltic plateaux in existence at this time were greatly disturbed, immense tracts subsiding to such an extent that they are now beneath the sea; while in places fragments of considerable height were left standing hundreds of miles apart. The fragments left standing in that part of the northern hemisphere where we now find Iceland, doubtless at the beginning of the post-tertiary period, formed a group of islands very similar in appearance to the Faroes of to-day, but scattered over a greater area. To judge by the existing coastal formation of Iceland, these islands subsequent to the glacial epoch were detached by the arms of a vast glacier occupying the space now the interior of the island, which stretching seaward through rifts in and the gaps between the mountain masses, deepened and widened them into the fjord inlets of this remarkably indented island. Amidst the scatter of mountainous isles left standing, existed a vast volcanic outlet that has remained active until this very hour; belching forth its fiery floods of molten rock to be deposited in the form of conglomerates and tuffs when they issued subaqueously or subglacially, and later on, subaerially, in the form of the vast sheets of lava composing the more superficial strata of the inland plateau. Not only in the large space inclosed by the fragments of the older plateau was the molten rock so deposited, but coursing between the rifts and gaps a certain quantity was left behind, the sea and ice thereby being gradually ousted, and the detached masses connected by lower lying tracts into one island, with an exceedingly irregular coastal outline, and thus was the foundation laid of the Iceland of to-day.

There is reason to believe that the sea-level over the northern hemisphere varied considerably towards the close of the glacial epoch, and likewise during the early ages of the post-tertiary period, at times being far higher than at others. This would account for the tuff-strata found alternating with the lava; as it is not very speculative to imagine that those portions of Iceland, including the interior, lowlying at that time, would be flooded; the volcanic vent converted for a period into a submarine volcano, and the molten rock that issued at such times be deposited in the form of tuffs and conglomerates. In the course of ages the whole of the spaces between the fragments of the older plateau were gradually upbuilded above the encroachment of the sea; the currents and tides carrying away the greater part of the disintegrated igneous rock that found its way beyond the outlying tertiary bulwarks that now form a considerable part of the coastal region; the climate became more temperate, no glaciers being found at a lesser altitude than 2,500 feet, and the later discharges of molten rock were deposited unchanged, save by congelation, in the form of the basaltic and other lava-strata that lie uppermost in the post-tertiary plateau forming the greater part of the interior.

The regularity and evenness with which these vast sheets have been deposited seem to point to a remarkably peaceful welling forth of the floods of molten rock, accompanied by the discharge of little or no fragmentary material, for no layers of ash interpose between the strata, thin layers of clinker-like crust alone being found. Their deposit, however, appears to have first greatly narrowed in, and ultimately to have sealed the vent whence they issued; and then came troublous times.

As to the site of this volcanic vent, I believe that immediately following the disturbances of the glacial epoch a rift in the earlier rock formations of the earth's crust extended from south to north under those portions of the island now known as the *Vatna Jökull* and the *O'dd'ðahraun* as far north as *Krafla*. Fragments of the older plateau being left standing on both sides of the southern end of the rift, it was narrower than in the centre, and the superincumbent masses of igneous rock now existing there were sooner piled up than where the rift was wider; as also was the case towards the northern end where it also was less in width, the volcanic vent being thus at a comparatively early period of its post-tertiary history narrowed down to the limits of the *O'dd'ðahraun*. The mountain masses lying upon these rifts on the north and south stand to this day, as a glance at the map will show. The greater number of the foundation strata of the island were probably deposited during the time the outlet extended north and south through the *O'dd'ðahraun*; and by the welling forth of the later sheets of molten rock, the outlet was still further narrowed down to the limits of the *Askja* crater. The *O'dd'ðahraun* lies higher than the deserts that surround it on the north, west and east, strong presumptive evidence that it lies nearer the vent whence the sheets of rock issued, and also that the later ones were less in bulk than those preceding, and consequently did not extend farther round the vent than the borders of the *O'dd'ȣahraun* ; the very last that issued prior to the upbuilding of *Askja's* mountainous periphery being the comparatively small ones, that form its widely extending base. One thing is certain, *Askja* is surrounded with a tract covered with lava which, subsequently to the deposit of the most superficial sheet of rock on the plateau, has issued from that crater, and welled forth from rifts and smaller volcanic mountains around it, having as large an area as the whole of the other tracts similarly overspread in the island ; and this fact in itself is strongly corroborative of the view taken that the *Askja* crater marks the focus of volcanic activity in Iceland.

The period following the close sealing of the great central vent was, beyond doubt, the most troublous one in the history of the island since the glacial epoch ; most of the mountains, not portions of the older plateau, now standing in the island being formed by the volcanic disturbances that succeeded.

It is an easy matter to trace the rift, of which *Askja* is the present great central outlet, for it forms to this very hour a covered channel running almost due north for a distance of forty miles, and another south to the coast, both clearly traceable by signs of active volcanicity in several places, where gases from the central vent force their way through the porous lava filling in the rift, and form solfatarar in spots where cracks and fissures exist. The *Fremrinámar* (Farther-solfatarar) lie upon the northern channel on the very verge of the *O'dd'ȣahraun*, and mark where an immense flood of lava in comparatively recent times burst forth through the overlying strata, roofing in the rift, at a weak spot between the site of former disturbance farther north, where volcanic mountains and vast lava-floods piled above offered more resistance, and another volcanic range, the Northern *Dýngjufjöll*, which mark the course of the rift through the *O'dd'ȣahraun*. Farther north, upon the line of this rift are also the *Hlí'ȣarnámar*, the solfatarar in which are situated the largest boiling mud wells in Iceland, *Leirhnúkr* and *Krafla ;* and it is possible at the latter place, which has been the scene of terribly violent eruptions, ramifications extend to the Þ*eistareykir* solfatarar and the *Uxahver* group of hot springs. From *Leirhnúkr*, and a number of fissures between that volcanic mountain and the *Fremrinámar* (all lying in a line running from south to north upon the rift), lava-flood after lava-flood streamed forth in the years A.D. 1724, 1725, 1727, 1728 and 1729, spreading over the plateau in both an easterly and westerly direction. That portion of the rift, south of *Askja*, runs nearly due south under the *O'ddŏahraun*, and the icy wastes of the *Vatna Jökull* to the coast, its course being marked by the *Kverkhnúkarani* and the *Kverkfjöll*, a range of volcanic mountains penetrating far amid the glaciers of the *Jökull*, possibly even as far south as the *Öræfa Jökull*, the volcano which marks the termination of the rift. From the *Kverkfjöll*, Mr. Watts saw smoke ascending during the *Askja* eruption in 1875. Further, and most convincing evidence that the volcanic vents on this rift are connected with a central vent, and with each other, is found in the phenomena of the eruptions in the years 1727, 1728, and 1729. It is recorded that the *Öræfa Jökull* took the initiative on the 3rd August, 1727, *Leirhnúkr* following suit on the 21st of that month, the *Jökull* remaining active until the spring of the following year, when a fresh outburst at *Leirhnúkr* on the 18th April, and the opening of rifts and the formation of erupting craters in the *Dalfjall*, in *Hrossadalr*, and at *Bjarnarflag*—all three spots close together on the rift between *Leirhnúkr* and *Askja*, and lying at a far lower altitude than the *Öræfa Jökull*—the lava-floods were diverted from the *Jökull* and found outlets in the four places mentioned. *Leirhnúkr* was active during the whole of the following year. It is also worthy of notice, that in 1728, when no less than five volcanic vents were active upon a clearly traceable rift or channel, running north and south from *Askja*, it is recorded that 'this same year volcanic action was going on in the lava wastes round *Hekla*;' and the fact that 'volcanic action was going on in the lava wastes round *Hekla*,' and not from the volcano itself, at the time that five vents upon a far distant rift or channel were erupting is, at any rate, something more than slightly corroborative of the opinion held by the author that a channel also runs in the direction of *Hekla* from a main central vent.

From the number of lava-floods that have burst forth at various times at a distance from volcanic mountains in the same way as the one in 1875, it is evident that innumerable channels exist in the post-tertiary strata; and, to judge from the phenomena of the eruptions in the three years from 1727 to 1729, and those in 1875, there is every reason to believe that these channels are connected with the great central volcanic vent beneath *Askja*.

A remarkable proof of the existence of radiating channels is found in the fact, that during the eruption in the vicinity of the *Skaptár Jökull*, in 1783, of the most prodigious lava-flood of which we have any record in Iceland or elsewhere, lava welled forth beneath the sea and built up an islet, *Eldey*, a few miles south-west of *Reykjanes*, over one hundred and fifty miles from the *Skaptár Jökull!*

It would not be a very difficult matter to propound a feasible geological theorem to account for the existence of subterraneous channels in the sub-strata of an island built up, as Iceland has been, chiefly by volcanic agency; but space cannot be spared to do so, this section having already run to a greater length than was intended. In Route 3 mention is made of several places where there is abundant evidence of their existence; notably in the *Ásbyrgi*, *Mývatns Öræfi*, *Snæfell* peninsula and the *Vatnsdal*. Mention, however, must be made of the eruption from the *Kötlugjá* fissure in the year A.D. 1660, as it is strongly corroborative of the theory as to Iceland's formation advanced by the author. The eruption 'began November 3rd; such was the quantity of sand, stone and débris borne down with the flood from the mountain, that a dry beach was formed where formerly people fished in a depth of twenty fathoms; the coast was pushed 1,000 fathoms out to sea; five or six farmsteads were destroyed' (Th. Thoroddsen's extract from the Icelandic annals). With one such eruption in every decade it would not take many centuries to unite a widely scattered group of islets into one large island! The geologically minded reader will find the genesis of Iceland more fully entered into in the monograph from which the foregoing is extracted; and to this the author must refer those who desire to extend their knowledge of the geology of this strange island.

The reader will be able to form some idea of Iceland from the foregoing brief topographical description, and the remarks upon the scenery in the introductory chapter. He will not find it difficult to picture in his mind the wild weirdness of many of its landscapes, where widely extending ice-clad mountains rise from fire-blasted deserts of lava, volcanic ash and sand; nor to imagine that as suddenly as by the stroke of an enchanter's wand, a scene as calm and peaceful, as the one left was the reverse, may open to his gaze upon descending to the margin of one of the still fjords, or tranquil lakes, lying embosomed amid the snow-clad remnants of the older plateau; whose rocky buttresses on the north have withstood the raging of the Arctic waves through sunlit summer's night and sunless winter's day, from a period when the hissing seething sea battled with floods of molten rock for possession of the channels between the islets, left standing here at the close of the glacial epoch.

SECTION II.—THE PEOPLE AND THE CLIMATE.

Two VERY, and equally important considerations for the tourist, are the character of the people among whom he proposes to sojourn, and the kind of weather he is likely to meet with. In this section it is purposed to treat of both only so far as they affect the summer visitant. First, the people:—

The Icelanders are somewhat reserved in the presence of strangers at first, but if the latter are affable and genial in manner this soon wears off. They are very hospitable; and a night's lodging is never refused travellers even at the humblest home. In at least two instances during his travels, the author had reason to suspect that the farmer at whose house he sought quarters late at night vacated his own bed that he might have it, and sought less comfortable quarters elsewhere—possibly among his hay. Both these farms were very poor ones, and many miles distant from the peopled districts. Upon another occasion the people could not boast of possessing sheets for the bed, but they had in the house some dozen yards of new calico, and this was hurriedly stitched together to supply the want. The people, as a rule, are moderate in their charges for food, accommodation, and services rendered. In the author's three summer tours there occurred but four cases of attempted extortion, two of which he regrets to say he was forced to allow to be successful.

Some recent writers have grossly libelled the Icelanders by saying they are addicted to drunkenness and dirty in their habits. This, however, is not the case, for one can travel about the country for months, staying every night at a farm, and never see a man the worse for drink. It is true that at the trading stations on the coast, and in the capital, a drunken man will occasionally be seen, but it must be borne in mind that such a one is in all likelihood a peasant come into 'town,' for a supply of necessaries, who has not tasted spirits for months, and who, consequently, is overcome by comparatively little drink. Neither are the Icelanders such a dirty race as they have been represented; it must be confessed there is room for improvement in the matter of cleanliness, but so there is with the working population of our own isles. Mrs. Blackburn says:—' I do not think any one who is familiar with the abodes of the Celtic population in this country, or who has been in a Spanish railway station, or, above all, who has visited Amalfi, would consider the Icelanders dirty. Cleanliness, after all, is only comparative, and must depend a good deal on circumstances.'

The Icelanders are a strong, hardy, muscular race, usually of middle height, though tall men are not rare. An Icelander treats a soaking with contemptuous indifference; and the traveller ere he has been a week on the island will probably see his guide wade waist deep into an icily cold river to drive the ponies across, and then remount and ride in his wet clothes the remainder of the day; and, what is stranger still, will not be a whit the worse for it on the morrow.

The author deeply regrets that he is not able to compliment the Icelandic women upon their good looks, a really good-looking woman being a great rarity; however, they carry warm hearts and modesty within their homely exteriors.

Both sexes frequently weather a good many winters and attain a ripe old age. The author saw last year, in the north, a hale old woman of ninety, and another woman seven years older, but she was breaking fast.

There is nothing picturesque in the every-day costume of the people, their garments in the country districts being usually of serge-like home-spun cloth; but there are two articles of dress which attract the attention of strangers, *viz.* the moccasin-like soleless slippers of undressed sheepskin worn by old and young of both sexes, and the small skull-cap of black cloth, with a long silk tassel of the same hue rove through a silver ferrule, worn by the women. It appears to be the fashion for the younger women to wear the cap with the tassel hanging down by the left cheek: and aliens are prone to think that the unmarried wear their cap in this manner, and the married theirs with its tassel hanging down against the right cheek; this, however, is not the case, the cap is worn with the tassel on either side at the will of the wearer. The ladies have a very pretty national dress, but it is only worn on special occasions, such as a marriage or a ball. It consists of a short black jacket, richly embroidered with gold or silver down the front, and round the collar, and a black skirt also embroidered down the front. The head-dress, worn at the same time, is known as the 'Faldr,' and is a high white cap, fixed within a golden or silver coronet, which encircles the brow of the wearer. A long white lace veil is usually worn with the cap.

The population of the island at the present time is said to be 72,000; over nine-tenths of whom gain their living by breeding sheep and ponies, and by fishing. The sole care of these pastoral farmers is to garner in as much hay as possible; as upon the greater or lesser quantity secured depends the number of breeding stock he will be able to keep through the winter. There are no agricultural farmers or arable land, but a small patch of swede-turnips and potatoes will be found close adjacent to most of the best farms. The priest is invariably a farmer, and he usually owns the best grass-land in the district. The farmer on the coast is always a sea fisherman as well as a breeder of sheep and ponies.

A few lines must be devoted to the Icelander's dwelling. Timber, having to be imported, is dear, and difficult to transport; therefore the Icelander makes use of as little as possible in building himself a house. With less than a dozen exceptions, all the better class farm-houses, whose interiors the author ventured to explore during his rambles in the wilds of 'Thule,' were built on the following plan. A long, low, dark passage, with walls built of rough slabs of lava bedded in turfs by way of mortar, runs from front to back the whole length of the house, a distance varying from fifty to eighty feet, on each side of which at the rear of the two front rooms, which are lighted by windows, are from two to four cave-like apartments, built wholly of the same rude materials as the walls of the passage, lighted only by a hole in the roof, which also serves as chimney, and what little light the doorways admit from the gloomy passage. These back rooms are utterly destitute of wainscot or plaster, and also the passage; which invariably terminates at the entrance to a large apartment quite at the rear of the premises, called the 'Baðstofa'; wherein the farmer, his family, and farm servants of both sexes, not only take their meals together, but all sleep in bunks ranged round the walls, similar to what one sees in the steerage of an emigrant ship. The two front rooms are frequently not only very comfortable wainscotted apartments, but are also fairly well furnished with a sofa, chairs, and other articles. These rooms are seldom used by the farmer and his family, save when festivities take place; being reserved for the accommodation of guests; and are always placed wholly at the service of travellers seeking a night's lodging. Most farmers are willing for moderate payment to accommodate sporting tourists who may wish to make a stay of some days to fish or shoot in the neighbourhood. The roof is usually of turf, resting on a layer of birch-bark to render it waterproof, and gabled. Approaching from the front, a house frequently presents quite an imposing appearance, for it is not an uncommon thing to find a house with seven gables; a number of buildings which serve as blacksmith shop, harness room, and store-houses being attached on each side of the main one. The fronts of these additions are sometimes boarded and painted, as well as the front of the chief building.

CLIMATE.—This will be alluded to but briefly, as it is only the summer weather that is likely to interest the tourist. Iceland enjoys a milder climate than that part of North America lying between the same parallels, but a colder one than that part of Norway lying immediately north of the Polar Circle. In the valley of the Alten, N. lat. 69° 70', corn is successfully raised, and besides the birch, the fir, alder and rowan grow and thrive; while in Iceland the only forest growth is some limited areas overgrown with stunted birch and willow bushes. The winters in Iceland are only occasionally so severe as the winters in the Alten valley, and the dearth of forest growth in Iceland is undoubtedly due to the fact that about once in every decade the Polar ice drifts southward in the spring to within a few miles of the northern coast, and remains there until late in the summer. Whenever this happens, and it happened last year (1881), there is a frost at night throughout the summer, and hail and snow-storms whenever the wind blows from the N.W., and all vegetation, save in sheltered localities, suffers severely. Last year the cold summer followed an unusually severe winter, and hundreds of square miles of moorland pastures were as utterly destroyed by the long continuance of the frost in the ground as they would have been had a fire swept over them. Usually the north and north-east parts of the island enjoy in summer far more settled and warmer weather than the southern parts and the north-west. In 1878 and 1880, in the six weeks between the middle of July and end of August, the author experienced respectively but four and six showery days, while last year scarcely a week passed without rain and snow; but the bad weather went out with August, and the month of September was delightful. South of a line drawn across the island due east from the *Snæfells Jökull*, the summer weather is closely akin to that of Scotland, but the months of July and August are generally finer and drier than in that country, or the western districts of Norway. The summer usually breaks up about the end of the first week in October, though sometimes, but rarely, it will do so a fortnight earlier, and winter may be said to last until the following June; spring and autumn having virtually no existence in Icelandic chronology. In fine weather the air, in the words of Capt. Burton, 'is a medium of matchless purity,' and mountains distant seventy to eighty miles can be seen plainly by any one with average eyesight; and in July, it is almost unnecessary to add, there is 'nightless night' in Iceland, while even in the latter end of August there are not many hours of darkness; so that the sportsman or tourist need never fear that he will be benighted should sport, or a wish to visit some distant object of interest, induce him to prolong his excursions. The atmospheric effects late in August, and in September are splendid; and it is no uncommon occurrence to see first all the mountain summits of the landscape, with their snow-fields and glaciers, glowing crimson masses in the evening aurora, the Alpenglow, and a few hours' later to behold, should there be strong or contrary upper air currents, the northern streamers, the true aurora, holding high revel in the sky. Every one who visits Iceland experiences benefit from the bracing, pure air, and Burton says :—'All the English travellers upon the island in the summer of 1872 agreed that Anglo-Indians on "sick leave" should prefer a tour in the north to the debilitating German Bäder, or to the fantastic hydropathic establishments, which are best suited to riotous health.'

SECTION III.—HISTORICAL NOTICE.[1]

To which is appended an Outline of the Njál Saga.

Prior to A.D. 874 Iceland was uninhabited, save by a few Culdee anchorites; monks who in the sixth century seceded from the Church of Rome, and retired to the outlying isles of the west of Europe that they might worship God in peace and simplicity.

[1] Works consulted in the compilation of this Historical Notice:—'The Thousandth Anniversary of the Norwegian Settlement in Iceland,' by Jón A. Hjaltalin, Reykjavík, 1874; and Dasent's Introduction to 'The Story of Burnt Njál.'

Some members of this sect found their way to Iceland long prior to the discovery of the island, in 860, by Naddoddr, a Norse Víking; and they left traces behind them in the cells in which they dwelt, and in a few simple articles of church furniture found therein. This sect was not likely to spread, 'being no lovers of women'; and it is not known for certain whether any of the anchorites were found actually living in Iceland by the Norsemen or not. There is some reason for believing that the Culdees who sought Iceland were Irish.

Naddoddr, while on a voyage from Norway to the Faroes, was driven to the north-west by a storm, and sighted Iceland, which he named 'Snæland' (Snowland). Four years later a Swede, Garðar Svafarsson, circumnavigated the island; named it 'Garðarsholm'; and, it is asserted, wintered at *Húsavík* on the north coast, where he built a house, hence the name Housewick. It was next visited, in 868, by Flóki Vilgerðarsson, a mighty Víking; who, finding the northern coasts invested with ice, gave the island 'its present grim and gristly title.'

The first permanent settlers of the Norse race were two foster-brothers, Ingólfr and Leifr (commonly called Hjörleifr = Sword Leifr). These two men, for the slaying of an enemy in a 'blood-feud' in Norway, had their estates in that country confiscated. They fitted out a ship and set sail for Iceland, of which they had heard from Flóki, where they arrived in the year 874, and settled in the south. Ingólfr, some three years later, removed to the south-west, and settled on the spot which is now the capital. Leifr, prior to this, was murdered by his Irish thralls. The assassins fled to the *Vestmannaeyjar* (Westmans, or Irishmen's Isles; to which that name was given in consequence), but were followed and killed by Ingólfr.

Harald Haarfager (the Fair-haired) at this time was extending his kingdom over the whole of Norway, and as he increased in power behaved in such a tyrannical manner that a great number of his subjects, including many powerful chiefs too proud to submit to him, quitted the land of their forefathers and sought a home in Iceland. This emigration attained such great proportions, that Harald attempted to check it by issuing an order 'that no one should set sail to Iceland without paying four ounces of fine silver to the Crown.'

The island was far different then to what is now, and had greater attractions to settlers. The climate must have been more temperate, for 'corn ripened, the tracts of grass-land were of greater extent, and there was considerable forest growth.' Accordingly we find it recorded in the Icelandic annals, that within twenty years after the landing of Ingólfr and Leifr, 'the island began to be thickly peopled'; and that sixty years after, 'the inhabitants numbered 50,000': and from that time until within the last twenty years, the population has varied but little in point of numbers. The majority of the settlers came direct from Norway; no inconsiderable number, however, came from the Orkneys, the north of Scotland, and from Ireland; but these were chiefly Norsemen who had previously migrated to the west, and in many cases intermarried with Scotch and Irish families; members of which, of pure blood, frequently accompanied their Norse relatives. Many localities, by the names bestowed upon the natural features and homesteads, bear witness to this day of their occupation by sons of the Emerald Isle. Thus a fjord in the N.W. is named *Patreksfjörðr*, after an Irish Bishop—not the Saint.

The earliest settlers had a peculiar way of determining the site of their future home, which space must be spared to notice here. On nearing Iceland, the head of the family threw overboard the pillars which had supported the high seat at his former residence. Wherever these were driven ashore, he considered the gods had directed him to fix his future dwelling-place. Sometimes it was necessary to search for years before a settler found his high-seat pillars, and could fix his permanent abode. Ingólfr's high-seat pillars drifted ashore in *Reykjavik* bay, and so rigid was the observance of this custom that he removed there from the south, quitting what was in that day one of the most fertile tracts on the whole island for one remarkably sterile. Possession was taken of as much land as the settler thought he would need 'by going round it with fire' in the following manner. A fire was kindled in one place, and then another within sight of the first one, until the whole area intended for occupation was thus surrounded. When the settlers became numerous, it was agreed that no new comer was to take possession of a larger tract in breadth, parallel with the coast, or length inland, than he could place within a quadrangle of fires in a day. A woman was not allowed to take possession of more than what she could make a two-year-old heifer go over between sunrise and sunset in the spring.

In the early days of settlement many of the Norse chiefs took possession of extensive tracts of country, and allotted portions to their respective friends and retainers, likewise to their freed thralls. It was a common thing for a thrall to be presented with his freedom and a farm for rendering a great service to his master. The chief also invariably built at his residence a temple, 'Hof,' to the Scandinavian mythological gods, placing under its foundations earth brought from the site of the temple at his old abode. He was himself priest of the temple, and performed the sacred rites. His retainers, or those who had fixed their abodes within the boundaries of his settlement, were to pay a tax to the temple—church-rates we see were an early institution—to help defray the cost of the sacrificial feasts and of keeping the temple in repair. All those who worshipped at a temple were expected to attend the chief and assist him in his quarrels with other chiefs. In return he had to adjust their quarrels, and to protect them against other chiefs and their retainers. Thus a kind of patriarchal government was early instituted, each chief being entirely independent of other chiefs; but there was no law but the sword, and might was right; therefore the later and less powerful settlers were in a manner compelled to seek the protection of one of the powerful chiefs, and show him a certain amount of allegiance, by worshipping at his temple and paying a tax for its maintenance.

The chief had unlimited power of life and death over his family and thralls; for in a word 'he was a priest in his own house and a king in his own home.' He could even rear his children or not as he pleased. 'As soon as a child was born it was laid upon the bare ground; and until the father came and looked at it, heard and saw that it was strong in lung and limb, lifted it in his arms, and handed it over to the women to be reared, its fate hung in the balance, and life or death depended on the sentence of its sire.'

As the island became more thickly peopled, the chief in each district would call together his neighbours to consult with them on matters of importance to the dwellers in that particular part of the island. Such a meeting was called a 'þíng' (Thing), and freemen could alone attend it. The meetings were usually held in the immediate vicinity of the temple of the chief. Many of the chiefs after a time ceased to act as priests, and such appointed a relative or friend to officiate as priest in his Hof; and to these subsequently was also conceded the right to preside at the meetings of the local þíng. All this time it must be borne in mind there was no written or universal law; neither was there any supreme authority, and quarrels between the members of one þíng and those of another could only be settled, as the quarrels of nations are settled, by treaty or an appeal to arms.

Naturally the utter absence of law and a supreme authority

was not found to answer with a race of people like the warlike Norse who had made a home in Iceland; so in the year 926 steps were taken by the principal men for the founding of a commonwealth, and the drawing up of a code of laws for the government of the whole island. A man well acquainted with the laws of Norway, Ulfljót, living at *Lón* in the south, was commissioned to frame the statutes. He was related to certain famous lawgivers in Norway, and he proceeded thence forthwith to take counsel with them. He remained in that country about three years, the chief part of the time at the home of Þórleifr the Wise, his mother's brother; the same who shortly after assisted King Hácon, the foster-child of the English King Athelstane, in framing 'The Gula Thing's Code.'

Ulfljót's foster-brother, Grímr 'Goatshoe,' was directed during his absence to seek out a natural fastness, easily guarded, where the 'National Assembly' might hold its meetings undisturbed. He selected a rocky islet, in the midst of a sunken plain, cut off from the surrounding country by deep fissures, which at that time were only passable in one place over rocky débris that formed a rude causeway. This spot is the now world-famous *Þingvellir* (Thing-fields). The plain at this time was the property of Þórir 'Cropbeard,' but he having just recently slain a man named Kol, his estate was confiscated. Besides the act of confiscation which happened so opportunely, the facts that the spot lay at the junction of the tracks across the desert interior, and within the Þing of the priesthood founded by Ingólfr, one of the first settlers, no doubt had some weight in determining its selection as the 'Thingstead.' The priest of this district, by reason of the 'legal capital' of the country being within his cure, became the 'Allsherjargoði' (Priest of the Whole Host), or high priest of the island.

'There then, on the great sunken plain between the two rifts, with the bright *Þingvallavatn* before it, and the huge Broadshield (*Skjaldbreið*) mountain looking down on it, was the Alþing set in the year 929, and Ulfljót's code solemnly adopted as the law of the land.'

There appears to be some question as to the number of members of this, the first Alþing, and Herra Jón A. Hjaltalín, a well-known Icelandic scholar, says: 'At the same time the whole island was divided into four quarters, east, south, west and north. The east, south and west quarters were again subdivided into three districts each, and the north quarter into four districts. Each district had three chiefs, or temple priests, as they are also called. All these chiefs had seats in the Alþíng, and each of them was to take with him two of his retainers.' Other authorities, on the contrary, say, and the author believes correctly, that this division of the country did not take place until about thirty years later. It is possible that the composition of the first Alþíng will ever be a matter of dispute; as in those days 'there were no books, everything was traditional; the law itself was committed to memory and the custody of faithful lips.'

The men who thus made the law their study, and 'learnt its traditional precepts by heart,' were termed 'Lögmen' (Lawmen). They were private persons 'invested with no official character,' but who enjoyed, it is evident from the Sagas, great influence; being consulted by their neighbours much as a solicitor is in our own land to-day; with this difference, there was no payment of fees. Njál was one of the most famous Lögmen of the latter part of the tenth century; and the author is under an impression gleaned from the Saga of which he is the hero, that a Lögmaðr could not plead at the Alþíng on behalf of another, he could only instruct him how to plead.

When the Alþíng was established, a 'Speaker of the Law' (Lögsöguma𝛿r) was appointed. To him all who were in need of a legal opinion, of information as to what was and what was not law, had a right to turn during the hearing of a case before the Alþíng. His term of office was restricted to three years, but he was eligible for re-election. Ulfljót, the framer of the statutes, was the first Speaker of the Law.

The Alþíng was both a deliberative and an executive assembly, it made new laws and administered justice, and 'was in a word both Parliament and High Court of Justice in one.' Every one who appeared before the court as a party to a suit or witness, and even the judges themselves, had, prior to the introduction of Christianity, to swear an oath on a sacred ring (brought from the temple of the High Priest) after it had been sprinkled with the blood of an animal sacrificed to the gods: 'So help him Njord, Frey and the almighty god, Thor (Þór), that his cause was, or that his witness or judgment should be, to the best of his belief, right and just.' The statute regulating the form of the court of justice said, that 'three twelves were to judge in all suits.'

Whether the country was divided into four quarters or not when the Alþíng was first established, we find it recorded that in the year 959–960 the island *was* divided into quarters; and it being found inconvenient that all petty cases should be taken before the Alþíng, it was arranged that the three subdivisions of each quarter should be judicial districts, 'Þíngsóknir'; the inhabitants of each of which were bound to attend a common place of meeting, 'Þíngsted,' which, as will be hereafter explained, was to be 'a court of first instance.' There was some trouble in the Northlanders' quarter about its subdivision, and it was finally settled that it should be divided into four 'Þíngsóknir. Each of the quarters had its 'Fjórðungaþíng' (Quarter-thing), and each of the subdivisions its 'Varþíng' (Vernal-thing); in the latter of which certain suits were to be in the first place set on foot, then carried to the Quarter-thing, and thence, if needs were, to the Alþíng. In each of the subdivisions there were three chief temples, 'Höfudhof'; and the Vernal-thing, or court of first instance, was composed of the three priests, who presided in turn; and these each named twelve men to assist them in trying cases brought before the court, for the time-honoured law demanded 'that three twelves were to judge in all suits.' The whole thirty-six, moreover, were bound to be unanimous in their judgments—to judge from the Sagas this did not occur very often. The Quarter-thing gradually fell into disuse, for in practice it was found that if an unanimous verdict was unobtainable at the Vernal-thing, it was almost certain to be the case likewise at the Quarter-thing. At this time it was further arranged that there should be four courts, 'Fjórðungs-dómar,' at the Alþíng for the trial of suits; and in the year 1004 was added, at the suggestion of Njál Þórgeirsson (the hero of the Njál Saga), a fifth, 'Fímtardómr,' or High Court of Appeal.

The Alþíng now, whatever its composition before, was thus composed. First of all thirty-nine priests sat in it, the northern quarter sending twelve and each of the other quarters nine. To counterbalance this inequality three men were chosen from each of the other three quarters by the priests who represented it, so that the whole number on the bench of the priests was forty-eight. Each of these chose two men as his assessors, therefore the national assembly consisted, with the Speaker of the Laws, now its President, of one hundred and forty-five. Later on, when Christianity spread throughout the land, the Bishops became *ex-officio* members of the Alþíng. With reference to voting, priests and assessors had an equal right.

Any one who had means and influence enough might still build a temple, and officiate in it, but his new temple would not be one of the recognised temples, nor would he who built it be a priest in the sense required by the constitution.

The chief men who owned the recognised temples and officiated as, or appointed, priests had great power. The priest could call upon a ninth part of his 'þíngmen'—the men residing within the jurisdiction of his þíng—to follow him to the Alþíng; and when there they were bound to back him in his suits and quarrels, while it was his duty to stand by them, and see them righted in theirs. The leading of bands of armed followers to the Alþíng led, as may well be supposed, to constant fights at *þíngvellir*, there being no supreme authority to hold the chiefs in check. The Sagas abound in instances where a suitor, dissatisfied with, or unable to obtain a decision at the Alþíng courts, attacked with his armed followers his opponent and his men, in the immediate vicinity of the Court of Laws. As party feeling usually ran high, it was not an uncommon occurrence for most of those present to embrace the cause of one or the other of the disputants, and then a most sanguinary battle would take place, in which sometimes as many as a thousand men would be engaged. One such conflict took place over the death of the hero of the Njál Saga, an outline of which will be given further on. As a rule, however, the more powerful chiefs combined to see matters settled according to the law of the land. If a case was lost through some flaw in the procedure—not an uncommon thing, by-the-bye, for never were men more expert in law quirks, or more formal in their legal proceedings, than the old Icelanders—it was frequently submitted to the arbitration of the combined chiefs. In order to induce hostile parties to submit their case to arbitration, these chiefs promised their armed assistance to him who was willing to do so.

The history of the Icelanders from the establishment of the Alþíng down to the commencement of the eleventh century records but one event of any great importance, that is, the discovery of Greenland, which subsequently led to that of America. About the year 980, a man named Gunnbjörn discovered Jan Mayen; and some years later Eiríkr Rauði (Eric the Red) went in quest of this island, but sighting Greenland he sailed there instead, and founded a settlement. The Icelanders sailing southward to explore the coast of Greenland discovered America in A.D. 981–1000, and in the year 1477 Columbus visited Iceland, and doubtless heard of the land lying to the westward, hence his voyage in search of it, and its *re*-discovery by him.

In the year 997 the first Christian missionary landed in Iceland, at *Gautavik* in the *Berufjörðr* (Bear-fjord). His name was Thangbrand, and he was a son of Willibald, a count of Saxony. He was sent by the Norwegian king O'lafr Tryggvasson, who at that time was preaching Christianity to his subjects with fire and sword; and Thangbrand, like his master, attempted to thrust the new religion upon the Icelanders more by the use of weapons than argument; for it is recorded that on his journey west in the spring of the following year he slew several men. In the introductory remarks allusion was made to an extraordinary legend respecting this journey, which says that as Thangbrand was riding over the *Arnarstakkshei𐌸i*, a sorcerer, Hedinn of *Kerlingardalr*, made a great sacrifice to the gods, and then 'the earth burst asunder his (Thangbrand's) horse, but he sprang off his horse and saved himself on the brink of the gulf.' It is interesting to learn that the sorcerer was immediately after slain by Thangbrand's Icelandic companion, Guðliefr. The object of Thangbrand's journey was to induce the Alþíng to adopt Christianity as the religion of the land, but he failed, 'his duels and bloodsheddings doing the cause much harm,' and returned to Norway.

However, two years later, on the 24th June, 1000, Iceland passed from Paganism to Christianity. This was brought about by the sound reasoning of Snorri, a converted Pagan priest, with the assistance of several powerful chiefs who had recently been on a visit to King O'lafr, who had loaded them with presents and honours, and thus gained them over 'to try everything in their power to establish Christianity in Iceland.' In order to make them the more zealous in the performance of their task, he retained a number of their sons with him as hostages, and there was every reason for anxiety, as to what would have been their fate, if the result of their fathers' mission had been different from what it was. Many a chief was thus moved as much by fear for the safety of a son as by persuasion to support the Christian party. In the Njál Saga we find it recorded that:

'During the debate a man came running and said, "that a stream of lava had burst out at *Olfus*, and would run over the homestead of Þórodr the priest."

'Then the heathen men began to say, "No wonder that the gods are wroth at such speeches as we have heard."

'Then Snorri, the priest, spoke and said, "At what, then, were the gods wroth when this lava was molten, and ran over the spot on which we now stand?"'

To this there was no reply; as the sunken plain of *Þingvellir* is one of the most remarkable lava tracts on the island, and doubtless the eruption when the molten rock burst forth took place ages before human eye ever rested on Iceland.

Sooner than might have been expected, Christianity became not only nominally, but really the faith of the Icelanders, and this without much bloodshed. The first Bishops were foreigners, but natives were soon educated to succeed them.

'Writing and materials for writing first came into the land with Christianity.' There is no proof that the earlier or Runic alphabet, which existed in Pagan times, was ever sued for any other purposes than those of simple monumental inscriptions, or to record short legends on weapons or sacrificial vessels, or horns and drinking cups.

In the early part of the eleventh century many Icelanders visited Europe to study at the principal universities. Schools were established on the island by the native Bishops, and were well attended. Soon Iceland became as famous under the Christian religion for its scholars, as it had been during Paganism for its adventurous sea-rovers. These at once began to write down the songs and legends of their Pagan ancestors, as well as the Sagas, which already 'had been formed in the mouth of the Sagateller, and handed down from generation to generation.' The literary productiveness of the Icelanders reached its culminating point during the last fifty years of the Commonwealth (1212–1262), the darkest period of the European 'dark ages.' Montgomery says:

> 'Iceland shone with glorious lore renowned
> A northern light, when all was gloom around.'

In A.D. 1117–18 the laws were codified and written down.

Towards the end of the twelfth century the peace of the little commonwealth was disturbed by several of the most powerful chiefs, and this ultimately led to no less disastrous result to the Icelanders than the loss of their independence. When two, or more, of these chiefs quarrelled, they refused to have their differences settled by law, and there was no supreme power to compel them to do so. They preferred an appeal to arms, and thus began family feuds which spread wider and wider as time went on, until nearly the whole of the inhabitants were involved in them. Some of the contending chiefs visited Norway and solicited the aid of the king, Hákon the Old. He was by no means displeased to hear of the quarrels between the more powerful of the Icelandic chiefs; as from the time the island was first colonised the kings of Norway had had a longing for its annexation. Hákon, therefore, rather endeavoured to foment than settle the disputes among the chiefs, and finally made proposals to a number of them that they should try to place Iceland under his sceptre; and many were ambitious

and short-sighted enough to listen to his persuasions; among them
being Snorri Sturlusson, the most famous of the saga-writers of
Iceland. After considerable bloodshed, Hákon gained his purpose;
and Iceland was incorporated with Norway in the years 1262-64.
'The Icelandic republic was no more,' says Herra Hjaltalín, and
adds, 'We may suppose that the immediate object of the Icelanders
was to obtain peace and tranquillity, and so far they were indeed
successful. But they had not counted the cost of this political
suicide, for it was a historical suicide as well.'

The subsequent history of Iceland has been a very mournful one
until within the last thirty years. Peace brought indolence and
apathy, because it was accompanied by the loss of independence
and the responsibility of self-government. However, since 1848
a band of patriotic Icelanders, under the leadership of Herra Jón
Sigurðsson (who, alas! died in 1880), have fought a manful battle
to raise Iceland from the political atrophy into which it had sunk.
Space can only be spared to briefly notice the more important events
from the loss of independence.

In 1380, Norway was united to Denmark, and Iceland was also
transferred to the Danish Crown. From 1540-51 is the date of
the Icelandic Reformation, when Lutheranism prevailed over
Catholicism. Both these changes took place without bloodshed,
and ever since the Icelanders have 'remained Lutheran to a man,'
and it is almost unnecessary to add that the island is still a Danish
possession.

In the year 1800 the Alþíng was abolished, and for forty-three
years Iceland was entirely under Danish government. In 1843 the
Alþíng was reestablished, but it was only a shadow of its former
self—a body of representatives to whom was denied the right to
legislate! Two years later it was determined that the Alþíng for
the future should hold its sittings at *Reykjavík*. It may be mentioned here, that last year (1881) a spacious stone building was
completed in which the Alþíng is for the future to deliberate,
hitherto that body has assembled in a large room in the College
('Latínuskóli'=Latin-school) at *Reykjavík*.

In 1848 a constitution was proclaimed for Denmark, and the
Icelanders petitioned that legislative powers should be restored to
the Alþíng. For many years the Danish Government refused to grant
this, but happily wiser counsel has prevailed and the King of
Denmark, Christian IX., wishing to commemorate the millennial
anniversary of the Norse colonisation of the island, signed a new
constitution for Iceland on the 5th January 1873, which was to

come into force on the 1st August the following year, when he himself visited the island, and, to the best of the author's belief, personally presented a deputation from the Alþíng with the new constitution, on the classic spot where the National Assembly formerly met at Þingvellir.

The most important features of this constitution, in the words of Herra Hjaltalín, are: 'Iceland is to have its own Legislature and administration for all local affairs. The legislative power is in the hands of the King and the National Assembly (Alþíng), and the executive in the hands of the King alone. So long as Iceland has no representatives in the Danish Rigsdag, it does not take part in legislating on general State affairs. On the other hand, it will not be required to contribute to the general State expenditure. There is to be a secretary for Iceland in Copenhagen, who is to be responsible for the maintenance of the constitution. This responsibility is to be further determined upon by legislation. The King appoints a governor for the island who is to carry on the government on the responsibility of the secretary in Copenhagen. His duties will be defined by the King. If the Alþíng complains of the governor, the King will determine how he is to be called to account. The Alþíng will consist of thirty members elected by the people, and six appointed by the King. It is to be divided into two houses—the upper and lower—the upper containing the six members appointed by the King, and six others elected from the general body of the Alþíng from among those of its members who have been sent to it by the constituencies. The Alþíng is to sit every other year.'

Herra Hjaltalín concludes: 'Although there are several objectionable points in this new constitution, it is on the whole a great improvement on the former schemes of the Danish government; and if it is worked in a fair spirit on both sides, it may become a blessing to the Icelanders and a credit to the Danes.' . . . 'We wish, however, that the old spirit and enterprising energy of its inhabitants may revive, so that they may successfully overcome the difficulties of their situation and long years of suffering.' . . . 'They must not any longer be absorbed in the contemplation of the past. They must not only educate themselves theoretically, as they do at present—and in this they are by no means behind any other nation in Europe—but they must also educate themselves practically; for in this respect they are sadly behind. Natural science, chemistry and political economy are almost unknown, and there is not a single architect or engineer in the whole island.

OUTLINE OF THE NJÁL SAGA. 65

They must also learn to be self-reliant, to make it clear to themselves that they cannot expect anything from others, and if they wish to thrive, they must do so with their own means.' . . . It is true 'Iceland has indeed many disadvantages. The large number of volcanic outlets have rendered extensive tracts uninhabitable. Thousands of square miles are covered with glaciers and snow-fields: and when the Polar ice comes drifting down upon the northern coasts, summer is turned into winter. In spite of these drawbacks, Iceland is not uninhabitable, if the resources of the island are properly worked and developed, which they are not. There are excellent pastures which if properly used might feed several times the number of sheep and ponies that are now on the island; while the sea round the coasts might be an unexhaustible mine of wealth, if the fisheries were not carried on in the most primitive fashion.'

THE NJÁL SAGA.

SIR GEORGE WEBBE DASENT, in his introduction to his admirable English version of the above, says:—'The Icelandic Sagas, narrating the lives, and feuds, and ends of mighty chiefs, the heads of the great families, were told by men who lived on the very spot, and told with a minuteness and exactness, as to time and place, that will bear the strictest examination. Such a story is that of Njál. Of all the Sagas, relating to Iceland, this tragic story bears away the palm for truthfulness and beauty!' It also abounds in rare pathos, and it is impossible to read this old-world story, which in the days 'lang syne' was handed down from one Sagateller to another, and 'told at all great gatherings of the people, and over many a fireside, on sea strand or river bank, or up among the dales and hills,' without feeling a strong desire to visit the spots where the stirring incidents recorded occurred, and those that figured therein resided.

The author of 'Six Weeks in the Saddle,' Mr. S. E. Waller, tells us in the introduction to his very readable little work:—'It was "Burnt Njál" that was at the bottom of it (his visit to Iceland). I had gone through Dr. Dasent's admirable version of the book with the very deepest interest, and was wild to visit the scene of such a tremendous tragedy.'

In Route 2 is laid down a tour to the most interesting of the spots mentioned in 'The Njál Saga'; and notwithstanding that it is unlikely any one will contemplate a pilgrimage through 'the Njál country' who has not read Dasent's version, a brief outline

of the main facts and incidents will be given, as, besides making
Route 2 intelligible, it may beguile an hour of unavoidable idleness,
or prove of interest to those contemplating a tour in Iceland
who have never even heard of 'The Story of Burnt Njál,' and
possibly lead them to read it before leaving England. Its perusal,
the author feels confident, will induce some of those who at first
merely purposed making a tour to the sights *de rigeur* to extend
it into the Njál country.

NJÁL ÞÓRGEIRSSON, the hero of the Saga, was born about the
middle of the tenth century. He was a 'Lögsögumaðr' (see *ante*),
and was a man wonderfully well acquainted with the laws and
customs of the land, and was held in high repute by his con-
temporaries. Njál's home was *Bergþórshvoll* (Bergthora's-knoll),
a farm situated on the southernmost point of the largest of the
Utlandeyjar (Outermost-isles, see map). When the story commences, he dwelt there with his wife Bergþóra, three sons
and three daughters. Njál himself was a very peaceable man ;
not so his sons, Skarphedinn, Helgi, and Grímr, and a friend of
theirs, Kári, who plays a most conspicuous part in the concluding
tragedies.

Njál had a 'true fast' friend, by name Gunnar, a noble-hearted
man, whose only fault was his over-readiness to give a blow when
angered. He has been termed 'the Bayard of Iceland, for whom
in goodness of heart, strength of body and skill in arms, no man
was ever a match in Iceland.' He resided at *Hlíðarendi* (Lithe-
end), a farm about twenty miles N.E. of *Bergþórshvoll.* Unfor-
tunately he had a wife 'with the form and beauty of an angel and
the mind of a fiend,' by name Hallgerða. As she was the exciting
cause of most of the bloodshed that follows, she claims to be
introduced at some length.

She was the daughter of a man named Höskuld, living at
Höskuldstaðir (*staðir* = stead), on the banks of the *Laxá* falling
into the *Hvammsfjörðr* (Coombe-fjord) in the west. He had a
brother, Hrútr, living close by. Hallgerða, when but a girl,
was tall and very fair to look upon, with hair as soft as silk
reaching to her waist. She had a 'wicked eye' and evil heart,
however, and this Hrútr, who seems to have been gifted with
great powers of perception, discovered when she was quite a child.
Her father one day asked Hrútr :—

'"What dost thou think of this maiden? Is she not fair?"

'Hrútr held his peace. Höskuld said the same thing to him a
second time, and then Hrútr answered :—

'"Fair enough is this maid, and many will smart for it; but this I know not, whence thief's eyes have come into our race."

'Then Höskuld was wroth, and for a time the brothers saw little of each other.'

Hrútr's prophecy was but too fully verified. In A.D. 955, her father, being tired of her at home, gave her, when but fifteen years of age, in marriage to a man named Þórvaldr, who survived his unfortunate union but a year; for the axe of Hallgerða's foster-father, Þiostólfr, at her instigation, put an end to husband No. One. She shortly after married again, a man named Glum, and he also fell under Þiostólfr's axe. We shall next hear of her as Gunnar's wife; but two more of the *dramatis personæ* must be first introduced: Mord, whose surname was Fiddle, and his only daughter, Unna, a fair, courteous and gifted woman, who was thought 'the best match in the Wrong-river valleys.' Mord dwelt near the *Rangá* (Wrong-river). He was a son of Sigvat the Red, and a mighty chief, and 'a great taker up of suits, and so great a lawyer that no judgments were thought lawful unless he had a hand in them.'

Unna became the wife of Hrútr, but she shortly after separated from him, and when her father died she took all the goods this wealthy man left behind him; but she was very lavish and unthrifty, so that her ready money and goods wasted away, and at last she had scarcely anything left but land and cattle.

Several chapters must be passed over, in which is told how Gunnar went a 'sea-roving' after compelling Hrútr to restore to Unna her dower; Unna's second wedding, and many other interesting incidents, graphically narrated, throwing light upon life in Iceland during the tenth century.

When Gunnar returned from his sea-roving, Hallgerða, with unbecoming boldness, came out to welcome him from the booths of her kinsmen, at that time encamped at Þingvellir, the Alþing being sitting. Gunnar was smitten by her beauty, proposed marriage against the advice of Njál, was accepted, and the marriage came off in due course.

All the intervening incidents must be passed over, until, in Chapter 35, we learn how Njál's wife made an enemy of this fiend in woman's form, Hallgerða. She and her husband visited Njál at *Bergþórshvoll*, from whom they received a hearty welcome. All went well until Helgi, Njál's son and his wife Þórhalla, came in. Then Bergþóra said to Hallgerða:—

'"Thou shalt give place to this woman."

'She answered:—"To no one will I give place, for I will not be driven into the corner by any one."

'"I shall rule here," said Bergþóra.

'After that Þórhalla sat down, and Bergþóra went round the table with water to wash the guests' hands. Then Hallgerða took hold of Bergþóra's hand, and maliciously said:—

'"There's not much to choose, though, between you two. Thou hast hangnails upon every finger, and Njál is beardless."

'"That's true," said Bergþóra; "yet neither of us finds fault with the other for it; but Þórvaldr, thy husband, was not beardless, yet thou plottedst his death."

'Then Hallgerða said, "It stands me in little stead to have the bravest man in Iceland if thou dost not avenge this, Gunnar!"

'He sprang up and strode across from the board, and said:— "Home I will go, and it were more seemly that thou should'st wrangle with those of thine own household, and not under other men's roofs; but as for Njál, I am his debtor for much honour, and never will I be egged on by thee like a fool."'

Upon the veriest trifle great events frequently hinge, is a truism, and this petty quarrel between two women not only resulted indirectly in the deaths of Gunnar, Njál and his wife and sons, and many of the noblest and bravest men in Iceland at that day, but at one time bade fair to bring about intestine war, most of the chief families espousing the cause of the Njál family or that of its enemies.

The first victim was Njál's 'house-carle,' Svart; Hallgerða's grieve, Kol, at her instigation, slew him while he was hewing wood in a tract of woodland owned in common by Njál and Gunnar. Bergþóra directed her new house-carle, Atli, to avenge Svart, and forthwith he slew Kol; and in turn was slain by Brýnjolfr the Unruly, a kinsman of Hallgerða's, by whom he was brought from the west to avenge the death of Kol. He fell next, and then Njál and Gunnar came to terms to secure peace between their households. Such a woman as Hallgerða, however, could not rest long out of mischief; and one day she said to Gunnar:—

'It is not good to be content with that hundred in silver, which thou tookest for my kinsman Brýnjolfr. I shall avenge him if I can': and notwithstanding that Gunnar himself warned Þórd—the foster-father of all Njál's sons, who had slain Brýnjolfr, he was attacked by two men, Sigmunðr and Skiolld—a third, `Þrain, standing by—and was killed.

Again Njál and Gunnar, as the heads of the two families, make peace, and Hallgerða will not let matters rest. At her suggestion Sigmunðr makes a poem, calling Njál 'the beardless carle,' and his sons 'dungbeardlings.' This is carried to the ears of Bergþpóra, and she tells her sons:—

'If ye do not take vengeance for this wrong, ye will avenge no shame.'

Njál's sons, at this taunt, lay in wait for Sigmunðr and Skiolld, and slew them; and Skarphedinn sent the head of Sigmunðr to Hallgerða with the message:—' She would know whether that head had made jeering songs about them.'

Peace was once more made between Gunnar and Njál; they were determined not to take arms the one against the other: but naturally, under circumstances so unfavourable for the maintenance of friendship, a coldness sprang up between these two worthy men.

Shortly after this, Gunnar was sadly disgraced by his wife. There was a dearth of provisions, and Hallgerða found a difficulty in obtaining food by purchase; accordingly she instructed one of her servants to steal. One day, upon Gunnar's return home, he noticed a quantity of provisions, and learnt that they had been stolen.

'Gunnar got wroth and said, "Ill indeed is it if I am a partaker with thieves;" and with that he gave her (his wife) a slap on the cheek.

'She said, "She would bear that slap in mind and repay it if she could."' And it was repaid in a fearful hour; it cost Gunnar his life, as we shall see in due course. These provisions had been stolen from *Kirkjubær* (Kirkby), the home of a man named Otkell, who does not appear to have been well disposed towards Gunnar. He first brought the latter before the Alþíng for the theft, and failing to obtain redress there, he subsequently galloped his horse through Gunnar's corn-field and rode over its owner himself, who was at work there at the time. The peaceful Gunnar took no notice of this insult, notwithstanding that Otkell made his boast over the country side—

'That he rode over Gunnar on his own ground, and that he shed tears like a child.'

These insults being taken so quietly, Otkell, with several companions, all armed, shortly afterwards set out for *Hlíðarendi*, bent on doing some injury to the place or its owner. The news that Otkell and a band of armed followers were approaching, was brought to Gunnar by a shepherd; and followed only by his brother, Kolskegg, he advanced to meet the party. A desperate conflict took place, which resulted in the death of Otkell, and his seven companions, at the hands of 'the man who shed tears like a child' when insulted, aided only by his brother.

This naturally led to a blood-feud between the relatives of the slain and Gunnar; and the following year at a horsefight (a popular amusement in those days) Gunnar, suspecting foul play towards his fighting horse, struck two men to the ground, and made more enemies. This began a fresh feud, and one of the assaulted, Starkaðr, determined to avail himself of the first favourable opportunity to take his revenge; accordingly, as Gunnar and his two brothers, Kolskegg and Hjort, were returning from a feast at *Túnga*, they were suddenly attacked, when near the Þríhyrningr (Three-horns) mountain, by Starkaðr and a band of thirty armed men. The three brothers, undaunted by the apparently overwhelming number of their assailants, fought so bravely that no less than fourteen of the latter bit the dust, when the survivors took to flight, exclaiming 'that they had to do with more than men.' Hjort, to Gunnar's great grief, fell in this conflict.

Otkell and Starkaðr having sons, it was only natural that they would seek to avenge the death of their respective fathers. Accordingly some three years later, Gunnar and Kolskegg, as they were returning from a visit to the south, were attacked by the sons of Otkell and Starkaðr, and twenty-three others. Gunnar and Kolskegg performed deeds of extraordinary valour that day, and defeated their assailants with great slaughter. Gunnar was summoned before the Alþíng, and the judges considering it somewhat extraordinary that he should be so constantly embroiled, sentenced him to banishment for three years. This sentence he disregarded, for he felt that he had been somewhat unjustly treated, and was loth to tear himself away from his home; and in consequence became an outlaw, whom it was lawful for any man to slay. One beautiful autumn evening Gunnar unexpectedly found *Hlíðarendi* surrounded by a great company of armed men. He would not have been thus surprised, had not his faithful Irish hound, Samr, been lured from the house by a neighbour who was on friendly terms with the faithful brute. The honest old hound's dying groan, however, awoke Gunnar in time to arm himself before his assailants were upon him. Bravely he fought for his life and homestead; arrow after arrow from his bow pierced man after man as they advanced up the slope to attack him; eight lay wounded and two dead, ere his opponents succeeded in making a breach in his stronghold, which they did by hauling the roof off with ropes: a sudden snap—his bowstring had been cut from behind by Þórbrand Þórleiksson, who had crawled along a rafter in his rear.

'Then Gunnar said to Hallgerða, "Give me two locks of thy hair, and ye too, my mother and thou, twist them together into a bowstring for me."

' "Does aught lie on it?" she says.

' "My life lies on it," he said; "for they will never come to close quarters with me if I can keep them off with my bow."

' "Well!" she says, "Now I will call to thy mind that slap on the face which thou gavest me; and I care never a whit whether thou holdest out a long while or a short." '

His foes closed in upon him; he wounded eight more, several unto death, and then, exhausted with wounds, he succumbed; and his dauntless spirit winged its way to Valhalla. His brave defence excited the admiration even of his enemies, and they interred him on the hill-side, and above his grave erected a cairn, which stands to this day. It is said that no man would enrich himself by despoiling his body, and that his armour and clothes, and even his golden ornaments, were placed beneath a huge block of lava.

With Gunnar's death the first fitte of the Saga ends. Of that portion the unfortunate Bayard of Iceland is rather the hero than Njál.

Skarphedinn, Njál's son, when he heard of the cowardly butchery of this brave old friend of his father, vowed to wreak a terrible vengeance; and well he kept his word; and right fraternally was he assisted by his brothers, Grímr and Helgi, and also by their friend Kári. Whenever these four men met with any of those who had had a hand in the death of Gunnar, they attacked and invariably slew them. Skarphedinn also slew Þrain, the man who stood by when Þórd, the foster-father of all Njál's sons, was killed by Sigmunðr and Skiolld, on the principle, we may suppose, 'that those who are not on our side must be against us.' The good-hearted Njál took no part whatever in these feuds, and did all that was possible to induce his sons to lead a peaceful life; he even took Þrain's son, Höskuld, as his foster-child. He in course of time became a Christian priest—the religion being then newly introduced, and Njál a convert—and in course of time married a young woman of good family, Hildigunna. Little did the kind-hearted Njál think when he befriended this fatherless boy that the act would add another brand to the burning which was to bring about his death, that of his wife and sons, and of some five-and-twenty members of his household.

A Pagan priest, Valgard, jealous of the spread of Christianity, was greatly embittered against all converts, especially the influential old law-giver, Njál, and his family; and he with great cunning matured a deep-laid scheme, which should not only bring about their destruction, but also the death of Höskuld, whom, being a Christian priest, he also hated. He was only too successful. He instructed his son, who was an acquaintance of Skarphedinn's, to urge on the latter that it was necessary for his own safety to slay Höskuld, as he was meditating Skarphedinn's destruction for having killed his father, þrain. The artful priest knew full well that if he could only bring about Höskuld's death at the hands of Njál's sons, his wife's powerful and warlike uncle, Flósi, would never rest until he had amply avenged him. After more than a year of intrigue, Skarphedinn was finally excited to protect himself from what was purely an imaginary danger, by killing Höskuld: the unfortunate priest being attacked and killed in his own corn-field by a party of five, Skarphedinn, his two brothers, Helgi and Grímr, Kári and Valgardsson.

An attempt was made to settle the feud, thus brought about, by law and the payment of blood money, but fruitlessly, as Valgard had foreseen would be the case with such a powerful and warlike man as Flósi: and terribly did the latter avenge the death of his niece's husband. He assembled one hundred and twenty men, and one night surrounded *Bergþórshvoll*, determined to take summary vengeance on Njál's three sons and Kári. Njál and his wife, the females of the household, were informed they might leave the house unmolested, but Njál declined to do so, and his wife refused to quit him. He said :—

'I will not go out, for I am an old man, and little fitted to avenge my sons, but I will not live on in shame.'

In those days revenge was a duty and a right, and a man preferred death at the hands of his enemies rather than swear an oath to forego revenge; therefore to Njál death was preferable to living on without the power to avenge his sons.

So dauntless were the besieged, that the assailants found it impossible to force an entrance into the house, and finally they piled the peat and haystacks up against its walls and set fire to them. Njál, perceiving that death was inevitable, lay down with his wife and a little child upon a bed, and dragged an oxhide over them; and beneath this they were found dead, but unburnt, when a search was made among the ruins of the house. A brave defence was made by the sons of Njál and the house-carles, but all three of the former perished. Helgi attempted to escape in woman's clothes, but was detected and slain. Kári was the only male who made good his escape. Under cover of the smoke, with his clothing in flames, he first got on to the roof and thence to the ground, when he ran down-wind to a little tarn wherein he extinguished his flaming garments.

The news of the burning—it is known and spoken of as 'the burning' to this day—of *Bergþórshvoll*, and the slaughter of Njál, with his wife and sons, spread like wildfire over the whole island, and a strong party of the friends of the late lawgiver determined to avenge their deaths. At the next meeting of the Alþíng the friends of Njál made an attempt to bring the men who had burned *Bergþórshvoll* to justice, but failing in this, they thereupon attacked and, although inferior in numbers, defeated the 'burners' in a desperate fight at *Þingvellir*. The conduct of a very powerful Christian priest at this juncture is rather amusing, and must be noticed, though this outline of the Saga is running to a great length. He could not be persuaded to take up arms for or against either party; but he agreed with the 'Njálites' that he and his strong band of armed followers would hold the pass from the 'Thing-fields' through the gap in the eastern wall of the *Almannagjá*, and should the Njálites be defeated—as they were likely to be, being greatly inferior in numbers—he would allow them to pass through, and then prevent their enemies from following them; but should the Njálites get the upper hand, and the opposite party try to escape to the rift, he would not allow them to do so until he thought a sufficient number of them had been slain to atone for the death of Njál, his family and people. As said, the Njálites got the upper hand, and, as foreseen, Flósi and his followers sought to flee to the natural fortress of the *Almannagjá*, but were turned back by the priest's followers into the hands of their victorious assailants, and being demoralised, great was the slaughter.

This conflict bade fair to bring about an universal civil war, as members of a number of the most powerful families were killed; but ultimately matters were settled by payment of blood-fines in some instances, and by the banishment for various periods of the survivors of those who had taken an active part in the 'burning,' and the affray at *Þingvellir*. One man, however, determined that only with his life, or the death of all the survivors of those who had a hand in the death of his old friends, Njál and his sons, should the blood-feud cease. This was Kári, a man 'thorough' enough to have pleased the author of 'Guy Livingstone.' He followed the survivors, who were outlawed, through many countries, and no less than fifteen fell to his hand. Space cannot be spared here to mention more than one of the many bold acts by which this very ample vengeance was taken.

On Christmas day, A.D. 1013, Kári strode into the banqueting-hall of Sigurðr, the great Earl of Orkney, and without looking to the right or to the left, or uttering a word, smote off the head of one of Flósi's band, and walked off unharmed, notwithstanding the command of the Earl that he should be followed and slain.

The next year fifteen of the 'burners' perish in a battle in Ireland, and Flósi and the remainder of his followers rest awhile in Wales, where Kári follows them and slays the worst of all the band, Kolþórsteinsson. With this deed 'the measure of Kári's wrath is full,' and he determines to forego further revenge, notwithstanding that Flósi is still living. He sets out for Rome to obtain absolution; and subsequently returns to Iceland, but is wrecked on *Ingólfshöfði* (Ingólfs-head), at Flósi's very door. He seeks a dwelling-house, the door is opened by Flósi; and the shipwrecked man and the foe he has followed for years to slay are reconciled. After a thorough atonement, Kári marries Hildigunna the Proud, and lives happily. In his old age Flósi is lost at sea; and 'The Story of Burnt Njál' is brought to a conclusion by the mention of this incident.

There are a number of highly-interesting historical events recorded in the Saga; but as the most important were mentioned in the preceding Historical Notice, there was no need to repeat them in this outline of the Saga.

CHAPTER III.

NOTES ON SPORT;

AND

A LIST OF SALMON RIVERS AND CHIEF TROUT STREAMS.

SHOOTING.

ICELAND IS THE NURSERY of a great variety of birds which, although not classed as game, are eagerly sought after in winter by English sportsmen when they have migrated to our shores. The chief of these are swans—the hooper (*Cygnus ferus*, Ray); geese—the grey-lag (*Anser ferus*, Steph.), the bean-goose (*A. Segetum*, Steph.), and the pink-footed goose (*A. brachyrhynchus*, Baillon); a variety of ducks, the eider (*Somateria mollisima*, Leach)—which must not be shot—the mallard (*Anas Boschas*, Linn.), king-duck (*Somateria spectabilis*, Leach), harlequin-duck (*Anas histrionica*, Linn.), teal (*A. Crecca*, Linn.), and a number of others; curlew, chiefly whimbrel (*Numenius Phæopus*, Lath.); golden-plover (*Charadrius pluvialis*, Linn.); and snipe, both the single (*Scolopax Gallinago*, Linn.) and double (*S. major*, Gmel.).

These birds are met with in the northern parts of Iceland till the end of August, the curlew, plover, and ducks in vast numbers; the two first named on the moors and in the fens, and the latter, save the eider-duck, also in the fens, and on the shores and islands of lakes, and in the still reaches of rivers. In the north, even in the first week in September, hardly a curlew or a plover is to be seen, these birds being the earliest of the migrants; the ducks take flight a fortnight or so later. In the south-western part of the island both curlew and plover are to be found in some numbers up till the middle of September, and the ducks for some three weeks longer. Woodcock, it is believed, are never seen in Iceland, at least the author has never heard of, or shot, one. Neither has he ever fallen in with geese, but in the valley of the *Skjalfanda-*

fljót and that of the *Jökulsá*, falling into the *Axarfjör'ŏr*, and on *Ljósavatn* and the *Svartárvatn*; but he is informed they are frequently seen in large flocks on the *Fiskivötn*, on the *Arnarvatn-sheiði* in the north-west, and on the *Lagarfljót*, in the east. Swans are far more common than geese, and are frequently seen early in August on all the larger lakes: the author once shot two on *Mývatn*, where these birds and geese only may be shot.

The bird that affords most sport is a variety of the grouse family, called in Icelandic Rjúpa, and in Danish Ryper. The author has said *a* variety, but there is little doubt there are three varieties, the ptarmigan (*Lagopus alpina*, Linn.), identical with the Norwegian Fjeld-ryper, the willow-grouse (*L. subalpina*, Nilss.), identical with the Norwegian Dal- or Scov-ryper, and a hybrid produced by the interbreeding of these birds. It is but seldom now that a bird of pure blood is fallen in with, the major part of the birds subsisting on the island being hybrids. In the wooded valley of the *Fnjóská*, and some other low-lying sheltered tracts overgrown with birch and willow scrub, a few of the willow-grouse are still to be found, and on the mountains in the interior a covey of true ptarmigan may yet be fallen in with. The majority of the birds that will fall to the sportsman's gun are undoubtedly hybrid, for the full-grown birds will be found, on examination by any one who has shot ptarmigan and willow-grouse in Norway, to be but little, if any, larger than the former, and yet have a plumage closely akin to that of the latter.

This interbreeding has probably been brought about in the following manner. Whenever one of the cold summers, caused by the settlement of Polar ice within a short distance of the Icelandic coast, has succeeded an unusually severe winter—as occurred as recently as last year (1881), the greater number of the ptarmigan which had come down from the mountains to the low ground for shelter did not return, but remained and interbred with their near relatives, the willow-grouse. That interbreeding is the true cause of the difference in the size and appearance of the Icelandic ryper from the two varieties found in Norway is, the author thinks, almost conclusively proved by the habits of the major part of the birds of this genus found at the present time in Iceland. They chiefly breed on sunny slopes at some elevation, where the snow melts earlier than in far less elevated and sheltered situations, as the ptarmigan do in the north of Norway on, and just south and north of, the Arctic Circle, and not on the low-lying tracts overgrown with birch and willow, raised but little above sea-level, as do the willow-grouse in that country in the same latitudes. The ptarmigan there, however, take their young ones, as soon as they are able to flutter, *up* to the summits of the fjelds, while in Iceland the birds, which the author believes to be hybrids, conduct their young families *down* to the low-lying tracts and less elevated moors. The willow-grouse in Arctic Norway are never found on the mountainous fjelds; but the hybrid birds of Iceland, when it happens that their plumage becomes light-coloured before the low-lying grounds are covered with snow, ascend to the snow-line of the mountains, and, broadly speaking, are only to be found there at such times. The exception is when the moors, where the birds have been in August, lie in the vicinity of lava-beds, for in that case many of the birds seek shelter among the rugged, piled-up and distorted masses of igneous rock. In August last year (1881) the moors around *Ljósavatn*, about 500 feet above sea-level, were alive with grouse; in September not a bird was to be shot on them, nor on the neighbouring fjelds at a less elevation than 2,000 feet, where there were patches of snow. This looks as if the willow-grouse instinct surviving in the hybrids teaches them that better and more palatable food is to be found on the low-lands, so they go there, while the surviving ptarmigan instinct teaches them that when their plumage begins to lighten there is greater safety on the snow-clad mountains, than on the 'bonny brown moors' and in among the scrub, so they do what the true willow-grouse never do as far north in Norway, betake themselves to the mountains. Here they remain, following the snow-line downward until the plains are covered with snow, when they seek sheltered low-lying localities.

The question will not be entered into more fully here, a guide-book being hardly the proper place to discuss it; and the reader of ornithological tastes is referred to 'The Field' of the 5th July, 1879, where, in a short paper entitled 'Notes on Iceland,' the author entered into it somewhat fully; and, it appears, proved to the satisfaction of the Icelandic ornithologists the existence of three varieties, for this is now pretty generally admitted by them to be the case, though in 1878 it was denied. At that time but one variety was recognised, and it was a disputed point whether the Icelandic bird was identical or not with either of the Norwegian ryper; and stuffed specimens in the Museum at *Reykjavik* were labelled *Tetrao Islandicus*. However, what the author has written here will be of service to sportsmen, as it shows where, under certain conditions, they are likely to find grouse.

A few words descriptive of the birds must be given. Most Englishmen are familiar with the so-called ptarmigan from Norway sold in poultry shops in winter; these are chiefly willow-grouse in their winter plumage, only the smaller full-grown birds being true ptarmigan, and fifty of the former come to England to one of the latter. The willow-grouse is one-third larger than the ptarmigan, has a thicker beak, and, it is said, the fifth wing-feather of both sexes is always longer than the second, while in the ptarmigan it is always shorter; both varieties become white in winter, save their tail feathers, and are then only distinguishable by these peculiarities. In summer and early autumn the plumage of the cock willow-grouse is a beautiful dark reddish-brown—that of the hen yellowish brown, both having black tail and white wing feathers. The ptarmigan of both sexes are at the same period bluish-grey mottled with black, but the hen's plumage has a somewhat yellower tinge than the cock's with tail and wing feathers of the same colour as those of the willow-grouse. The full-grown hybrid birds found in Iceland, as before said, are but little, if any, larger than the ptarmigan, yet the plumage of both sexes, especially of the cock birds, resembles in a very marked degree that of the willow-grouse, except that the feathers on the back are of a much darker brown, approaching a chocolate colour. The wing-feathers of the three varieties are at all times white.

In the month of August grouse are found more or less numerous on all the moors, the lower fjeld slopes, and old moss-covered lava-beds in Iceland. The author, speaking from personal experience, recommends the following localities to the sportsman. In the north-east, the *Hvammsheiði*, south of *Húsavík*; the moors west of the *Skjalfandafljót*, from Þingey southward for eight miles; also the vast extent of moorland on the east, between that river and *Mývatn*; the valleys on the *west* of the volcanic range north of *Reykjahlíð*; the extensive moors around *Svartárkot*; and the moors on the north coast around *Garðr*. In the north-west, the author is only personally acquainted with two places, the moors north-west of the *Laxárvatn*, and those east of *Borg*, south of the *Hóp*. It is said, and the author believes with truth, that the *Víðidalsfjall*, west of the *Vatnsdal*, is one of the best places in all Iceland for grouse. Route 3 will conduct the sportsman to all the places mentioned. However, the best and most economical plan, owing to the difficulty and cost of transporting heavy baggage about, is to select one of the localities mentioned, and, after visiting the 'lions' in the south, take the Danish steamer from *Reykjavík* to the nearest trading post, and proceed thence direct to the shooting ground selected. In the south, the author has only shot in the vicinity of Þingvellir, and in the lava-beds between the capital and *Hafnarfjörðr*, and in neither place was game abundant in October. In August, however, it is said that the sunken plain at Þingvellir is literally alive with grouse, and the author believes this to be the case, and that when he was there, the ground being bare of snow, the birds were on the mountains.

For wildfowl shooting, the *Fiskivötn* on the *Arnarvatnsheiði* (Route 3) are spoken of as the best place in all Iceland, though it is possible the scatter of lakes bearing the same name a few miles west of the *Skaptár Jökull* are equally as good. Ducks may be shot in any river where they do not breed in any great numbers, but where they do so in the vicinity of farms is generally a proclaimed 'egg ground,' and it is not allowed to shoot ducks in such localities. This is the case on *Mývatn* and in several places on the *Laxá* flowing therefrom. The valley of the *Jökulsá*, north of the *Dettifoss*, is the most likely place the author is acquainted with for geese; and an eagle or a falcon is generally to be seen near the islands chosen by the *Anser* genus as breeding grounds. Duck, curlew, plover and grouse are said to be very plentiful in the *Mýrarsýsla* (Fen-county) in the west, just north of the *Borgarfjörðr* (Routes 3 and 4). Also in the east, in the valley of the *Lagarfljót*, and the author believes that on some of the moors in this district grouse are very plentiful indeed, for he is informed that a great number are shipped off from *Seyðisfjörðr* every autumn. The author has never found snipe very numerous anywhere in his travels, a brace in the course of a day's grouse shooting, now and then, being all that he has ever bagged.

REINDEER.—These animals are not indigenous to Iceland, but are the descendants of a small herd brought from Norway. There are three herds known to exist on the island, and it is possible there is a fourth. Each herd has a separate habitat; the largest herd, numbering about 200, is chiefly found on the fjelds south-west of the *Lagarfljót* and north of the eastern *Snæfell;* but these deer, or another herd, sometimes pay a visit to a smaller herd that has chosen a home among the mountain range north and south of *Krafla*. The third herd, which now numbers about a score only, is found in the range of volcanoes running N.E. from *Krisuvík*, in the south, to Þingvallavatn.

SEALS.—The *Phocæ* are very numerous on many parts of the coast, and are private property. They are usually caught in nets, as this does not disturb the 'ground' so much as shooting them would. Before shooting at one, be sure and obtain the permission of the owner of the shore, as very heavy penalties are recoverable for disturbing a man's 'proclaimed' seal-ground. Many farmers, on whose foreshore seals are only occasionally seen, readily give permission for one to shoot at these aquatic mammals, while others will not permit a gun to be fired within a mile of their seal-ground upon any account.

Neither hares nor rabbits are found in Iceland.

ANGLING.

THE TROUT FISHING in Iceland is remarkably good in nearly all the rivers that do not drain glaciers; but, as stated in the introductory remarks, no salmon fishing, worth a journey to Iceland for the sole purpose of obtaining it, is procurable without renting a river or buying the nets off a portion of one. The following 'List of Salmon Rivers' was, in somewhat different words, originally contributed by the author to 'The Field,' and by the gracious permission of the publisher of that paper is here reproduced, with some additional information.

LIST OF SALMON RIVERS AND CHIEF TROUT STREAMS.

ELLIÐAÁR (Ellidi—a famous Víking war-ship—river). This river issues from a lake, the *Elliðavatn*, distant about three hours' ride from *Reykjavik*, and falls into a deep indentation of the *Faxafjörðr*, but a few miles from the capital. All the fishery rights are claimed by Herra Thomsen, a merchant living at *Reykjavik*, and he allows English tourists to fish at the by no means moderate charge of ten *kroner* (= 11s. 3d.) per diem. The best water for rod-fishing can be reached in an hour and a half's ride from either of the hotels, therefore anglers can sleep there, riding out to the river in the morning and returning late at night. But the better plan, early morn being the best time for fishing, would be to hire a room at the house, half-farm half-inn, on the eastern bank of the river near the ford; but as half-inn in Iceland does not promise much in the way of cleanliness or comfort, it would be well for the anglers to bring their own beds, potted provisions, etc.

The salmon in the *Elliðaár* run very small, one weighing 10lbs. being a rarity. The coastal indentation at the mouth of the river swarms with sea-trout at times. In one week, in July, 1878, the farmer living at *Gravarvaug* caught over 2,000 lbs. weight of sea-trout and salmon. It is said there is good trout fishing in the lake, but the author is inclined to the belief that only char are found there. If so, it is doubtful whether they will take artificial flies.

THE SOUTHERN HVÍTÁ (White-river).—This is a large river, and, as usual with all such in Iceland, is a *Jökulsá—i.e.* fed by glacier water. Naturally, the waters of such rivers are too cold and turbid to be the haunts of the Salmonidæ, and therefore they are fishless streams, save when they have tributaries fed from other sources; as when such is the case the salmon—the author is not sure whether sea-trout do so, or not—brave the turbid milky-white water of the lower reaches of the rivers, and make their way to the tributaries, in whose clear water they can find congenial quarters. About twenty-five miles from the debouchure of the *Hvítá* the river makes a sharp bend, and receives several tributaries, the two easternmost of which are said to be good salmon rivers. The smaller of these, the one nearest the main channel, is named *Minni Laxá* (Lesser Salmon-river) and the easternmost the *Stærra Laxá* (Greater Salmon-river). The best houses at which quarters are obtainable are *Gröf* farm and *Hruni* parsonage. In every case in Iceland the permission of the owner of the land, upon which it will be necessary to go to fish, must be obtained ere wetting a line. At the present time, with but few exceptions, it is readily accorded upon the bulk of the fish being handed over to the farmer owning the land abutting on that part of the stream where they were caught. It will be as well to offer to pay for the fish reserved for the angler's own consumption, but in most instances no payment will be taken. Both *Gröf* and *Hruni* are distant two longish days' ride from the capital *viâ Þingvellir* (See Route 1). Several parties of Englishmen are said to have had good sport both in the *Minni* and *Stærra Laxá*.

THE LAXÁ FALLING INTO THE HVALFJÖRÐR (Whale-fjord).—Distant one day's journey from the capital; good quarters at *Reynivellir* parsonage. Nothing is known by the author of the sport to be had in this *Laxá*. It is, however, worth a visit, as it lies *en route* to the two rivers which bear the name of being the best salmon rivers in Iceland, though he believes they are excelled by the northern *Laxá* near *Húsavík*.

THE LAXÁ FALLING INTO THE LEIRÁRVOGAR (? Lair-river-voes).—A small river unvisited by the author. An excursion can be made to this *Laxá* from *Reynivellir* parsonage by riding to *Hals* farm, thence by boat across the Whale-fjord, whence a walk of five or six miles will bring the angler to its banks. Should it be found worthy of a sojourn of several days, the guide could be sent back to *Reynivellir* to bring round the ponies and baggage.

GRIMSÁ AND NORÐRÁ—Two tributaries of the Western *Hvitá*, a large river falling into the *Borgarfjörðr* (Burg-fjord). Like the southern river of the same name it is a *Jökulsá*, and the remarks respecting the ascent of salmon in that river apply likewise to this. The *Norðrá*, as its name implies, is the northernmost, and it is also the largest of the two tributaries, and bears the name of being the best salmon river in all Iceland. The catch was so large in 1877 that Mr. Ritchie, a Scotch fish merchant, thought it would pay to have a steam launch running between the mouth of the *Hvitá* and *Reykjavik*, and accordingly he had one there in 1878, when the author was at the capital. The author's guide in the south that year was a native of this part of the island, and earlier in the summer he had accompanied a party of Englishmen who had fair sport in these rivers. They were also by the author's advice visited in 1880 by Capt. M., Royal Artillery, and the author was told by the Captain of the Camoens, by which vessel he returned, that he caught twenty-seven salmon. The best farm at which to stay to fish the *Grimsá* is *Hvitárvellir*, owned by a farmer named Andreas, who speaks English, and is willing to accommodate visitors. To fish the *Norðrá*, the best farm at which to seek quarters would be *Þverá*, the residence of Jón Norðtúnga, who is also, it is said, very obliging to English sportsmen. Either of these farms can be reached in one day from *Reynivellir*. A few miles farther up the valley the *Hvitá* receives another tributary, the *Þverá*, which the author's guide said is worth a trial in cold summers, when the water in the main river is clearer than in warm ones, and the salmon consequently ascend to tributaries more distant from the sea than they do when the river is in full flood, with milk-white turbid water from the glaciers. The *Þverá* is a good trout stream, it is said.

North-west of the *Borgarfjörðr*, three largish streams, the *Lángá* (Long-river), *Álftá* (? Swan-river), and the *Hitá* (Hot-river), enter the sea; but, when questioned by the author, his guide said, although he had been in all three of the valleys through which the streams flow, he had never heard that the farmers in either valley caught any salmon, and therefore concluded that none were caught. Excursions can be made up the valley of the *Hvitá* to the *Fiskivötn*, mentioned when treating of shooting, which abound in trout and waterfowl. (See Routes 3 and 4.)

THE LAXÁ FALLING INTO THE STRAUMFJARÐAR O's (Stream-fjords Outlet).—The O's is a peculiar-shaped inlet on the south coast of the promontory terminating in Snæfells Jökull. This Laxá is a small but good salmon river, and is distant about one and a half days' journey from the farms on the Norðrá and Grímsá, and four from Reykjavik. Good accommodation at Miklaholt parsonage. It is but a day's journey hence to the famous basaltic caverns at Stapi, and likewise to Stykkishólmr, a trading town on the Breiðifjörðr, at which the Danish steamers call. (Route 3.)

THE LAXÁ FALLING INTO THE HVAMMSFJÖRÐR (Coombe-fjord).— This river is distant but four hours' ride from Borðeyri, a trading post at the head of the Hrútafjörðr (? Hrútr's-fjord), a day's journey from Stykkishólmr, and five days' from the capital. Several very fair farms in the valley. An English angler tried this river in the summer of 1878, but the author did not hear with what result. The Camoens occasionally calls at Borðeyri, but the Danish steamers do not call—at least they have not hitherto.

One day's journey south of Borðeyri lie numerous lakes, which are so abundantly stocked with char and trout that they are named Fiskivötn, Anglicè Fish Lakes. They can also be visited, as previously mentioned, vid the valley of the Hvitá, by proceeding up the valley of the Norðrá, and also through the Reykholtsdalr. (See Route 3.) There are no farms within many miles of the lakes, nor boats thereon; therefore a party of sportsmen would need a tent, and a Berthon folding-boat would greatly increase the sport they would have. Grouse are said to be very numerous in 'good Rjúpa years' on the Arnarvatnsheiði, the moor around the lakes, while the latter are the breeding grounds of a variety of water-fowl; and also, in the latter end of July and early part of August, are much frequented by swans. A party of sportsmen, selecting this portion of the island for a sporting ground, should make Borðeyri their head-quarters, arrange for a room with the farmer at either Hvammr or Dýrastaðir, two farms in the upper part of the valley of the Norðrá, and camp out on the moors in fine weather, retreating to the farm should they encounter a spell of bad weather. By arranging thus, salmon fishing could be had in the Norðrá, and trout fishing in the lakes, during the month of July, and swan, wild-duck and grouse shooting during the month of August.

MIÐFJARÐRÁ (Mid-fjord-river).—A river in which a considerable number of salmon are annually caught, but no rod-fishing is obtainable without buying off the nets. The pastor at Melstaðr

(Meal-stead) and the farmer at *Reykir* (respectively five and four miles from the fjord) so effectually stop the ascent of the fish, that the pastor at *Staðarbakki*, a mile or two above *Melstað*r, had not caught a single salmon in 1880, when the author visited the river. The pastor and farmer at the two places first mentioned own respectively the land on the west and east side of the lower reaches of the river, and divide the fishing by using their nets on alternate days; and the river not being deep, the *modus operandi* is to drag down-stream from about 'half-flood' and meet the fish running up with the incoming tide. The night that the author stayed at *Reykir* it was the farmer's turn to fish, and he caught eleven fine salmon, and three grilse of about 5 lbs. Up to this date, 26th July, 1880, he had caught 202 salmon, and the pastor at *Melstaðr* had caught about the same number. *Melstaðr* is one day's ride from *Borðeyri*; two from *Sauðdkrókr*, a trading post at the head of the *Skagafjörðr*, called at by the Danish steamers; four from *Akureyri*, and about a week from the capital. (Routes 3 and 4.)

VÍÐIDALSÁ (Wooded-valley-river).—A day's ride east of the *Miðfjarðrá*. Salmon are very numerous in this river, but are very capricious, and it is believed that none have ever been caught with the artificial fly. The author one evening carefully fished a pool that was literally full of salmon and did not get a fish. The net five minutes after he ceased fishing brought to land sixteen large salmon. Very comfortable quarters indeed at *Borg*, whose owner, Pétr Christophersson, speaks capital English, and is a very genial, hospitable man. Trout are to be caught in the upper waters of the river, and in a tributary flowing from the *Vestrahópsvatn*. Good grouse, curlew, and plover shooting in the neighbourhood.

VATNSDALSÁ (Lake-valley-river).—Two hours' ride east of *Borg*. Arrangements have been made with the farmers owning the best stretches of water on this river for the sole right of fishing.

LÁXA FROM THE LAXÁRVATN.—A small stream a few miles east of the last-named river. It is well stocked with salmon in those years when the summer is not exceptionally dry. The pastor at *Hjaltabakki* catches a great many salmon every year, and the farmer at *Syðrnes*, not far from the *Laxárvatn*, also catches a few. There is said to be excellent trout-fishing in that lake, and likewise in the *Svinavatn*, a few miles off. Grouse plentiful in this neighbourhood in August. For fishing the lakes, *Auðkúla* parsonage would be the most comfortable quarters; and for the river, *Hjaltabakki*.

BLANDA (Bland).—A large river falling into the *Húnafjörðr* (Bearcub-fjord). Salmon are never seen in this river until September, and but few then; it being glacier-fed and its water in summer as white as milk. In the *Svartá* (Black-river), tributary to this river, trout and char are to be caught. There is a trading post and inn at the mouth of the *Blanda*, but the Danish steamers do not call.

A LAXÁ falls into the *Húnafjörðr* about six miles north-east of the debouchure of the *Blanda*. Salmon have not been caught in this river for some years, but the author cannot help thinking that a fish or two are to be found in the pools below the bridge. Trout up to 8 lbs. in weight have been caught in the stream flowing through the *Hallardalr*, a valley about five miles north of the *Laxá*

Os LAXÁ.—A few hours' ride due north of the river last mentioned will bring the angler to this small but, it is said, well-stocked salmon river. This is the only *Laxá* in the north that was not visited by the author. Midway up the fjord is *Skagaströnd* trading post, where the Danish steamers call.

THE LAXÁ FALLING INTO THE SKAGAFJÖRÐR.—A fair-sized stream, but the salmon have been utterly exterminated by netting. A good day's trout fishing is obtainable, however, and some excellent duck, curlew and plover shooting.

THE LAXÁ FALLING INTO THE SKJÁLFANDI 'BUGT' (Shivering or Shimmering Bay).—In the author's opinion the best salmon river in Iceland, though, as before said, the *Norðrá* in the west has the credit of being superior. The waters belonging to three farms on this river were taken on lease for five years by two Englishmen in 1878; but the author believes the lease has been thrown up; at any rate no one has been on the waters leased for the last two summers. The lessees only caught six salmon, it is said, in 1879; whereas in the two previous years they caught respectively seventy-five and sixty-eight fish. This would be a splendid river for salmon fishing for any one who could afford to buy the nets and traps off the lower waters belonging to the farmer at *Laxármýri*, who now catches 999 out of every 1,000 fish that enter the river. Excellent trout fishing obtainable under the falls abreast of *Grenjaðarstaðr*, and also in the upper waters, especially among the islands about a mile from the river's outlet from *Mývatn*.

LAXÁ, S.E. OF THE VATNA JÖKULL.—It is said salmon are caught in a tributary to a *Jökulsá*, draining the *Vatna*, that falls into the *Papafjörðr* near *Lónsvik*. Quite unknown to the author.

This closes the list of salmon rivers that the author has visited or heard of during three summers in Iceland. It is possible that on the east coast there may be one or two streams in which salmon are caught—the *Lagarfljót* would be a likely one, but it is doubtful, for in three voyages to *Seyðisfjörðr*, one to *Eskifjörðr* and *Vopnafjörðr*, the three chief trading posts in the east, the author never saw any salmon brought to the steamers for sale, pretty conclusive evidence, he thinks, that not many are caught in the rivers in this part of the island.

TROUT STREAMS.—The *Sog*, draining Þingvallavatn; the *Brúará*, tributary to the southern *Hvítá* (Route 1); the stream draining the *Skorradalsvatn*, in the west (Route 4); the Þverá, tributary to the western *Hvítá*; the *Haukadalsá*, falling into the *Hvammsfjörðr* (Routes 3 and 4); the *Svartá*, tributary to the *Héraðsvötn* falling into the *Skagafjörðr* (Route 3); the *Svartá*, tributary to the *Blanda* (Route 3); the *Hörgá*, and the lower part of the *Fnjóská*, respectively west and east of the *Eyjafjörðr* (Route 3); and the *Svartá* from *Svartárvatn* in the interior. There are doubtless many others, for it is said that every stream having its source in a lake, or fed by feeders from one, abounds in trout or char, unless the water is impregnated with mineral matters from thermal springs or noxious volcanic deposits.

Two kinds of trout are caught, pink-fleshed and white, besides the sea-trout. The latter caught by the author have run very small, six ounces to half a lb. being the largest, but the river and lake trout run large, 2 lbs. to 4 lbs. being common, while one up to 7 lbs. is not a rarity. Char are numerous and run large in the lakes, up to 8 lbs., but seldom, if ever, take artificial lures. In the rivers, on the contrary, char seldom exceed 2 lbs. in weight, and greedily take artificial flies. In 'The Home of the Eddas,' a recently published work on Iceland, we find (p. 312) red char described as ' sea-trout, or salmon-trout '!! and are informed that they ' swarm in every lake, pool, and stream, except those fed directly by glacier water.' To this piece of original information, it would have been well if the author, who poses as a very learned and critical · individual, had described how the ' red char (sea-trout, or salmon-trout)' ascend the river falls to reach the lakes lying at a considerable altitude, where the red char are found in great numbers.

CHAPTER IV.

THE CAPITAL; AND EXCURSIONS IN ITS VICINITY.

REYKJAVÍK, the capital of Iceland, has a population of about 4,000. It is pleasantly situated on the shore of a shallow bay on the north of a headland, *Seltjarnarnes* (Seal-tarn-naze), jutting in a north-westerly direction for about eight miles into the wide *Faxafjörðr*. An excellent sheltered harbour is formed by this headland on the south-west, and three islands—*Akrey* (Acre-isle), *Engey* (Meadow-isle), and *Viðey* (? Wood-isle)—to the northward of it, and two or three rocky holms lying within the islands. To the nearest of the holms it is possible to walk dryshod at low water along a reef. About 300 yards from the beach at the centre of the small bay is an oval sheet of water, some 300 yards in width by 600 yards in length, the *Tjörn* (Tarn); and upon each side of this the ground slopes upward, while the tract between the tarn and the waters of the bay is level and but little above high-water mark. The central part of the town stands upon this level tract, and its wings extend west and east up the slopes of the rise on either hand. Seen from a vessel in the harbour, the town has rather a pretty colonial appearance, with its white painted wooden stores built round the curve of the shore, with their little wooden jetties stretching far out into the harbour. And when one lands, he finds the metropolis of Iceland by no means the dirty place, offensive to the olfactory senses, it has been represented; for the streets are broad, and cleanly kept, and the drying of codfish is mainly confined to the shore.

It is the residence of the Governor-General (Landshöfðingi), Bishop, Judge Sheriff and Chief of the Revenue Department in one official (Stiftamtmaðr), Head Doctor, and several other officials.

The chief buildings, none of which can boast of any architectural beauty, are the Cathedral, the newly-erected Senate House, the College (Latinuskóli), Hospital (where a warm bath is obtainable), Government House, a large wooden store known as 'Glasgow,' and a building, said by a recent writer to be used as Jail and Museum. In 1878, when the author was at *Reykjavik*, the Antiquarian Museum and a Free Library were located in a large loft under the roof of the Cathedral, and a Natural History Collection in a room at the College. Near the Cathedral, in the centre of the town, is a grassy plot on which stands a monument to Albert Thorvaldsen, the great sculptor—who was of Icelandic descent and born at sea between Iceland and Denmark. A short distance out to the rear of the town, on the west of the tarn, is a neatly kept cemetery; and near by a rifle range. On the rise to the east, a short distance out of the town, is a small tower erected as an Observatory; but it is said to have been built on magnetic rock, and to be useless for the purpose for which it was erected; it is therefore closed. On the east rise in the town is a Windmill used for grinding the imported cerealia.

There are two hotels, Smith's—formerly a club-house—ranking first, and Japhetsson's, smaller, but clean and comfortable; a number of stores, where everything required by the Icelanders is sold from a needle to an anchor; a post-office; two booksellers; a like number of silversmiths, printers, harness-makers, and photographers; one druggist, a hatter, and several other handy-craftsmen, and last, but not least, there is the very fair dealing man who makes a business of furnishing foreign visitors with guides and ponies, Geir Zœga.

What strikes the stranger most is the entire absence of wheeled vehicles, for, with the exception of one or two carts used for the carting in of peat from a bog beyond the tarn, there are none in the Icelandic Metropolis.

The founder of the town may be said to have been Ingólfr, one of the first Norse settlers, who, it will be remembered, found his high-seat pillars stranded in the bay, in the year A.D. 877, three years after he landed in Iceland. Naturally in the vicinity of the dwelling of a powerful chief like Ingólfr and his descendants a number of men would have their dwellings—retainers, freed thralls, boatmen, boat-builders, fishermen, and others, and thus sprung up a village which in the course of time became the capital of the island.

The Antiquarian Museum, the Ornithological and Mineralogical Collections, and the Library, whether located in the Jail or still in their old quarters in the Cathedral loft and College, will well repay a visit. Among the many objects of interest in the first named, is a rude wooden crucifix, which was found in a lava-cave and is believed to be a Culdee relic. The white marble altar-stone, blackened above by use, from *Skálholt* Cathedral, is preserved here; as also are several enamelled and jewelled crucifixes of the thirteenth century, and many richly-embroidered ecclesiastical garments and altar-cloths. There are a number of weapons, which date from A.D. 1050 to 1400, chiefly old spears and halberds, battle-axes, and daggers. Excellent specimens of the embroidered female national dress, with a number of gold and silver ornaments in filigree work, are also to be seen. As well as a variety of old drinking cups, which in days 'lang syne' doubtless figured in many a wassail. The best are of walrus ivory. Horse furniture is well represented: prettily worked saddle-cloths, and a number of old stirrups of wood and bone, are the most noticeable. There is some tapestry work, and a number of boxes on which are carved and painted knights and ladies, in quaint old-fashioned costumes, riding with hawk and hound.

In the Ornithological and Mineralogical Departments are respectively an interesting collection of the birds indigenous to Iceland, and of the minerals, metals, etc., found on the island.

In the Library are preserved many old works in MS.; also the first Bible printed in Iceland, at *Hólar* in A.D. 1584. This work was printed by Bishop Guðbrand Þorlaksson, who not only made a translation from the German version by Martin Luther, but carved with his own hand the blocks for the large number of plates and woodcuts that illustrate the volume. There is a very curious old illustrated Book of Magic, and many other old works, including two versions of the New Testament, dated 1540 and 1609; likewise the second Bible printed in Iceland, date 1644. There is an excellent collection of modern books on all subjects, chiefly presented by Americans on their visit to the island in 1874, at the celebration of the thousandth anniversary of its colonisation by the Norsemen.

The new Senate House must not be neglected; nor should the Cathedral, although it is a very plain building, whose outer walls of brick were in a sad state of repair in 1878. Inside but little is to be seen, save the Font by Thorvaldsen, presented by him, and a full-length figure of the Saviour, above the Altar.

EXCURSIONS.

THE LAUG (Hot-Spring, pron. *Lurg*).—Tourists visiting Iceland for the first time, especially those who have not hitherto seen any volcanic phenomena, invariably turn their footsteps first in the direction of the small hot-springs, distant two miles east of the town; the steam rising from which gives to the capital its name, Reek-wick. The pleasantest route thereto is to walk out of the town over the rise on the east, descend close to the shore, which follow for about a mile, and then strike across the boggy moor to the springs. It will take about an hour to reach them. The springs rise in and close to the margin of a small brook; the water is scalding hot, and the stream, warmed by the supply from these natural hot-water taps, is utilized by the poorer *Reykjavik* people as a laundry. The steam is strongly impregnated with sulphuretted hydrogen; and to the geologist the mineral deposits in the vicinity of these thermal springs will be interesting.

ENGEY AND VIĐEY.—An equally favourite excursion is one by boat to these islets, to see the eider-ducks which breed there in great numbers. They are very tame, and the hen will allow her back to be gently stroked by one's hand when sitting. The eider-duck is preserved for its down, and it is not permitted to fire a gun within a mile of those parts of the coast and islets whose owners have proclaimed at the local þíng the spots as eider-duck breeding grounds. The down, which the parent birds tear from their breasts to line their nest with, may be removed twice without the birds deserting the nest; but if a third time, it is said it is abandoned. The down is worth at the present time about 12*s.* per lb.; it was formerly much dearer. It is a very interesting sight to see the nests in every hole and nook and cranny among the rocks; and also to watch the earlier hatched broods of dark downy ducklings swimming about near the shore, jealously guarded by the mater; who will occasionally be seen calmly sitting on the water with one of her young ones perched on her back. A great many terns—Icelandic name Kría—also have their nests upon these islets; and the old birds circle over and swoop down upon intruders in a very menacing manner, coming within a foot of one's head frequently.

On *Engey* there is now a fish-curing establishment, and to avoid its aroma, which is none of Rimmel's, be sure and land, if possible, to windward of it. *Viðey*, however, is far the most interesting of the islets on which to land, as, in addition to the eider-ducks and their nests, there is, to the west of the substantial stone residence of the owner of the islet, a chapel that was part of a monastery founded in A.D. 1226. Burton describes it as 'a solid box of rough basalt, squared only at the corners, with rude arches over doorway and windows; the dwarf "campanile," a shed perched upon the roof, shelters three bells. In the massive red door was a huge iron key, which may date from the days of the ghostly owners. The roof is supported by heavy solid rafters, and the furniture is older and more ornamental than usual; the benches are carved, and the colours are the tricolor, blue, red, and green.'

To HAFNARFJÖRÐR (Haven-fjord).—A trading town of some 400 inhabitants, at the head of the fjord which gives the town its name, distant two hours' steam from the capital. The Danish steamers every voyage, during the interval between their arrival at *Reykjavik* and departure therefrom, make a trip to *Hafnarfjörðr*, and usually return the same day. If one of the steamers should happen to be in the bay at the time of the tourist's arrival, inquiry should be made of the Agent at *Reykjavik* as to what day the trip will be made and it may be that this excursion will fit in with other arrangements made by the tourists. The fare is a mere trifle. The scenery around *Hafnarfjörðr* is very wild and volcanic, bristling lava-floods in every direction.

The pleasantest way to visit this little town is to hire a guide and pony for a couple of days and ride to *Hafnarfjörðr* the first day, and sleep there. Small, but clean, inn. Make an early start the next morning and return *via*

BESSASTAÐIR (? Bear-stead) on *Álftanes*, the headland north of the *Hafnarfjörðr*. *Bessastaðir* is a large building said to have been built about the middle of the thirteenth century by Snórri Sturluson, the author of the 'prose Edda,' who, it will be remembered, was also one of the traitorous chiefs who plotted with King Hácon of Norway to place Iceland under his sceptre. From 1805 to 1846, when the present College at *Reykjavik* was established, *Bessastaðir* was used as the College. Prior to 1801 there were two Colleges, one near each of the Cathedrals, *Hólar* and *Skálholt*; but that year it was arranged that there should be but one bishopric instead of two, and that the Cathedral should be in the capital.

One can ride from *Reykjavik* to *Hafnarfjörðr* comfortably in three hours, so that the return journey can easily be made the same day if wished, and another day devoted to the excursion to *Bessastaðir*, which may be reached from the capital in a little over two hours.

To visit either place, one quits the capital and crosses *Seltjarnarnes* by a good made road, which brings him to the head of what would be called in Shetland a 'voe,' the head of which is ridden round on the beach. After crossing a small naze, the head of a second voe is ridden round; and if the traveller is bound to *Hafnarfjörðr*, he now rides almost due south through vast lava-beds where masses of rock are distorted and piled up in a manner that appears perfectly chaotic to any one who has not previously seen a flood of igneous rock. If bound to *Bessastaðir*, the traveller turns to the right and rides out on the *Alftanes*. An excursion to either place passes a day very agreeably. As also will one to the *Elliðaár* salmon river, if the tourist is an angler (See List of Salmon Rivers in preceding Chapter). When the author visited *Bessastaðir* in October, he made a good bag of a variety of waders, which were very numerous round the shores of the voes and the shallow inlets on *Alftanes*.

ROUTES.

ROUTE I.

REYKJAVÍK TO ÞÍNGVELLIR, GEYSIR, GULLFOSS AND HEKLA; RETURNING VIÂ KRÍSUVÍK, HAFNARFJÖRÐR AND BESSASTAÐIR. A TWELVE DAYS' EXCURSION, WHICH MAY BE EXTENDED TO EIGHTEEN; SUITABLE FOR THOSE WHO ONLY CONTEMPLATE REMAINING IN ICELAND DURING THE INTERVAL BETWEEN THE ARRIVAL OF THE CAMOENS ON ONE VOYAGE AND HER DEPARTURE ON THE NEXT.

THE PONIES should be ordered to be at the hotel at 9 A.M. punctually; as in all probability it will be two hours later before the tourists get away, such a number of things will have to be seen to—perhaps one or two of the ponies may have to be shod, and, if saddles are borrowed, new cruppers and stirrup leathers bought, etc., etc.

Somewhat less than an hour's ride, most of the way over a good made road, will bring the party to the ford over the *Elliðaár*, the salmon river mentioned in 'Excursions from *Reykjavík*.' The ford, save immediately after heavy rains, is a very shallow one. The farm-house on the eastern bank is a primitive inn much frequented in summer by the townspeople. At the river the made road terminated, in 1878 (but it is possible the made road is now extended farther from the capital), and deep ruts worn by years of pony traffic formed the bridle path. This winds upwards over a range of hills, amidst which nestle several small lakes. In a fine clear day the view looking westward over the *Faxafjörðr*, with *Snæfells Jökull* rising like a pyramid of ice from the sea, beyond the range of mountains forming the peninsula of which it is the western termination, is charming. It is said the nearest chain of mountains in that direction, *Esja*, when the light is favourable, 'appear covered with flourishing vegetation. Their steep arid sides owe this appearance to the beautiful green tint of the rocks (? clay) which compose the greater part of the chain; their upper strata present a great variety of colours.'

Shortly after the largest of the lakes, the *Hafravatn* (Goat-lake), is passed, the *Seljadalr* (? Shieling-dale) is entered, and the bridle-path abruptly comes to an end in the bed of a shallow stream. This is bordered on either hand for some distance by morass, down through which it has worn a channel to a sub-stratum of sand and shingle, which affords firm footing for the ponies, and the bed of the stream is utilized as a road. The author forded this stream twenty-three times (Capt. Burton twenty-five times) to avoid the deeps and enable his pony to keep on the belts of shingle fringing the stream. How the natives manage to traverse this part of the country during the early summer floods is a puzzle to every stranger who has ridden up the *Seljadalr*. At the head of this valley a halt will be made for half an hour or so, to pasture the ponies and partake of luncheon ; and on the journey being resumed the saddles and baggage will be shifted on to the relay ponies, that were previously driven on ahead by the guide. A path will again be met with, and it leads still upward till the plateau of the *Mosfellsheiði* (Moss-fell-heath) is attained ; before reaching which a wild rocky glen will be passed. In this the stream which furnished a roadway through the morass has its birth-place. The *Mosfellsheiði* is a dreary stony waste, which it will take nearly two hours to traverse: a road was being constructed over it in 1878. Early in August the sportsman will find that curlew and plover and an occasional grouse are to be bagged while crossing the heath. The somewhat monotonous ride over the dreary waste has its advantages, however ; for, like the gloomy scene which invariably precedes the transformation scene of a pantomime, it enhances the beauties of the charming landscape which is shortly, and as suddenly as if by enchantment, to be opened to the view of the travellers. First the monarch of the Icelandic lakes, *Þingvallavatn*, comes in sight; an imposing sheet of water covering an area of close on forty square miles ; its surface broken by two small islands, said by Burton to be crater-islets, and picturesque headlands jutting outward from the eastern and western shores. Quite unexpectedly, while the traveller is riding slowly onward gazing admiringly at the lake, his pony comes to a halt, and looking for the cause, the ground appears to have suddenly opened at the very feet of his steed, and he beholds a vast rift stretching away in a north-north-easterly direction for over two miles. This is the famous *Almannagjá*, or All-men's-rift, so named because, when the Alþing held its meetings at Þingvellir, it was the custom of the people to assemble on the outer slope of the eastern wall of the rift, whence they could command an excellent view of the proceedings below; whether it was to witness a peaceful meeting of the 'House of Representatives,' or the warlike one of two of the chiefs of the people settling their dispute by a mortal combat (Holm Ganga) on an holm in the *Öxará* (Axe-river) flowing at the base of the slope, or the drowning of a woman guilty of adultery in the pool below the cascade formed by the river where it leaps through a gap in the eastern wall of the rift.

The traveller descends into the All-men's-rift by a steep rocky causeway, 'formed by nature and improved by art' (up and down which a recent writer says the best native ponies could gallop, but the author would beg to be excused from riding one while it was trying the experiment), and proceeds between its cliffs for a short distance when a further descent is made through an opening in the eastern cliff to the banks of the Axe-river; crossing which a few minutes' ride brings him to the door of Þingvellir parsonage. Here he will find a kindly welcome, the newly-appointed pastor being an exceptionally genial gentleman, reasonable in his charges and obliging. The sleeping accommodation at the parsonage is limited, therefore if the party is a large one the tent brought for use at the *Geysir* will have to be pitched; but an abundance of coffee, milk, pancakes, and delicious fresh char from the lake will be procurable.

SECOND DAY—AT ÞINGVELLIR.—It will be agreeably passed in the exploration of this highly interesting and classic locality. Þingvellir is a tract about four miles in length from S.S.W. to N.N.E., and rather less in width, lying at a lower level than the country on either side; from which it evidently broke away during a terrible volcanic convulsion in prehistoric times. The line of disruption on each side is marked by a rift, the *Almannagjá* on the west, and the *Hrafnagjá* (Raven-rift) on the east. The tract between slopes gradually upward as it recedes from the lake, which borders it on the south; the rifts decreasing in depth and width as the depth of the subsidence becomes less. The formation of this part of the island appears to be vast horizontal sheets of basaltic lava underlying a thin superficial stratum of soil, and these evidently at the spot where the subsidence took place roofed in an abyss of some kind, into which the disrupted mass descended.

Irrefragable proof of the correctness of the subsidence theory is found in the presence of horizontal stratification in the perpendicular walls, not only of the two main rifts, but also in those of the fissures in the sunken tract itself. Moreover, numerous similar subsidences have taken place in many parts of the island, notably in the *Mývatns Öræfi*, where one occurred as recently as 1875 during an eruption of an immense lava-flood. (See Route 3.)

The disrupted tract at Þingvellir in its descent fissured deeply in many places, and chiefly in the same direction as the two outer rifts, viz. from N.N.E. to S.S.W. Some six or seven hundred yards east of the *Almannagjá*, and about a mile from the lake, one of these fissures divides into two arms, which diverge from each other and reunite at a distance of about a hundred yards or so, inclosing a long narrow rocky islet. This is the spot where, in the lawless days of old, the Alþíng held its meetings. In olden times it was possible to cross its engirdling chasms in one place only, where masses of rock formed a rude causeway; but at the present time any one of ordinary activity can cross in at least two places, where frost and earthquakes have shattered the cliffs and choked the rifts with débris. The natural stone-mound near the northern end of the island is said to be the *Lögberg* (Law-rock), where new laws were proclaimed and judgments pronounced; and further south on the brink of the eastern rift a detached fragment of rock, about twelve feet in length, is shown as the 'Blood-stone,' on which for certain offences the backs of criminals were broken, the victims being hurled backward and allowed to fall into the rift. It is recorded that several men attempted to seize Flósi, the leader of the 'burners' of Njál, during a meeting of the Alþíng, and that he escaped by taking a very risky leap across the rift hard by the Blood-stone. In the Sagas mention is made of many a stormy debate and remarkable trial that took place here, ending in blood-shed and life-long feuds. It will be remembered that in the Historical Notice allusion was made to the ready wit displayed, and the remarkable incidents that occurred during the debate with reference to the adoption of the Christian religion.

From the meeting-place of the Alþíng the tourist will probably turn his footsteps towards the picturesque, though not large, fall formed by the *Öxará*, where it leaps in a single bound from the elevated moorland west of the Thingfields into the *Almannagjá*; through which it flows for a short distance until it finds a gap in the eastern wall of the rift, and leaps in two bounds to the plain beneath. In the pool below this cascade it is said unfortunate women convicted of adultery or infanticide were drowned; while on a knoll close by those found guilty of witchcraft were burned.

In the *Almannagjá*, and at the foot of the outer slope of its eastern wall, are to be seen low, rude walls of unhewn stones, now used as folds for sheep. Within these, it is said, members of the Alþíng pitched their booths of wadmaal ('Buðir') when they attended its meetings; but the fact is disputed.

The church will repay a visit: the altar-piece, a Last Supper, is old, and the pulpit dates from A.D. 1683. In the churchyard stands a block of vesicular lava, the marks upon the eastern face of which, it is alleged, were used in olden times as a standard measure by which the ellwands and other measures in common use were to be regulated.

The Thingstead and its surroundings, notwithstanding the disparaging way in which a recent writer has spoken of it and them, is a charming landscape. On three sides it is guarded by mountains of considerable altitude; to the north-west are to be seen the *Súlur* pinnacles 'bristled as with trees: the fretted peaks about Gagnheiði; the dull black heap of Ármannsfell, so called from Orman the Irish giant, who there lies in his grave; and the ridgelet of Jornkliff, crouching below it. There to the north-east stands Skjaldbreið, shield-shaped, as its name says, ending in a snowflaked umbo which suggests a crater. The peaks of Tindaskagi at its foot apparently connect with the great Hrafnabjörg; and far behind them, but brought near by the surpassing atmospheric clearness, sparkle the snows of Lángjökull' (Burton). The most striking of these mountains is *Skjaldbreið*, and well does it deserve its name Broad-shield; at least the author thought so when he saw it one clear October morning after a fall of snow which remained only on the mountains, when it appeared like a giant genie's shield, formed of silver and barred with steel, so bright was its sunlit face and 'steely-blue' its shadows.

South-west of the lake there is also a very striking group of mountains, from the nearest of which, at an altitude of about a thousand feet, a cloud of steam ascends, giving the mountain—which is named *Hengill*—a very volcanic appearance. Chalybeate, carbonated, sulphureous, and siliceous springs, it is said, are found on the slopes of this mountain and at its base. The famous Dr. Hjaltalín, of *Reykjavík*, proposed some years ago the erection of a small Sanatorium on the mountain at an altitude of 1,500 feet, but hitherto the money has not been forthcoming to carry out the project.

Lord Dufferin says of the Þingvellir landscape: 'A lovelier scene I have seldom witnessed. In the foreground lay huge masses of rock and lava tossed about like the ruins of a world, and washed by waters as bright and green as polished malachite. Beyond, a bevy of distant mountains, robed by the transparent atmosphere in tints unknown to Europe, peeped over each other's shoulders into the silver mirror at their feet; while here and there, from among their purple ridges, columns of white vapour rose like altar smoke toward the tranquil heaven.'

The Saga reader will probably regard this classic locality much as Waller did, who says: 'It is almost impossible to give any idea of the feelings of deep interest with which I regarded every inch of this romantic spot, and tried to imagine what an appearance it must have presented 900 years ago. I wondered where Hallgerða's booth was. I know that it was just down by the water that Gunnar first saw her sitting in the doorway. Njál's booth, too, was some two or three hundred yards down the river on the other side. It was here that the desperate battle took place between Njál's assassins and his avengers, and it was between the water and the lava that so many of them were killed.'

Altogether Þingvellir is a charmingly romantic old-world spot; which pen cannot describe; a spot where scenery wild and weird is found hallowed by historical associations of no common order. It is indeed a spot, if such exists on earth,

> 'Where two foes each other meeting
> Would exchange a friendly greeting:
> Where a man, intent on spoil,
> Would stop short 'shamed of approaching
> As if fearful of encroaching
> On a consecrated soil.'

The simple plain wooden church, and the parsonage, mainly built of turf and rugged blocks of lava, owing to their very simplicity, are in keeping with the surroundings: a huge modern church would be an anachronism.

With reference to the *Hrafnagjá*, though longer it is not as wide nor deep as the western rift, and as an hour can be devoted to its examination on the way to the *Geysir* on the morrow, it is hardly worth while to ride three miles each way to see it.

Respecting the sporting capabilities of the neighbourhood, grouse are most years very plentiful in the month of August among the birch scrub, which flourishes over the tract lying between the rifts, it being sheltered by the more elevated country on either hand. As to fishing, those anglers who have tried to beguile the finny inhabitants of the lake have been very unsuccessful, landing but a few small 'foreller' (*Ang.* trout). Thus the author believes the char here, like those in *Mývatn* (which he has several times tried to allure, but in vain), will not take the artificial fly. A goodly number are netted at times by the pastor near the mouth of the *Öxará*, and the author can testify that they are excellent eating. Burton has the following about angling in the *Sog*, the outlet of the lake, which may be reached in four or five hours' sharp riding from Þ*ingvellir* : 'Here in July any quantity of salmon-trout may be caught; the fish lie above the first foss thick as water-plants. My informant had taken twenty-five in one day; the heaviest was 7lbs., and only two weighed under 6 lbs.; but he had been almost blinded by the plagues of gnats and flies, which covered his pony with blood-points.'

THIRD DAY.—The halting-place for the night will be by encampment at the *Geysir*, or at *Múli* or *Haukadalr* farms, a short distance off. The scenery between Þ*ingvellir* and the *Geysir* is far more interesting than that between the capital and the first-named place.

A quarter of an hour after leaving the parsonage a deep fissure will be passed, and less than an hour's ride across the sunken plain of Þ*ingvellir*, within a short distance of the lake, will bring the traveller to the *Hrafnagjá*. As before observed, it is not as wide nor deep as the *Almannagjá*, and therefore it is not descended into, but crossed on a causeway of fallen lava-blocks. Half an hour can be spared for its examination, if wished, the journey to the *Geysir* taking seven to eight hours only. The path, almost immediately after leaving the rift, winds through an extensive bed of rugged lava, to the north-east of which lies a range of jagged volcanic mountains. Do not fail to observe at the base of a hill, on the left, a peculiar extinct crater; for it is Bryson's 'Tintron,' respecting which 'Umbra' penned the following : 'This is the mysterious Tintron, the puzzle of geologists, the Lava Spout, the only one known to exist in the world, like unto the blackened stump of a tree, ten feet or so in height, through which the fluid flame is supposed to have once soared in air, as water from the hose of a fire-engine.' Had the author of the above ever visited the lower part of the *Laxárdalr*, near *Húsavík*, in the north, he would never have penned 'the only one known to exist in the world,' for he would have seen there a plain thickly studded with Tintrons, many twenty to thirty feet in height. (See Route 3.)

The path next leads through a defile in a volcanic range, with three peaks on the left, named the *Kálfstindar* (Calf-peaks); and it will be seen that this region has frequently been the scene of volcanic disturbance. A steep descent will bring the travellers into an extensive and almost circular grassy amphitheatre surrounded by hills. Here a halt will be made to bait the ponies, partake of lunch, and shift saddles. It is remarkable that there is no farm here, for many a one may be seen elsewhere surrounded with far less pasture.

Remounting, a short gallop will bring the party to the fertile *Laugardalr* (Hot-spring-dale), a valley containing many hot springs, and an extensive lake. As the path runs within a short distance of the north-western corner of the *Laugarvatn* (Hot-spring-lake), travellers usually dismount to visit a group of hot springs which bubble forth merrily within a foot or so of the water's edge. An efflorescence of alum and a little sulphur will be found around the springs. The large columns of steam ascending from the midst of an extensive marsh on the opposite side of the lake mark the sites of other groups of hot springs, but these are seldom visited, as a lengthy detour would have to be made, and a number of similar ones are to be seen in the vicinity of the *Geysir*. A cup of coffee and excellent pancakes are procurable at the farm near the lake, if the travellers wish to halt for refreshments.

Two hours' ride, fair path, passing through a tract of birch and willow scrub (in which a covey or two of grouse may generally be found in August) near *Miðdalr* (Mid-dale) church, will bring the travellers to the famous *Brúará* (Bridge-river), so named from a peculiar bridge here, which is situated in the river, not bridging it over. At the spot where the bridge is placed, the river in summer is usually sixty or seventy yards in width and of no great depth, save in mid-channel; but both width and depth vary according to the season of the year and the state of the weather. The river-bed is a rugged tract of lava, in the centre of which is a deep wedge-shaped crevasse extending up stream from an equally deep pool, lying some feet below the level of the river-bed above, into which the water falls. The river abounding in deep holes above the crevasse, while it is but a foot or so deep between it and the banks, except when flooded, some eight or nine stout planks have been placed across the chasm, with strong iron-clamped hand-rails on each side, and form a somewhat singular bridge, twelve feet by eight. It is, however, only possible to cross by this when the river is in its normal condition, as during the floods the planks of the bridge are several feet beneath a foaming cataract, and travellers have to cross in a boat at the ferry a short distance down stream.

An hour and a half's ride will bring the party to *Múli*, two hours' to the *Geysir* or *Haukadalr* farm. Accommodation for two travellers at *Múli*, for several at *Haukadalr*. The people at both places are obliging, but have somewhat expansive ideas on the subject of remuneration. In Ultima Thule, as elsewhere, English tourists have evidently rendered the people living near the 'lions' avaricious. It will be as well to repeat here what has been before observed in the introductory information, there is but the most remote chance in the world of seeing the *Geysir* erupt unless a tent is brought and pitched in its vicinity, its eruptions taking place with great uncertainty. It has been known to remain quiescent for a week, and unlike its irritable neighbour, the now equally famous *Strokkr*, it is not to be bullied into an eruption at the will of visitors by drastic herbal treatment in the shape of huge doses of turf. It speaks but little for the enterprise of the farmer at *Haukadalr*, who is a comparatively rich man, that he has not long ere this erected a house in the immediate vicinity of the *Geysir* for the accommodation of tourists.

FOURTH DAY.—This will be passed awaiting an eruption of the *Geysir*, forcing *Strokkr* into activity once or oftener in the meanwhile. Should the day be fine, the time will pass away very pleasantly, there being over fifty boiling springs within, at the most, half a mile of the principal ones, and a remarkable grotto filled with water, but little below boiling-point, named *Blesi* (Blaze—as on the face of a horse), whose roof is broken in, allowing a glimpse of the interior.

A brief description will now be given of the sights of this interesting locality. The two chief geysirs are the *Geysir* 'par excellence,' and the *Strokkr*. The first named, as just said, is very uncertain in its eruptions, sometimes ejecting enormous columns of boiling water to a height approaching a hundred feet at intervals of a few hours, while at other times it remains quiescent for several days. The *Strokkr* lies ninety paces nearly due south of its world-renowned neighbour, and, fortunately for sight-seers, can at all times be excited into an eruption by partly choking up its pipe—a hollow like a huge test-tube in a bed of siliceous sinter—with a considerable quantity of turf. The *Geysir*, on the contrary, evinces contemptuous indifference to such indignities. The *Strokkr* also 'spouts' voluntarily at uncertain intervals.

The Geysir and its satellites are situated at the base of an eminence of no great height, the *Laugafjall*—not lofty mountain-range as shown in engravings—in a tract of hot viscid clay and mineral earths of various colours, red and yellow are conspicuous, raised a few feet above the level of the grassy plain lying between the *Laugafjall* on the west and the *Túngufljót* (Tongue-flood) on the east, a river tributary to the great southern *Hvitá*, which drains the glacier-covered mountains to the northward. The extent of the tract in which the thermal springs abound is about 700 yards in length by 300 in width. Burton says:—Here 'we may still study the seven forms of Geysir life. First, is the baby still sleeping in the bosom of Mother Earth, the airy wreath escaping from the hot clay ground; then comes the infant breathing strongly, and at times puking in the nurse's lap; third, is the child simmering with impatience; and fourth, is the youth whose occupation is to boil over. The full-grown man is represented by the "Great Gusher" in the plentitude of its lusty power; old age, by the tranquil, sleepy "laug"; and second childhood and death, mostly from diphtheria or quinsy, in the empty red pits strewn about the dwarf plain.'

The *Geysir* lies towards the northern end of the 'dwarf plain,' and its basin is at the summit of a mound built up to a height of about forty feet of silica, a mineral that the *Geysir* water holds in solution, and which is deposited in thin layers of a beautiful enamel from the water which is constantly overflowing. The mound is ever increasing in size from the continuous deposit of silica; and fragments of stone left on its slopes will in a short time be found attached to the surface by newly-formed layers of siliceous sinter, the name by which the enamel is known to mineralogists. The basin is nearly circular; and except immediately after an eruption is full of water to the brim: four measurements taken twice on the surface of the water gave the average diameter at 66 feet. In the centre of the basin is a cylindrical well or tube 10 feet 4 inches in diameter, and 82 feet in depth. A recent writer made a curious discovery. He says, By standing with his back to the sun and looking into the basin, the spectator will see 'his face and head clear as in a mirror, surrounded by a halo of bright prismatic colours. The coloured rays extended round the head to the distance of two or three feet, forming two-thirds to three-fourths of a circle, the lower portion wanting. The observer could only see his own likeness, not that of his neighbour.'

The author was not fortunate enough on his visit to witness an eruption of the *Geysir*, therefore not being able to describe one from personal observation, he begs permission to further quote the writer of the foregoing, premising that an eruption is preceded by a trembling of the earth and a noise like subterranean thunder:
'The water in the basin was as smooth as glass, the slight vapour rising being carried to the south-west, when suddenly in the centre

of the basin over the well or pipe the water rose, through the water in the basin, to the full circumference of the pipe (31 feet), to the height of about three feet.

'The column appeared for an instant as if a solid body, immediately falling into the basin, and ruffling its surface with a series of waves.

'Again, the water rose 5 or 6 feet, falling as before, creating a little storm in the basin, and rushing out at the two openings in the rim, the one on the north-east, the other on the east. By the third and fourth rise of these columns, following each other with increasing rapidity, the boiling water came tumbling like a cataract over the basin and down the mound on all sides. Compelled to retire a little distance, columns of water were now dimly seen following each other with loud noise, as they rushed through the tube into the air, each succeeding column higher than the one before it. There were now a series of explosions, giving off enormous clouds of steam, black from their density. . . . The display lasted for about seven minutes from the commencement.

'Immediately after the last and highest explosion, the flow down the sides of the mound suddenly ceased, and running up and into the basin, we found it empty, and the water standing some ten feet down, the tube gradually filling again.'

The writer was fortunate enough to see another eruption the next morning. He was roused by the underground thundering, and with his friends had attained the position from which he had observed the eruption the previous day, before the 'explosions had attained their highest elevation. . . . Rising above the dense clouds of vapour, the water in columns was distinctly seen opening out at the top into separate shoots at varying heights, the lower curving outwards, the higher shot up perpendicular, and shattered into diamond drops, sparkling in the sun. The well opens up trumpet-shape into the basin, the diameter of the curve being about 2 feet 6 inches. To this it appears to be due that most of the water falls outside its margin.

'From one of the columns about a third broke off, and, bending between me and the sun, left his image quite black upon the retina.

'Prepared for the close, we had reached the basin in time to see the last portion of its contents running into the well, leaving the basin burning hot, and not a drop of water in it. The water was standing in the well about 12 feet down, and slowly rising, taking about 15 minutes to again fill the basin.

'During these eruptions the rush of boiling water never ceased;

but uniting to the east of the mound, it flowed down to the river in a continuous stream, in some places twenty yards in breadth.

'Taking the average height of the columns of water at 45 feet, and eight shoots in a minute during a period of eruption of 7½ minutes, the discharge is 1,410,600 gallons; or take one column 80 feet by 10 feet 4 inches diameter, gives 41,797 gallons at one discharge; a shot weighing 186 tons 11cwt. 3qrs. 17lbs. from this great gun, to which the Woolwich Infant is but a babe.'

Of all unpunctual exhibitions the Geysir is the most uncertain. Shepherd (the author of 'The North-West Peninsula of Iceland') vainly waited six days; a French party seven, and it is said by Burton 'there are legends of a wasted fortnight'; but as a general rule three days seldom elapse without an eruption. In A.D. 1770 it is on record that the *Geysir* spouted eleven times a day, and in A.D. 1814 every six hours.

STROKKR does not possess any basin around its well, which is shaped like a rugged test-tube, about 8 feet in diameter at its mouth, and, it is said, 36 feet deep. Burton furnishes it with a basin, or rather a 'saucer,' and a most extraordinary one too: 'The outer diameter of the saucer is only 7 feet, the inner about 18' (vol. ii. p. 181). After the eruption witnessed by the author, the level of the water in the tube was at a depth of 25 feet, and here were to be seen, partly submerged, or in nautical phraseology awash, the mouths of two pipes entering at different angles close together on the side nearest the *Geysir*. From these pipes steam belched forth at intervals with considerable force, churning the water in the well round rapidly. Directly steam ceased to issue from these pipes the rotary motion of the water gradually lessened, but never entirely ceased, the intervals between the jets of steam being too brief. About half an hour after the close of the eruption the jets of steam increased considerably in volume, and some water was injected through the pipes into the well, for they were shortly after submerged. The water did not commence to rise until water issued from the two pipes, accordingly there is reason to believe that the well has no other inlets. It is important that the existence of these two pipes should be recorded; as it is seldom, the author was told by his guide, that the water in the well is so low after an eruption as it was upon this occasion. Normally the water fills the tube to within 10 feet of its mouth, and is violently agitated and churned into continuous rotary motion (hence the name *Strokkr* = Churn), presumably by jets of steam entering from the pipes at different angles.

For the privilege of digging the turfs necessary to excite this 'gusher' to action, and for the loan of a spade—usually found lying on the grass close by—two *kroner* have to be handed over to the farmer at *Haukadalr*, who owns the site of the *Geysir*. Most writers say that about a quarter of an hour after a dose of turf has been administered, the *Strokkr* feels the effect of the emetic. However, the author waited nearly an hour, after tumbling in a heap of close on fifty large-sized turfs, without any signs of a display; but an additional dose, supplemented (contrary to 'the statute in that case made and provided') with a few small slabs of rock, evoked one with such suddenness that he and his guide, who were standing close to the edge of the well—fortunately to windward—peering down at the seething waters, narrowly escaped a severe scalding. An immense column of water was ejected, without the slightest warning, to a height of about 60 feet, and was followed immediately by dense jets of steam and water, which ascended with deafening roars and such great force that the ground trembled beneath our feet at a distance of a hundred yards. The eruptions continued for sixteen minutes and a half minutes, and clouds of steam ascended at intervals for half an hour afterwards.

It is recorded that a party of French naval officers worked the *Strokkr* several times between noon and eight in the evening without being able to exhaust it, for the water was ejected, 'the last time we excited it, nearly into our tent, and to a much greater distance than the preceding ones. It appeared to have redoubled in fury.'

What is very strange, the eruptions of the *Strokkr* do not in any way affect the water in the well and basin of the *Geysir*, though it is less than a hundred yards distant; while, it is asserted, that an eruption of the latter causes the water in the tube of the *Strokkr* to subside considerably.

BLESI lies fifty paces from the *Geysir* in the direction of the *Laugafjall*. At a first glance this appears to be but two pools of hot water separated from each other by a narrow wall of siliceous rock—the Blaze; but by standing on the margin of one of them, a little distance on either side of the seeming dividing wall, and peering down into the limpid water, it will be seen that this is a natural bridge with its arch submerged, under which one can see through the surface of the water on one side into the still crystal depths of that on the other. He can also see that where the water is exposed, two holes exist in the rocky roof of a beautiful grotto; and it is easy to trace from either side the curve inward of the silica-frosted craggy roof until it fades away in the depths, where the water imperceptibly loses its crystalline appearance and becomes of a beautiful pale cobalt tint. Were it not for the wreaths of steam that curl from the surface of the water, where exposed, one could fancy he was gazing into the beautiful cool depths of a grotto amid the rocks of some sheltered bay, into which were he to plunge and its mystic chambers explore, he feels, so fairy-like is its appearance, that if a mermaid or a sea-nymph exists, it is therein he would find her.

A couple of hours can be pleasantly spent examining the numerous hot springs and miniature geysirs south of *Strokkr*, and studying 'the seven forms of Geysir life.' The 'Little Strokkr' of the older travellers, in the centre of the 'dwarf plain,' has long ceased to spout, having degenerated into a simple laug, or a hot spring in which the water merely bubbles forth. The 'Little Geysir,' a gusher situated a short distance south of *Strokkr*, that has a tube about two feet in diameter and thirteen feet in depth to where it branches off laterally, occasionally spouts to the height of ten or twelve feet. There are also, Burton asserts, a 'gusherling' which discharges red-water, and another which 'spouts like an escape pipe, brown, high and strong.'

An ascent of the *Laugafjall* will well repay the trouble, for 'up on the hill-side are springs which do not boil and spout now; and still higher old tubes and crater-cones that once were the outlets of Geysirs of considerable size;' and a charming view is obtainable over the Alpine country to the south. *Hekla* with its mantle of snow is distinctly visible beyond the range of hills on the opposite side of the *Hvitá*; as also are the more distant ice-clad summits of the *Jöklar* near the south coast. When one turns his attention from the extreme distance to the foreground of this peculiar landscape, what a contrast! There, 'in icy pomp the glaciers tower' and a volcano sleepeth mantled in snow; here, in heated domes of ruddy clay and mounds of rock are embosomed Geysirs and wells of boiling water from which rise clouds of steam; speaking of the subterranean fires slumbering below, which every few years awaken and send fiery floods of molten rock coursing over this strange volcanic isle.

FIFTH DAY.—*Geysir* to *Hruni*, *Skálholt* or *Hrepphólar*, visiting *en route* the *Gullfoss*. Should the party have been so fortunate as to have witnessed an eruption of the *Geysir* during their first day's sojourn at its site, or it be decided not to await one, a start will be made this morning in the direction of *Hekla*. If the party be a

ROUTE I.—TO GEYSIR AND HEKLA. 107

large one, there are two courses open to them: (1) To keep together, and take the tent or tents brought for use at the *Geysir* on to the farm of *Næfrholt* or *Selsund*, the nearest farms to *Hekla*, where a guide will be obtained for the ascent; or (2) Separate into parties of about four, each to proceed by a slightly different route, agreeing beforehand as to which of the three above-named parsonages each division will select for night quarters, that the demand for sleeping accommodation at either one of them may not exceed what is procurable. The two farms near *Hekla* are not only too distant from the *Geysir* to be reached in a day, visiting the *Gullfoss en route*, but also afford very poor accommodation; therefore it is advisable to sleep the second night at *Stóruvellir* or at one of the numerous farms in its vicinity, setting out early the next morning for either *Næfrholt* or *Selsund*.

GULLFOSS.—There is no regular road to this fall; consequently if the guide hired at *Reykjavik* has not previously conducted a party thither, it will be necessary to engage at *Haukadalr* a local guide, to show the party through the swampy region that lies between that farm and the *Hvitá*. The fall is from three to four hours' ride distant, the time taken depending in a great measure on whether the summer has been a wet or dry one; and the head waters—three arms—of the *Túnguftjót* will be forded. The Goldfall was not seen by the author, therefore he must crave permission to describe it from the pen of one who paid it a visit. 'I was more than charmed as the full grandeur of the tumbling river burst upon us. To compare it with its rival the *Dettifoss*, I should say that it is superior as regards the volume of water, but inferior on the score of depth. All the great falls of Iceland have a distinct peculiarity, they are V-shaped, that is to say, the river falls from two opposite sides into a cleft of that form, the angular termination of a *gjá* or lava rift. In this instance, too, as in most others, the angle is marked by an islet of basalt, which thus forms two distinct bodies of water. I roughly estimated each arm at about 100 feet in width, the deepest of them, about 80 feet, falling into a fissure scarce ten feet wide at the bottom, and not more than fifty feet wide at the top, shaped somewhat like a funnel. Immediately above the main fall, the river descends in a series of cascades, in all perhaps forty feet in depth, and some 600 feet broad. The widest part of the river I judged to be not less than 500 yards, narrowing to about 300 as the rapids are reached. It is possible to scramble down to the level of the stream below the fall, whence a good view can be obtained, while behind one the black wall rises 150 feet sheer. From the basin that receives the fallen waters, . . . the imprisoned torrent foams and plunges with maddened rage twixt towering buttresses of palagonite (?) and basaltic lava, that frown upon it and bend over it as if longing to prevent its escape, and indeed from one point it is impossible to imagine that any but a subterranean exit can exist, so closely do the black walls approach each other.

'There are many grim, grand beauties in the foss itself, but these are far surpassed by the landscape northwards. In the foreground is the wild barren waste which forms the basin of the river, backed by the *Bláfell* (Blue-fell), a bulky-looking fellow with steep side and flattish top, behind which we know lies the glacier-fed and floe-covered *Hvítárvatn* (White-river-lake), whence issues the river, a matured and muddy flood. Beyond, on the one hand, the snow-fields of the *Lángjökull* tower in pristine whiteness, relieved by the sharp peaks of the *Járlhettur* (Earl's-hoods), rising from their base, while to the right or eastwards we can see the *Kerlingafjöll* (Carline-mountains), marking a scatter of hot springs, and over-topping them are the spurs of . . . the icy giant that guards two of the mid-island paths.'

After seeing the fall, the whole party will still keep together and ride southward close to the river as far as *Bræðratúnga* (Brother's tongue) farm; and the local guide had better be retained until this place is reached. Here a halt should be made for coffee; and if the party is large, and it has been decided not to bring the tents from the *Geysir*, the divisions will each take a slightly different route. Of course, if but two people are travelling together, they may select which route they please. If there are three divisions, two should cross the river here, and one ride southward east of the river nearly to its junction with the *S. Laxá*, and then branch off for *Hreppholar*, while the other will strike eastward to *Hruni*. The third division will ride southward (Route not shown on map) on the west side of the *Hvítá* to *Skálholt*—once the site of a cathedral and the residence of a bishop. The two parties proceeding southward will have the advantage with respect to scenery, for there is many a charming piece in this wild river valley. At *Hólmi* (Holm) a tall pillar of rock stands in the midst of the roaring torrent, which here bounds between the walls of a black ravine. A little to the south of the holm is the spot where a natural stone bridge spanned the river in olden times, which, according to some stories, was destroyed by the orders of the wife of a certain Bishop of *Skálholt*, that beggars might be kept from her doors. From *Bræðratúnga* to

ROUTE I.—TO GEYSIR AND HEKLA.

Hruni or *Skálholt* will take between two and three hours; to *Hrepphólar* about four. The *Minni Laxá* will have to be forded by both the *Hruni* and *Hrepphólar* party. Obliging people and fair accommodation at all three places, but rather dear at *Hruni*. Salmon fishing to be had in both the Lesser and Greater *Laxá*.

SIXTH DAY.—To *Stóruvellir*, or a farm near. An easy one for all three divisions, therefore a late start may be made. The *Skálholt* party will cross the *Hvítá* by ferry, and the *Hrepphólar* party will ferry or ford the *Stærra Laxá*, shortly after setting out, and the *Hruni* party likewise, but higher up the river. A ride of about an hour in the first instance, about half in the second, and an hour and a half in the third, will bring the three parties to the ferry over the *Þjórsá* (Bull-river). A visit should be paid to a little islet in the river, where one of the ancient local Things, the *Árnesþing*, held its meetings. There are two farms near by, at one of which a man and boat will be obtainable. An easy hour and a half's ride from the river will bring the party to *Stóruvellir*. The good old dean, Síra Guðmundr Jónsson, is famous for his hospitality, and tourists are always made exceptionally comfortable. The ladies of the now reunited party should seek quarters here, and the males at the farms in the vicinity.

SEVENTH DAY—ASCENT OF HEKLA.—An early start *must* be made. A guide for the ascent will be hired either at *Næfrholt* or *Selsund*; the farm first named is the nearest to *Hekla*, and is the one generally selected. The hire of a guide is usually 6 *kroner*. On the way a small river, the *Vestri Rángá* (West Wrong-river), will be forded. From *Næfrholt* the journey to and ascent of the mountain takes about four and a half hours, and the descent and return journey somewhat less; the ponies can be ridden for some distance.

The apex of *Hekla*, 5,108 feet, is the north-east lip of the northernmost of the two craters upon its summit. This volcano is credited with seventeen eruptions, but it is doubtful if so many have taken place, eruptions in any part of Iceland usually being placed to *Hekla's* credit. The dates of the eruptions recorded are given in the tabulated list of volcanoes in the right-hand upper corner of the map attached to this work. Eruptions of lava occasionally take place in the vicinity, while the mountain itself is quiescent; and the author believes the lava wells forth from fissures torn in the rocky strata roofing in a subterranean channel connecting the volcanic vent of *Hekla* with the vast central vent beneath *Askja* (See Chapter II. p. 47). The last eruption of lava took place in 1878, some miles north-east of *Hekla*; others are recorded in 1554 and 1754.

The first eruption of *Hekla* after the settlement of Iceland was brought about, according to a mythical legend, by a man named Sæmunðr, who threw a casket into a crater at the summit and 'awoke the sleeping lion.' The following were the most violent of the eruptions :—

A.D. 1294.—'Fifth eruption from *Hekla*. Violent earthquakes, huge chasms opened in the earth; wells and fountains became white as milk for three days; *Rangá* (Wrong-river) changed its course; rivers were covered with pumice. Some new hot springs came into existence, others vanished.'

A.D. 1300. 'Sixth eruption, July 13th, one of the most violent on record. The ashes were borne by a S.W. wind over the North country and covered a large portion of it. Great earthquakes. Famine and great loss of life followed.'

A.D. 1436. 'Ninth eruption—Eighteen homesteads destroyed.'

A.D. 1510. 'Tenth eruption, July 25th; great fall of ashes, huge blocks of lava were cast at a long distance out of the mountain; many people were killed by these falling.'

A.D. 1597. 'Twelfth eruption, excessively violent, began January 3rd; the loud reports were heard for twelve successive days even in the northernmost parts of the country; eighteen columns of fire were seen rising from the mountain . . . the ashes covered about one-half of the country, from *Borgarfjörðr* (Burg-fjord) in the West to the district called *Lón* (Wash) in the East, and North as far as *Bárðardalr* (Bard's-dale). The same spring there occurred earthquakes about *Olves*, through which many farmsteads fell in. . . .'

A.D. 1845.—The seventeenth and last. 'Commenced on the 2nd September and continued for seven months. The ashes were carried over to Shetland, and the column of smoke rising out of the mountain reached a height of 14,000 feet (Danish). The lava which this eruption produced contained a mass of 14,400 millions of cubic feet (Danish).' It is asserted that during this eruption the mountain lost 500 feet in height, so much of the summit having been blown away by the explosions. Burton laughs at the writers, saying: 'They forget or ignore the fact that the new crater opened laterally, and low down.' The forgetfulness is on the part of Burton himself, who ignores the fact that ashes, scoriæ and rock were ejected from the craters at the summit, whose remains are now to be seen, and that the crater low down was the one whence issued the lava.

In making the ascent, a little over an hour's climb after leaving the ponies (the spot where these will be left will probably depend a great deal on the guide: Burton says, 'We rode up half-way.... At an impassable divide we left our poor nags to pass the dreary time without water or forage') will bring the party to the 1845 lava crater. Owing to the action of 'frost and fire' it is in a very ruinous condition, but the lava-flood which here found exit well marks its site. Burton says: 'The only remnant is the upper lip prolonged to the right; the dimensions may have been 120 by 150 yards, and the cleft shows a projecting ice-ledge ready to fall. ... A little beyond this bowl the ground smokes, discharging snow-steam made visible by the cold air.' A quarter of an hour's climb distant is another crater, known as the Southern Crater. 'It is a regular formation about 100 yards at the bottom each way, with the right (east) side red and cindery, and the left yellow and sulphury; mosses and a few flowerets grow on the lips; in the sole rise jets of steam, and a rock-rib bisects it diagonally from north-east to south-west.' (Burton).

From this to the northern or 'Red Crater,' the walk is not difficult along a snow-covered ridge, with here and there hot patches of earth showing through. The north-east lip of this crater, as mentioned before, is the highest point of the mountain. Burton, who speaks very disparagingly of *Hekla* and terms it 'a common-place heap' and 'a mere pigmy' (a pigmy of 5,108 feet!), thus describes the view from its summit. 'Inland, beyond a steep snow-bed unpleasantly crevassed, lay a grim photograph all black and white; Lángjökull looking down upon us with a grand and freezing stare; the Hrafntinnu Valley marked by a dwarf cone, and beyond where streams head, the gloomy regions stretching to the Sprengisandr, dreary wastes of utter sterility, howling deserts of dark ashes, wholly lacking water and vegetable life, and wanting the gleam and the glow which light up the Arabian wild. Skaptár and Oræfa were hidden from sight. Seawards, ranging from west to south, the view, by contrast, was a picture of amenity and civilisation. Beyond castellated Hljóðfell and conical Skjaldbreið appeared the familiar forms of Esja, and the long lava projection of the Gold Breast country, melting into the western main. Nearer stretched the fair lowlands, once a broad deep bay, now traversed by the network of Ölfusá, Thjórsá, and the Markarfljót; while the sixfold bunch of the Westman Islands, mere stone lumps upon a blue ground, seemingly floating far below the raised horizon, lay crowned by summer sea. Eastward we distinctly traced the Fiskivötn. Run the eye along the southern shore, and again the scene shifts. Below the red hornitos of the slope rises the classical Threehorned, not lofty, but remarkable for its trident top; Tindfjall (tooth-fell) with its two horns, or pyramids of ice, casting blue shadows upon the untrodden snow; and the whole mighty mass known as the Eastern Jökull, Eyjafjall (island-fell), so called from the black button of rock which crowns the long white dorsum; Kátlá (Kötlugjá), Merkrjökull, and Goðalands, all connected by ridges, and apparently neither lofty nor impracticable. I venture (as also does the author) to predict that they will succumb to the first well-organised attack.'

After the descent a halt will be made at *Næfrholt* or *Seleund* for milk and coffee; and somewhere about midnight the party will arrive back at their previous night's quarters.

EIGHTH DAY.—Unless pressed for time, a day's rest will be welcome to the travellers, and doubly so to the ponies.

NINTH DAY.—*Stóruvellir* to *Eyrarbakki* (Beach-bank) —Longish day's journey. If the guide has not been this road before, a local one will be necessary from *Stóruvellir* to the *Þjórsá*. This river will be ferried in the vicinity of *Kálfholt* (Calf-holt), distant about eighteen miles from *Stóruvellir* by a route unshown on the maps. *Villingaholt* parsonage, on the west side of river, will be made a half-way house for the usual refreshment—a cup of coffee and a draught of milk. From here the path leads south-west to the coast, and follows the coast-line to *Eyrarbakki*, the only trading post on the south coast. The factor here, Herra Þórgrímsson, is a very obliging, hospitable man, who does all in his power to aid travellers in this part of the island. Steamers do not touch at *Eyrarbakki*, there being no harbour.

Anglers having a few days to spare may profitably employ them by making an excursion from here to one of the farms on the *Álftavatn*, there being excellent trout fishing, it is said, in the *Sog* north and south of that lake. (See *ante* p. 99). *Reykjavik* can be reached *viá Reykir* (Smoke) in a longish day's ride from the farms on the west shore of the *Álftavatn*. The mountain due north of *Eyrarbakki* is *Ingólfsfjall*, and, although of no great size, is full of interest, for upon it Ingólfr, one of the two first settlers, desired to be buried, 'that he might behold all his vast possessions from its summit, at the last day'!

TENTH DAY.—*Eyrarbakki* to *Krisuvík*.—About eight hours' ride. Shortly after setting out the outlet of the *Ölfusá*, a large sheet of water formed by the *Hvítá* and five other rivers where they fall into the sea, will have to be ferried at *Oseyri* farm. The path skirts the coast thence to the parsonage and church of *Strandar-kirkja* (Church-by-the-Strand), where a halt may be made for coffee. Shortly after leaving here the bays of the *Hlíðarvatn*, a brackish sheet of water, formerly an inlet from the sea, will be waded through. Four hours' ride thence, through a grim volcanic region, intersected with old lava-flows, will bring the travellers to *Krísuvík*. There is no parsonage here, the church being a chapel of ease; therefore quarters must be sought at the farm near by, whose owner, a widow, does all she can for travellers, and is moderate in her charges. The accommodation is very rude and limited, but there are several other farms—also rather poor ones—in the vicinity.

ELEVENTH DAY.—Should the travellers wish to reach *Reykjavík* to-night, early rising will enable them to devote four hours to the exploration of the solfatarar here and yet get away by midday, and eight hours later will see them safely back in the capital. A day, however, can be pleasantly passed here by those with a taste for geology. The *Krísuvík* solfatarar have been thus described:—

In a valley, bordered by high mountains, is a green and extensive morass, interspersed with a few lakes. In the midst of the morass ' are cauldrons of boiling mud, some of them fifteen feet in diameter, numberless jets of steam, and boiling mud issuing from the ground, in many instances to the height of six or eight feet.' Mr. Charles W. Vincent, F.C.E., the writer here quoted, further says :—' Sir George Mackenzie . . . . in his justly celebrated " Travels in Iceland" gives a vivid word picture of the scene : "It is impossible," he writes, "to convey adequate ideas of the wonders of its terrors. The sensation of a person, even of firm nerves, standing on a support which feebly sustains him, where literally fire and brimstone are in incessant action, having before his eyes tremendous proofs of what is going on beneath him, enveloped in thick vapours, his ears stunned with thundering noises—these can hardly be expressed in words, and can only be conceived by those who have experienced them."'

' The actual extent of the sulphur beds it is quite impossible to calculate; but from Krísuvík to Hengill (the steaming mountain S.W. of *Þingvallavatn*) forty-seven have been discovered. . . . . The deposit of sulphur I personally saw at Krísuvík must amount to many thousand tons (the mines are now worked by a Scotch firm, so that probably not so much sulphur will be seen); hitherto the sulphur taken away has been reproduced in two or three years (?), all the mines, or nearly all, being in a living state.' (Captain Commerell's Reports, July, 1857.)

'In the valley itself the springs are not always visible at the surface, being so completely covered by the earth that it is only by piercing through the crust of indurated sulphur earth, that their presence is discovered. Sometimes the explorer is made unpleasantly aware of the insecure nature of his footing by falling through, and thus opening up a fresh thermal spring. The late Sir William Hooker, when visiting this place, in endeavouring to escape a sudden gust of strongly odorous vapour, jumped into a mass of semi-liquid hot earth and sulphur, and but for his presence of mind, in throwing himself flat upon the ground, would have sunk to a considerable depth; as it was, the difficulty of extricating himself was very considerable.

'Less than a quarter of a mile from the hot springs is a lake, Geslravatn (?), formed by the filling up of an extinct crater. This the inhabitants describe as being fathomless (Mr. Seymour, last year, found no bottom at five-and-twenty fathoms). The depth is, at any rate, very considerable. Although so close to a spot where the ground is, even at the surface, scorching to the feet, the water in this lake is ice-cold' (Vincent).

The foregoing will show what an interesting locality the *Kriswvik* region is; a detailed account of the solfatarar here by Mr. Vincent will be found in 'The Journal of the Society of Arts' for January 17th, 1873. Travellers here in the month of August, by making a stay of a few days, might get a shot at a reindeer, a small herd having its habitat on the range of hills extending from *Kriswvik* to *Þingvallavatn*. The herd is frequently seen in the vicinity of the *Kleifavatn* (Cliff-lake), near the place first named. Grouse are some years found in great numbers upon the hills.

The distance to *Reykjavik* is about twenty-five miles; the path first descends a hill, and then, after crossing a boggy tract, skirts the western side of the *Kleifavatn*. Quitting the lake, tremendously rugged beds of lava will be traversed, with small oasis-like grass-patches lying amidst them, in one of which the ponies will be allowed to graze for half an hour or so, and a shift of saddles take place. Six hours' ride will bring the party to *Hafnarfjörðr* (alluded to in 'Excursions from the Capital'), where a cup of coffee, or a bottle of light Danish ale, may be obtained at the inn. If the party wish to visit *Bessastaðir* (also mentioned in Excursions from the Capital), they should stay at *Hafnarfjörðr* for the night, and visit the house built by Snórri Sturluson *en route* to *Reykjavik* on the morrow. From *Hafnarfjörðr* a three hours' ride, the first part of the way through another grim lava-covered tract, and subsequently, after rounding the heads of the inlets, over an excellent newly-made road, will bring the party back to the capital after, as will be admitted by all, a highly interesting twelve days' excursion.

In conclusion, the author would observe here that if a tourist has a couple of days to spare, they cannot be passed in a more agreeable manner than by making an excursion to *Reykjanes*, the south-west extremity of Iceland. Accommodation will be obtainable at *Staðr* parsonage, five hours' ride from *Krísuvík*. From here, the next morning, a short ride will bring him to a tremendous fissure, the *Hauksvörðugjá*, at the southern extremity of which are several hot springs. North of this fissure is another of less extent. The whole of this region has been subjected to great volcanic disturbance; and the vast lava floods that have here issued at various times cover an area of over 500 square miles! In all probability the volcanic outlets here mark the course of a subterranean channel running in a south-westerly direction from the centre of the island, connected with the great central volcanic vent there. Mr. Vincent, in his excellent paper above alluded to, says: 'The living sulphur mines of the Krísuvík region are all ranged on lines evidently corresponding to the great volcanic diagonal line stretching from Cape Reykjanes to the Lake of Mývatn.' This channel extends beneath the sea for a considerable distance, eruptions having taken place forty-five miles to the south-west of the coast. About twelve miles from *Reykjanes* in that direction are a group of islets, the *Eldeyjar* (Fire-isles), which are craters that frequently erupt. It was mentioned in the geological description of the island, that the existence of a channel running in this direction, connected with a central vent, was proved in a marked manner in 1783, when the eighth recorded eruption off *Reykjanes* took place at the same time that the vast lava-floods burst forth in the vicinity of the *Skaptár Jökull*.

The first recorded eruption in the *Reykjanes* district occurred in A.D. 1211. It was accompanied by terrible earthquakes, and eighteen people lost their lives. A list of the recorded eruptions will be found in the right-hand upper corner of the map.

Should the weather be calm, a boat and men should be hired at *Staðr*, and an excursion made to the Fire-isles; where it is believed no Englishman has yet set foot. On the journey from *Staðr* to *Reykjavík*, the northernmost fissure may be visited, the path passing close to. It is a longish day's ride, from *Staðr* to the capital, but may be done by making an early start.

ROUTE II.

A MONTH'S EXCURSION FROM REYKJAVÍK, RETURNING TO THE CAPITAL.

AN EXTENSION OF ROUTE I. THROUGH THE 'NJÁL COUNTRY' TO THE MÝRDALS JÖKULL, IN WHICH IS SITUATED THE KÖTLUGJÁ VOLCANO, AND TO ÞÓRSMÖRK, ONE OF THE MOST ENCHANTING PIECES OF SCENERY IN ICELAND; THENCE TO THE VAST LAVA-FLOODS IN THE VICINITY OF THE SKAPTÁR JÖKULL, TO THE GRAND GLACIAL SCENERY OF THE VATNA JÖKULL, AND TO THE MONARCH OF THE ICELANDIC MOUNTAINS, THE ÖRÆFA JÖKULL; RETURNING viâ THE SOUTH COAST AND KRÍSUVÍK.

THE FIRST SEVEN DAYS will be occupied as described in the preceding route, in visiting Þingvellir, Geysir, Gullfoss and Hekla; and the evening of the seventh day (if the stay at the Geysir is not prolonged to witness an eruption) will find the tourists back at Stóruvellir after the ascent of Hekla.

EIGHTH DAY.—*Stóruvellir to Breiðabólstaðir.* An easy day's ride, fording both the *Vestri* (W.) and *Eystri* (E.) *Rángá*, but the pony track is said to be not very good. On the way will be seen on the left hand the three peaks of the *Þríhyrningr* (Three-horned), in the vicinity of which the noble, but unfortunate, Gunnar and his two brothers, Kolskegg and Hjort, encountered and defeated a band of thirty armed assailants, fourteen of whom bit the dust—as also did Hjort, to Gunnar's great grief; as told in the Outline of the Njál Saga in the introductory portion of this work. To the southeast, across the *Markarfljót*, will be seen a hill standing on an island in the river; it is the *Stóra Dímon*, amongst whose crags Njál's sons concealed themselves when they fell upon Þrain and slew him.

Breiðabólstaðir parsonage lies right in the heart of the Njál country, and it was the home of several of the island's most famous men in the tenth and eleventh centuries. It stands a short distance north of the *Þverá*, a large river connecting the *Markarfljót*—which drains the *Torfa, Merkr* and *Góðalands Jöklar*—with the *Þjórsá*. The *Markarfljót* finds its way to the sea by several channels, thus creating a group of largish islands, the *Útlandeyjar*, the chief of which are bounded on the south by the sea. The easternmost channel retains the name of the parent river, but the centralmost is called *Álar* (Reins), and the westernmost *Affall*. These islands and the vicinity, besides being the scene of many of the events recorded in the Njál Saga, are rich in historical interest, for it was here some of the most famous chiefs and others dwelt in the early days of the Norse settlement.

The people at *Breiðabólstaðir* are very obliging. If one's guide has not accompanied a party through the Njál country before, it will be necessary to take a man from here on the morrow.

NINTH DAY.—To *Hlíðarendi*, 'where the peerless Gunnar dwelt, and fighting, fell;' and thence push on to *Barkarstaðir* or *Fljótsdalr*, two farms south of the *Tindfjalla Jökull*, to pass the night. The quarters are rather rough, but with the 'Garnet Wolseley,' or the box bed described in the chapter on Outfit, the travellers will pass the night pretty comfortably. *Hlíðarendi* is about two hours' ride from *Breiðabólstaðir*, and the same distance from the farms where it is recommended to seek night quarters; several streams will have to be forded *en route*.

Gunnar's home stood upon the southern slope of a range of low green hills, a short distance north of the Þverá. It is said that the foundation walls of the old hall are still traceable; but the farm buildings now standing on the site are mere hovels; for the farm is now a very poor one, but a miserable remnant of the fertile level grass land, which made the spot so dear in Gunnar's eyes, now remaining. In his day *Hlíðarendi* was surrounded with rich pastures, and corn-fields were not unknown, where we now find a wilderness 'howling in desolation'; while the fells were clad with forest. The whole face of the country in the eight and a half centuries that have elapsed since his time has completely changed; volcanic eruption after eruption has converted the rich grass meads into cindery wastes; while flood after flood of water from the glaciers has eaten away mile after mile of the plain, and torn it asunder to seek the sea by many outlets. Waller thus beautifully expresses the impression made upon his mind by a visit to 'these haunts of old romance': 'This wilderness was of all places in the world the most touching to me. It really seemed as if the beauty of the spot had cared to exist no longer since the hero was dead, and had let the elements work their destruction upon the scene, to obliterate it utterly, and to leave, like its master, but a memory behind.' He further says: 'We then pushed up the hill for some little distance, and found a cairn. "It is Gunnar's grave," said my companion, an old Icelander, "Here they buried him; and beneath yon boulder of lava-rock they put his bright clothes and armour, and no one has dared to touch them to this day. But though his body was laid here in its grave, his spirit rested not in the stony chamber, for on the starlit nights the war-songs he had sung in life were heard again upon the hill-side, and magic lights were seen to burn within the cairn."[1]

TENTH DAY.— Excursion to Þórsmörk, and thence to Ásar (? Gods); a long and roughish day's work, and an early start and local guide indispensable. This day's journey must, and the subsequent ones should, be made in the lightest possible marching order; therefore guns, ammunition, rods, and all dispensable baggage should be sent by a man and ponies, obtained here or at Breiðabólstaðir, down to Kross (25th day), to await the travellers' return. The Markarfljót will have to be ferried or forded shortly after setting out. This excursion is said to be one of the grandest that is to be made in Iceland. The author has never ceased to regret that circumstances—ice-fringed rivers in the month of October— prevented him paying a visit to a place that is described as 'the most charming and romantic spot in all Iceland.'

Þórsmörk is a remarkably wild portion of the valley of the Markarfljót, at a spot where it is narrowed in by the Tindfjalla Jökull, on the north-west, and the Góðalands and Merkr Jöklar, on the south-east, and it boasts one of 'the finest woods in Iceland.' Waller says:—'Inside of this extraordinary valley the contortions and shapes assumed by the lava are really wonderful. On one side can be imagined a line of gigantic fortresses running on for miles, and on the other great churches and temples mixed up in most curious confusion. Above these come the towering crags, topped by precipitous green glaciers, piled up and up until they are lost in the clouds; and from the junction of rock and ice, leaping like rainbows out of the sky, shoot countless waterfalls, making a series of exquisite arches as they fall into the valley below. At the extreme end of this place . . . . Between the gigantic rocks come sweeping down to the river the loveliest green slopes, some hundreds of them covered with birch-bushes and underwood.'

The tourist must not fail to ask his guide to show him on his way to Þórsmörk 'the largest tree in Iceland,' a solitary mountain-ash, at least thirty feet high, standing on the edge of a tremendous chasm, completely sheltered from the weather by huge lava cliffs.

From *Þórsmörk* the route will lie over the *Mælifellssandr* (Measure-fell-sand), north of the *Merkr Jökull*, and thence by a track known as the south *Fjallabaksvegr*, passing through wild scenery, to *Ásar* parsonage. The time taken to accomplish this day's journey will in a great measure depend upon the state of the tributary streams draining the glaciers. The traveller will probably be in the saddle at least ten hours.

ELEVENTH DAY.—At *Ásar*. The ponies will need a day's rest after the fatigues of yesterday's journey, and the travellers, doubtless, will also find one welcome. *Ásar* is situated on the western border of the vast floods of lava that burst forth in the vicinity of the *Skaptár Jökull* in 1783, and is a capital base for their exploration; it is also the best place from which to make an assault upon the hitherto, it is believed, unvisited *Kötlugjá* crater amidst the glaciers of the *Mýrdals Jökull*.

TWELFTH DAY.—*Kötlugjá* (*Kötlu*, genitive of Katla = Kettle; *gjá* = rift). An attempt should be made to visit this volcano; about which little is known save its dread doings. In Zurcher and Margollé's work on Volcanoes we find: 'The crater of *Kötlugjá* is an immense fissure which crosses the mountain, split in two during an eruption.' This huge volcanic outlet is situated in the eastern part of the *Jökull;* and is credited with thirteen eruptions, the last in 1860. The first was in A.D. 894, when a vast extent of country was laid waste. The ninth, in 1660, was of an extraordinary nature. Such was the quantity of sand, stones, and débris borne down by the flood from the melting glaciers on the heated mountain, 'that a dry beach was formed where formerly people fished in a depth of 20 fathoms; the coast was extended 1,000 fathoms out into the sea, and five or six farmsteads were destroyed.' As the author observed in the Geological Account of Iceland, it would not take many centuries, with one such eruption in every decade, to unite a widely-scattered group of islets into one island! The tenth eruption, in 1721, was a very violent one: 'It began on May 11th with excessive floods and glacier-slips; the ice-blocks grounded in a depth of from 70 to 80 fathoms three (Danish = $13\frac{1}{2}$ English) miles out at sea. A grass-grown neck of land was swept away, and in its stead was left a polished slab of rock 6,750 square fathoms in extent. The ashes were borne westward, and fell so thick the first day that at homesteads 25 (Danish = 110 English) geographical miles distant from the crater the light was obscured to such an extent as to make reading of print impossible' (Thoroddsen). In 1755 the eleventh recorded eruption occurred. Fifty homesteads were destroyed, and the surrounding country was covered with a layer of ashes from six inches to two feet in depth. In 1860 there is no mention of any farms having been destroyed, although the eruption was followed by earthquakes.

After the assault on the *Kötlugjá* the exploring party will return to *Asar*, and the

THIRTEENTH DAY had better be allowed as a day of rest, one will probably be needed by both men and ponies after the fatigues of an ascent of the *Mýrdals Jökull*.

FOURTEENTH DAY.—May be pleasantly and instructively employed exploring northward the westernmost of the vast lava-floods which burst forth in the vicinity in 1783. These eruptions were of a magnitude 'unparalleled on the earth in historic times.' Great eruptions of lava about the *Varmárdalr*, the valley of a river tributary to the *Skaptá*, began in June; and later on others burst forth about the sources of the *Hverfisfljót* (Wharf-fleet), a river lying farther east. The lava that issued formed two enormous torrents of molten rock, which, according to Zurcher, 'spread to a distance of from forty to fifty miles, with a breadth of seven to fourteen. The depth of the lava was in places 150 yards, and it was calculated by Professor Bischoff that the mass of igneous rock which issued during these eruptions exceeded in bulk the cubic contents of Mont Blanc.' During the eruptions 'a whirlwind of ashes' swept over the face of the country, and the rivers were charged with fetid waters; the first causing a famine, by destroying the pastures, and the latter a pestilence; and 'these proved fatal to 9,000 human beings, 21,000 cattle, 233,000 sheep, and 36,000 horses' (Thoroddsen).

The river valleys filled in with these lava-floods now present a terribly grand sight, with a background of ice-clad mountains covering an area of over 3,000 square miles; in places the lava is known to be 500 feet thick; and where the fluid rock leaped over precipices, it presents the appearance of petrified glaciers or cataracts.

FIFTEENTH DAY.—*Asar* to *Kálfafell*. At *Búland* (Home-land) church the *Eldvötn* (Fire-waters) will be forded, and shortly after a large sheet of water, nestling among some hills, will be skirted, and the lava-filled valley of an arm of the *Skaptá* entered. A halt will probably be made at *Kirkjubær* (Kirkby) for a cup of coffee, about half the distance to *Kálfafell* being accomplished. After leaving here the track will lie through a thickly peopled and tolerably fertile stretch of country till the vast lava-bed in the lower part of the valley of the *Hverfisfljót* is reached. The path winds through this for about eight miles, and then again enters a peopled district, watered by several rivers, which will have to be forded ere *Kálfafell* is reached.

SIXTEENTH DAY.—*Kálfafell* to the 'Forest' nestling amid the glaciers of the *Vatna Jökull*. A most interesting excursion; but a local guide is indispensable. A halt should be made at *Núpstaðr* (Peak-stead) for a cup of coffee. It was from this farm that Mr. Watts started upon his perilous journey across the *Vatna Jökull* in 1875. The path to the Forest passes close under the *Lómagnupr* (Loon-peak), a towering wall 2,400 feet high. North of the Forest, amidst the glaciers, are some lakes, *Grimsvötn*, which it is believed are craters; and an attempt should be made to visit them. It is recorded that eruptions took place from them in A.D. 1598, 1685 and 1716. An excursion should also be made to the *Seljalandsfoss*, a fine fall on the *Hverfisfljót*.

SEVENTEENTH DAY.—*Kálfafell* to *Svinafell* (Swine-fell) or *Sandfell*, respectively a farm and parsonage lying at the base of the *Öræfa Jökull*, an ice-clad volcano that is said to be the monarch of the Icelandic mountains. An easy day's ride over the *Skeiðarársandr* (Swift-river-sand), a vast extent of sand and gravel, the detritus of the glaciers. Several glacier-fed streams to ford at the commencement, and towards the close, of the day's journey. The accommodation at *Svinafell* is said to be fair; it is the nearest farm to the *Jökull*.

EIGHTEENTH AND NINETEENTH DAYS.—An assault should be made upon the *Öræfa Jökull*, 6,455 feet, which, it is believed, is a virgin peak. The second will be a day of rest before setting out on the return journey. If wished, from this point the travellers, instead of returning to *Reykjavik*, can proceed on to *Berufjörðr*, *Eskifjörðr* or *Seyðisfjörðr*, three trading posts on the east coast, called at by the Danish steamers. (See dotted route line on the map.)

TWENTIETH DAY.—Return to *Kálfafell*.

TWENTY-FIRST DAY.—*Kálfafell* to *Ásar*.

TWENTY-SECOND DAY.—*Ásar* to *Vík* (Wick). Nearly the whole of this day's journey will lie across the *Mýrdalssandr*, an extensive tract of detritus brought down from the *Jökull* after which the waste is named. A number of glacier-fed streams will have to be forded. Just before reaching *Höfðabrekka* church, the four forks of the *Miklakvisl* (Mickle-forks) will be forded. These insulate a triangular-shaped island with its base seaward. On the south side of this island is a headland named *Hjörleifshöfði* (Sword-Leifr's-head), which is said to be the second place where the two first settlers landed, the first being further to the eastward and named *Ingólfshöfði*. A detour may be made to visit the spot. Immediately after leaving *Höfðabrekka*, where a halt should be made for coffee, the *Kerlingardalsá* will be forded. It was in this dale that Hedinn the sorcerer resided, who, according to the Njál Saga, by his invocations brought about a volcanic eruption as Thangbrand, the apostle of Christianity, rode over the *Arnarstakksheiði*, a heath on the west side of the river. A half hour's ride hence will bring the travellers to *Vik*, a farm where exceptionally good quarters are procurable.

TWENTY-THIRD DAY.—*Vík* to *Holt*. A glorious, but rather long day's ride along the coast, with glacier scenery inland. A halt should be made at *Dyrhólar* to visit the *Loptsalahellir* (Air-hall-cave), a grotto in which the local þing formerly held its meetings. Off the headland to the south is an enormous natural stone arch, *Dyrhólaey*, through which it is said a ship might sail. A day may be pleasantly spent here, if the travellers are so minded, making a boating excursion to *Dyrhólaey*, etc. Quarters obtainable at *Dyrhólar* parsonage. Two hours' ride westward we come to the *Fúlilækr* (Foul-brook), a *Jökulsá* which bears the name of being the worst river in all Iceland to cross, it being liable in summer to frequent and sudden floods from the glaciers. After fording this, an hour's ride over the *Skógasandr* will bring the traveller in sight of a fine waterfall, the *Skógarfoss* (Grove-fall), and three hours later he will arrive at *Holt*. The time taken to accomplish this day's journey will depend greatly on the state of the rivers; but every effort should be made to reach *Holt* for the night, as the next day will be an easy one. Good accommodation, it is said, at *Holt*.

TWENTY-FOURTH DAY.—*Holt* to *Seljaland* (? Shieling-land). Less than three hours' ride. Before setting out examine the remarkable grottoes in the vicinity, *Hrútshellir* (Hrútr's-cave) is the most famous. Turn your ponies out to pasture directly you arrive at *Seljaland*, and set out on foot to visit the *Seljadalsfoss* (Shielingdale-fall), 'a magnificent cascade, at least 400 feet high' (Waller).

TWENTY-FIFTH DAY.—*Seljaland* to *Kross*. The distance is not great, but two wide rivers, the *Markarfljót* and *Álar*, will have to be ferried or forded. The pastor at *Kross* entertained Waller exceedingly well. Here the heavy baggage sent down from *Breiðabólstaðir* will be recovered.

TWENTY-SIXTH DAY.—*Kross* to *Bergþórshvoll*, and thence to *Oddi* (Triangle). A swampy ride to the *Affall*, which will be forded. Close by, on its eastern bank, is the far-famed *Bergþórshvoll*, the home some nine centuries since of the peaceful Njál, and his doughty sons, and the scene of the 'burning' in which they perished. A very poor farmstead now stands upon the site of the good old lawgiver's commodious home, a knoll of a longish shape which terminates about a bowshot from the *Affall*. On the opposite side of the knoll to the river is *Káratjörn* (Kári's-tarn), the little pool wherein Kári extinguished his flaming garments when he made his escape from the burning house. Not a vestige of the old buildings, it is said, remain; but a few years since, during an alteration to one of the buildings here, many ashes, charred turfs, and stones were brought to light, also a few small articles; but the latter were eagerly bought up. Notwithstanding that so little is to be seen now at the spot where so much was done in the days 'lang syne,' one who has read the Saga must feel a strange delight at standing on the very spot so long the home of the hero of the story; and it cannot require a very vivid imagination to picture in one's mind the scene enacted here on the day that he preferred to die in his burning home, so valiantly defended unto the death by his sons and retainers, rather than live on in the autumn of his life unable to avenge their deaths.

> But though the heroes are dust, and the good swords are rust,
> Still the land rings with the deeds that were done.

It is not possible to pass the night in the hovels at *Bergþórshvoll*; therefore a man should be taken to show the way over the island to *Oddi* parsonage, on the north bank of the *Þverá*. It will take about three hours to ride across the island to the river, which will be ferried opposite *Oddi*. A short ride from the river will bring the travellers to the door of the parsonage. Obliging people and good accommodation.

TWENTY-SEVENTH DAY.—*Oddi* to *Eyrarbakki*. Two hours' ride will bring the travellers to the ferry over the *Þjórsá*. After crossing which they will strike the bridle-path running south-west to the coast. From this point all particulars relative to the remaining three days' journey to *Reykjavík* will be found in Route I.

ROUTE III.

A SUMMER'S TOUR IN ICELAND.

THE MOST COMPREHENSIVE TOUR PRACTICABLE WITH PLEASURE IN THE COURSE OF AN ICELANDIC SUMMER, STARTING FROM REYKJAVÍK AND QUITTING THE ISLAND AT AKUREYRI, IN THE NORTH, OR SEYÐIS-FJÖRÐR, IN THE EAST. FOR LIST OF PLACES VISITED ON THIS TOUR, SEE ROUTE 3, AT END OF INTRODUCTORY SECTION (p. 21).

THE FIRST SEVEN DAYS will be occupied as described in Route I., in visiting Þingvellir, Geysir, Gullfoss, and Hekla; and the evening of the seventh day (if the stay at the Geysir is not prolonged to witness an eruption) will find the tourists back at Stóruvellir after the ascent of Hekla.

EIGHTH DAY.—*Stóruvellir to Skálholt.* An easy day after the fatigue of the preceding one. Iceland was formerly divided into two bishoprics, *Skálholt* and *Hólar*, but there is now but one, and the Cathedral and residence of the Bishop are at *Reykjavik*. *Skálholt* was the oldest, it was established in A.D. 1057; *Hólar*, fifty years later. The two cathedrals of Catholic days were destroyed by fire; the one at *Skálholt* being replaced by a very humble wooden building, while a more pretentious stone one was erected at *Hólar*.

NINTH DAY.—*Skálholt to Uthlíð.* About three hours' ride due north over the tract between the *Brúará* and *Tungufljót* rivers. This, like yesterday, is an easy day, and will admit of the ponies being in good condition for a long journey on the morrow.

TENTH DAY.—*Uthlíð to Reykholt.* A long day's ride through magnificent scenery. An early start advisable. About two hours after leaving *Uthlíð*, the party will pass through the *Hellisskarð* (Cave-pass) to the lava-beds surrounding *Skjaldbreið* and *Hlöðufell*. The scenery here is remarkably wild. The snow-crowned *Skjaldbreið* and *Hlöðufell* are the portals of a landscape the like of which is seldom seen. In the foreground, chaotic lava-beds fractured and upheaved in most fantastic forms; beyond, the extensive icy wastes of the *Geitlands* and *Skjaldbreiðar Jöklar*; and further off still, the *Ok* (Yoke) stands out boldly by itself, a mighty ice-clad rocky buttress. After traversing the lava-beds, the path winds close round *Skjaldbrei'ð* on the north to a number of small lakelets, *Brunnar* (Wells), whose grassy banks are frequently the halting-place of travellers, as the Wells lie at the junction of three tracks between the north and south parts of the island. It will probably take six hours to reach this halting-spot, even if the travellers have good pack ponies, not too heavily laden; and two hours' 'halt should be made there, as it will take four hours' rather sharp riding to bring the party to the first farm in the *Reykholtsdalr*, and about another hour to reach the parsonage. The travellers with their 'Garnet Wolseleys,' or box-bed arrangement, would doubtless be able to pass the night, should the ponies be greatly fatigued, at one of the farms in the upper part of the valley, but it is believed the houses are somewhat poor ones. There is probably, however, a large decent room at *Búrfell* (Bower-fell), a farm lying higher up the valley than the parsonage, for here the local Þíng holds its meetings.

ELEVENTH DAY.—At *Reykholt*. This should be a day of absolute rest for the ponies; but the travellers may pass their time very pleasantly examining the numerous hot springs in the valley. There is very fair accommodation at the parsonage. Here, in the first half of the thirteenth century, lived Snórri Sturluson, the most celebrated Saga-writer of Iceland, the author of the prose, or elder, Edda. He was one of the traitorous sons of Iceland who conspired to hand over the island to King Hákon of Norway, but he did not live to reap any reward at its annexation, for the project set the whole island in a blaze, and he was slain here in his own dwelling. A mound near the present parsonage, it is said, 'covers the chamber in which the poet was attacked and murdered.' It might, from an archæological point of view, repay the cost and trouble of excavation. Close by is 'Snórri's Bath,' a primitive piece of masonry circular in form, and about fifteen feet in diameter, in a sad state of decay, into which water from a hot spring near is conveyed by an underground duct. Here the traveller will be able to enjoy the luxury of a warm bath at any temperature he pleases, by diverting the supply and awaiting the cooling of the pool.

The most interesting of the hot springs in the valley, and the only one probably that the traveller fresh from the *Geysir* and *Strokkr* will care to see, is the *Árhver* (River-hot-spring), which bursts forth from a rocky islet raised but a few feet above the icy cold waters of the river. There is also a group of hot springs, the *Túnguhverir* (Tongue-hot-springs), a few miles from the junction of the river flowing through the valley with the *Hvitá*, which are well worth a visit; for the two largest of the geysirs here are known as the Alternating Geysir, as formerly, when one ceased to play, the other commenced to do so. Shepherd says, in his pleasant little work, 'The North-West Peninsula of Iceland':—'It (the Alternating Geysir) is situated on a mound of red clay, some sixty yards in length, at right angles to the river bank. . . . At the end of the mound furthest from the river were the two largest springs. They were partly on the side of the mound, which at that end was not nearly so steep as at the river-side, nor was it so high. These two jets appeared to me to have been formerly the alternating geysir; but, if so, they both, while we were there, played away together. I perceived no cessation in either of them during the twenty minutes we were watching them. The various jets were not at all regular in height, but varied from two to five feet.' He thus describes the other springs here:—'A more wonderful sight I never beheld. . . . The surface of the earth near the springs was covered with a thick coating of silex. Boiling water was issuing from holes and cracks in every direction. In one place was a single monster, emitting a jet several feet in height. In another place was a geysir, surrounded by a dozen smaller ones. Others were in little caves; and some in ledges on the silex-hardened face of the mound. All were making a sullen bubbling splash. . . . The cracks, holes, and fissures, from which this boiling water is emitted, must, I should think, be from eighty to one hundred in number.'

The view up the valley has much of beauty in it: the island in the river forms an interesting foreground, with the steam ascending from the geysir on it, the valley a middle distance, and beyond, for a background, stand the ice-crowned *Ok* and *Geitland's Jökull*,

'Like giants clad in armour blue
With helmets of a silver hue.'

If the members of the party are not anglers, and have no wish to visit the basaltic caverns at *Stapi*, or *Snæfells Jökull*, but desire to reach the north as quickly as possible, all the intervening days in this Route to the twenty-fifth day may be passed over. The party, should they determine to explore the *Snæfell* peninsula and make an assault upon the *Jökull*, will do well to leave all their heavy baggage at *Reykholt* or *Stafholt*, and take with them only what is absolutely indispensable for the fortnight's excursion westward, as to reach the north their route will lie up the *Reykholtsdalr*.

ROUTE III.—A SUMMER'S TOUR IN ICELAND. 127

Any pony which shows signs of giving in should be allowed to remain here until the party return, as there will be no need to take all the ponies on if some of the baggage is left behind. The excursion is strongly recommended, for it would be difficult to find a series of coastal landscapes to surpass those that are to be met with on the peninsula. Campbell says, in 'Frost and Fire':—'All down the Snæfell peninsula, on both sides, are cones and craters of many shapes. . . . At the head of the regiment of volcanoes is Snæfell, with its plains of basalt,' and, the author may add, basaltic caverns. The traveller will be unfortunate indeed if during his ten days' excursion on the peninsula he is not favoured with a view of the *Jökull*, and its connecting chain of mountains, with one of those gorgeous midnight sunset skies that are only to be seen in the far north; and at such a time even Burton thought the landscape, when seen from the sea, 'a "thing of beauty," even though the incomparable scenery of Magellan's Straits, rendering me not a little fastidious, was still fresh within my brain' (vol. ii. p. 100).

TWELFTH DAY.—*Reykholt* to *Stafholt* (Staff-holt). An easy day. The *Hvitá* will have to be ferried. If the travellers are anglers, they will probably make a stay of several days in the vicinity, as there are two salmon rivers close by, the *Norðrá* and *Þverá;* and a third, the *Grimsá,* within a few hours' ride. These three rivers are tributary to the *Hvitá,* which is a glacier-fed river. (See List of Salmon Rivers.)

THIRTEENTH DAY.—*Stafholt* to *Staðarhraun* (Stead-lava). Three rivers will have to be forded or ferried on this day's journey. *Staðarhraun* parsonage is situated on the borders of an ancient lava-flood; from which it derives its name. There is a more direct route than that shown on the map, viz. over the fens between the rivers, but this is not always practicable, even under the guidance of a local guide.

FOURTEENTH DAY. — *Staðarhraun* to *Miklaholt* (Mickle-holt). Three rivers will have to be forded; and after passing the second, the *Kaldá* (Cold-river), *Eldborg* (Fire-burg) will be seen. According to the Annals this is the first of the Icelandic volcanic outlets that erupted subsequently to the settlement of the island. It is about 200 feet high, stands in the midst of a plain, and is surrounded on all sides by lava. Campbell, in 'Frost and Fire' (vol. ii. p. 431), says:—'At a guess the crater at Eldborg may be about 400 yards wide, and 200 feet deep. No measurements were taken, but sketches were made. At the bottom of this great cup is a boss

of hard lava, the crown of a solid pillar, which froze in the tube.'
After examining *Eldborg*, the travellers will descend to the sea-
shore, and the heads of several shallow bays will be waded through.
Upon quitting the shore, a very swampy path leads up to *Miklaholt*
parsonage. 'Umbra' gives an amusing account of the passage of
the morass here, too lengthy to quote in full. He says: 'We
could not make straight for it (the parsonage), but had to stalk it,
as the sportsman on Scottish hills stalks the stag. . . . A narrow
causeway of rough, loose stones exists in places; which, detestable,
as it is to ride on abstractedly, is the only chance of safety.'

The people at *Miklaholt* have been found by travellers very
obliging. The river near here is a *Laxá*, which has seldom been
fished with a fly. The ponies should be allowed a day's rest here.

FIFTEENTH DAY.—*Miklaholt* to *Búðir* (Booths). A charming
day's ride along the shores of the *Faxafjörðr*, with the *Snæfells
Jökull* towering like a gigantic snow-covered pyramid to the westward. *Staðastaðr* parsonage should be made a half-way house for
a cup of coffee.

Búðir is, or was, a trading post, and Burton says: 'is far-famed
for chalybeate springs. Huts for invalids have been run up at this
well-known (?) "Kur-ort."'

SIXTEENTH DAY.—Excursion to the *Stapi* Basaltic Caverns.
Return to *Búðir* to sleep, as the accommodation there is superior
to the fishermen's dwellings at *Stapi*; or, if it is wished to ride
round the base of the *Jökull* on the morrow, push on to *Laugarbrekka* parsonage for the night. The latter course is recommended,
as the scenery is said to be superb, and the traveller may see—it is
to be hoped at a safe distance—an avalanche of rocky débris come
thundering down from the mountain near where the track passes
under *Enni* (the Brow), a precipice just west of *O'lafsvík* (Olafs-
wick). If an assault on the *Jökull* is contemplated, *Laugarbrekka*
should be made one's head-quarters. Burton says (vol. ii. p. 97):
'The Beruvík farm (near *Laugarbrekka*) appears to be a good starting place.' He also pens the following respecting the attempts
made to scale the icy giant: 'The earliest climbers seem to have
attempted the ascent from the east and south-east, where the snow-
line extends much lower. Such were Eggert Olafsson (1755);
Mr., afterwards Sir, John Stanley (1789); and the three Britishers
who "wrote their mistresses' names in the snow—the emblem of
their purity." Sir George Mackenzie (1810) remained below, and
Drs. Bright and Holland went stoutly up. . . . They were followed
by Henderson (1814), by Gaimard (1835), and by Forbes (1859).

'Of course (why 'of course'?) none reached the very summit. The Frenchman sensibly attempted it from the north, and found the slope easy. . . . Remains only to try the west, where the snow lies much higher up, and where the angle does not exceed 25°; here also the distance to the cusps or peaks is notably shorter. . . . . But Alpines who love "climbing for climb" must remember that without ropes and ladders, perhaps kites also, and very likely with them, it will be impossible to do more than has been done by their predecessors.'

SEVENTEENTH DAY.—*Laugarbrekka* to *O'lafsvik*: or *Búðir* to *Grundare*, if the travellers determine not to ride round the western termination of the peninsula. In the latter case the peninsula will be crossed by the pass known as the *Arnardalsskarð* (Eagle-dale-pass) to the head of the *Grundarfjörðr*. *Grundare* farm lies at the head of the fjord, between it and a pretty little lake; the accommodation is said to be very good. The route round the head of the peninsula to *O'lafsvik* has been alluded to. It is a fair day's journey, with good accommodation at the end of it. If this route is chosen, the

EIGHTEENTH DAY will be occupied in riding between that place and *Grundare*. It is a charming ride, skirting for many miles the shores of a deep bay. At *Hallbjarnareyri* (Hallbjörn's-beach) a couple of ancient grave tablets, with Runic inscriptions, are to be seen.

NINETEENTH DAY.—*Grundare* to *Helgafell* (Holy-fell). Another charming day's ride, with grand scenery, fell and fjord alternating. About midway, the traveller will pass through the *Berserkjahraun* (Berserks-lava) by a 'well-planned smooth road.' In the Eyrbyggja Saga is a legendary account of the making of this road by two Berserks. 'Umbra' tells the story at some length, and it may be condensed as follows: Two Berserks, named Halli and Leiknir, brothers, were anxious to obtain for one of them the hand of Ásdísa, the daughter of a neighbouring chief, Arngrímr, surnamed Víga Styr— the Stirring or Restless one. 'Whether the elder brother had priority, or whether they were to toss up,' 'Umbra' says, 'I do not know. The father, afraid of offending two such men of prowess, gave his consent, but enacted as a condition that they should first make a road through this lava in a week's time, which he judged an impossibility.' However, the work was completed within the allotted period; and the day was appointed for the wedding. The arch-villain Arngrímr was determined, notwithstanding, it should never come off, so he invited the Berserks to take a warm bath before proceeding to church. Having got them into the bath, he secured them therein by barring the door, turned on the hot water, and presently one of the brothers was a boiled Berserk! The other, severely scalded, broke through the barred door of the bath-room *in naturalibus*, but only to slip on the raw hide of a newly-slain bull, placed there in anticipation of an attempt to escape, and as he lay in that recumbent position a spear was ruthlessly thrust through his back.

Two mounds by the wayside will be pointed out by the guide as the graves of the Berserks; and it is said that these were opened by a Dr. Backmann, who really found in each a skeleton.

The Holy-fell is situated on a peninsula jutting northward into the *Breiðifjörðr*, which is connected with the mainland by a narrow isthmus between two miniature fjords. In the old heathen days the hill was sacred to the god Thor; and no one was allowed even to gaze on the holy height without having first subjected himself to bodily ablution. The hill itself is curious, being formed of irregular columnar basalt, and from its summit, a fair view over the Broad-fjord and its countless volcanic isles is obtainable. This famous Fell was chosen as a site for one of the earliest Christian churches erected in Iceland. In the Eyrbyggja Saga is a lengthy account of the intrigues, cruelties and murders of Snórri Goði, a priest of Thor, who officiated here. A mound is pointed out as the tumulus of Arnkell, the 'good boy' of the story.

An excursion will probably be made to *þórsnes* (Thors-ness), a headland about three miles N.E. of *Helgafell* church, to see an ancient Thing-stead, where traces of an old heathen Doom-ring and the Sacrificial Stone are still to be seen. There is some dispute, however, as to the exact site. Burton says (vol. ii. p. 104): 'We found a shepherd lad (at a cottage hard by) who steered us through the swamps to a rise on the west, a site marked by a Varða of rock. The "Stone of Fear" was a bit of basalt, six feet long by six feet two inches broad, and half-buried in the ground: at least such was the article shown to us. South of it lay the Doom-ring, a circle of rough rocks, twenty-five feet in diameter. Between the two were buried the criminals whose backs had been broken upon the stone. In these forensic and sacrificial circles the judge, still called "Deemster" in the Isle of Man, faced eastwards, with his back to Holy Hill, at which man might not look without ablution.'

Burton adds, in a footnote: 'Henderson (ii. 68) places the stone in the swamp, not on the hill-side; Forbes (219) adds that it was in the centre of the Doom-ring. If so, we did not see it: moreover, Mr. R. M. Smith heard from Hr. Thorlacius that we were misled. I cannot help believing in the shepherd-boy; and there was no mistaking the Doom-ring. For the most part, the instruments of death stood in the fens where certain classes of criminals were drowned.'

Less than an hour's ride from *Helgafell* to *Stykkishólmr*, the town that should rank fourth in importance in Iceland; it is a port of call for the Danish steamers. There are several merchants here; therefore biscuits and small stores are procurable. The travellers should endeavour to obtain quarters at the farm by *Helgafell* church for the night, visit *Þórsnes* the next morning, and subsequently ride into the town, taking a man with them from *Helgafell* to bring back the ponies; having first arranged with the farmer—the incumbent resides in *Stykkishólmr*—to find them pasturage during the two or three days that the party decide to stay in town, and to send in the ponies when required. Herra Clausen, a merchant here, speaks capital English, and is ever ready and willing to assist visitors in every way: he will furnish information as to a boat excursion to the most interesting of the crater-islets in the *Breiðifjörðr*. We will allow two days' sojourn in *Stykkishólmr*, and set out therefrom on the

TWENTY-THIRD DAY for *Breiðabólstaðr* (? Broad-built-stead). An easy day's journey, it being unlikely that an early start will be made—one seldom is from a town, the ponies having to be brought in from a farm. An excursion can be made from *Breiðabólstaðr* into the N.W. peninsula. Six hours' ride eastward will bring the party to *Hjarðarholt* (Herd-holt), and the next day's journey to *Borðeyri* (Board-beach), a trading post on the *Hrútafjörðr*; from whence northward see Route IV. On the opposite side of the river to *Hjarðarholt* is *Höskuldstaðr*, the birth-place of Gunnar's wife (See Outline of Njál Saga).

TWENTY-FOURTH DAY.—*Breiðabólstaðr* to *Hitárdalr* (Hit-river-valley). An easy day's journey southward across the peninsula. The lava-bed around *Eldborg* will be traversed just north of the volcano; and subsequently the *Kaldá* and *Hitá* will be forded. *Hitárdalr* parsonage stands on the eastern bank of the last-named river. In the valley is shown a huge feminine face carved in stone, which is 'said to represent Hit, the *Ás* or guardian goddess of the dale: a "Plutonic affection" exists between her and *Bárð* or Snæfell's *Ás*' (Burton, vol. ii. p. 96). In all probability this 'Plutonic affection' extends from *Snæfells Jökull* considerably farther inland than the *Hitárdalr*, for the presence of the two extensive tracts of lava in the interior, in a direct line with the peninsula eastward to *Askja*, seem to point to the existence of a volcanic channel running due west from that great central 'Plutonic' outlet. (See Geological Description of Iceland, Chapter II.)

TWENTY-FIFTH DAY.—*Hitdrdalr* to *Reykholt*. An hour's ride down the valley will bring the party to *Sta'barhraun*, and thence they will proceed to *Reykholt* by the same route as was travelled going westward. It would not be a bad plan, if any of the travellers have rods with them, to halt at *Stafholt* and have two or three days' fishing before going on to *Reykholt*, that the ponies may recruit. We will therefore allow two days. The party can return from here to *Reykjavik* in three days. See Route IV.

TWENTY-EIGHTH DAY.—*Reykholt* to *Kalmanstúnga* (Kalman's-tongue). Before quitting the *Reykholtsdalr*, a tent should be borrowed from the pastor or one of the farmers, and an additional man and ponies to transport it to and from the *Arnarvatnshei'ði* (Eagle-lake-heath), where it would be advisable to camp out the second night after leaving *Reykholt*. It is seventeen hours' journey, with pack-ponies, from *Kalmanstúnga* to *Haukagil*, the first farm on the east side of the elevated plateau that has to be crossed, and there is no farm on the way. A hut built as a hospice stands on the heath near the largest of the lakes, the *Arnarvatn*; but a recent, and not over-fastidious, traveller says he found its interior in such a filthy state that it 'forbade intrusion.' If a tent is not procurable, this hut might be cleaned out, and the travellers in their ' Garnets ' and box-beds will surely be able to tolerate one night there. This is the only occasion when a tent is really needed between *Reykjavik* and *Akureyri* by this route. A few days can be agreeably spent among the Fish-lakes on the *Arnarvatnshei'ði* (See Chapter III.). There is no farm nearer than *Kalmanstúnga*. The author was told by a party of Cambridge men, who encamped near the lakes last summer (1881), that they caught as many as seventy large trout in a day.

At *Kalmanstúnga* the accommodation is very poor, and the farmer is said to be extortionate; but those who complain at his charges should remember that the coffee, sugar, meal for the bread, and every article of food not produced on the farm, has to be brought a two to three (—to four and six, going and returning) days' journey from the nearest trading-station. The farm is situated in the midst of rich grass land, surrounded by surpassingly grand Alpine scenery.

TWENTY-NINTH DAY.—*Kalmanstúnga* to the *Arnarvatnshei'ði*;

visiting *Surtshellir* (Surtr's-cave) *en route*. It is a cavern in the lava of the *Hallmundarhraun* (Hallmundr's-lava), a short distance from the track. Entrance is obtained by means of one of several rifts in the lava forming its roof; and lights are necessary for its exploration (a pound of candles therefore should be bought at *Reykjavik* before setting out). The rift generally used as a means of entrance expands into a chamber about twenty feet high and thirty wide, and the cavern extends a considerable distance. It has been explored for about a mile, and it is believed it owes its formation to the congelation of the surface of a flood of lava, which retained its fluidity below and continued to flow in a sort of interior canal, from which it found an outlet at a lower level. This is very probable; for it is said: 'The large one (cavern) extends along the lava-stream, and is at the edge of a slight fall in the ground.' The following is a description of the interior from a French work, 'The Voyage de la Recherche'[1]: 'Its walls are hung with lava-stalactites. Toward the middle of the canal, under a kind of dome, the visitor is arrested by a dazzling mass; it is snow, which has accumulated there, after having penetrated into this hollow, lighted with a mysterious light by means of a little opening which time has made in the roof of the vault. At the time of our visit, a ray of sunlight penetrated obliquely through this passage, lessening the light of the torches with which we were provided, and rendered the interior still more gloomy. Quite at the accessible extremity of the canal, which falls a little, we penetrated into a gallery of fairy-like magnificence, everywhere hung with the purest crystal, which the light of our torches reflected in a thousand ways. The ceiling was covered with brilliant spangles; and to the right, on the side, we noticed a set of, as it were, organ-pipes, or very beautiful stalactites and stalagmites of ice.'

The track after leaving *Surtshellir* passes within two miles of *Eiriksjökull*, a vast ice-crowned detached mass of rock that at one time was believed to be the monarch of the Icelandic mountains, and the outlook south, over the group of *Jöklar* behind, suggests very vividly to the mind the fact that one is travelling in Iceland. The party will probably select for a camping ground the shore of the *Arnarvatn*, in the vicinity of the hut before alluded to. On a peninsula jutting out into the lake, Grettir the Strong, the hero of the 'Grettur Saga,' lived for some time in a rude stone house he built there. There is in summer very fair pasturage for the

[1] Extracted from Zurcher's work, 'Volcanoes.'

ponies; and, as before observed, sportsmen can pass the time very satisfactorily here. Swans are at times very numerous on the lakes. A Burthon boat sent by steamer to *Stykkishólmr*, and brought up here, would enable a party of anglers to make such a catch of trout as is seldom heard of in these days.

THIRTIETH DAY.—*Arnarvatn* to *Haukagil* (Hawk-gill). That is, if a stay is not made for fishing and shooting. Send back the tent to the *Reykholtsdalr*. The greater part of the day's journey will lie across the *Víðidalstúnguheiði* (Willow-dale-tongue's-heath), an elevated tract of moorland lying a thousand feet or more above sea-level. In the autumn grouse are very numerous here. A longish day's ride. At *Haukagil* farm and *Grímstúngur* (Grimr's-tongue) parsonage, there is very fair accommodation; and fishing, with the remotest possible chance of a salmon and the certainty of large trout, in the *Vatnsdalsá* (Water-dale-river). A pleasant day's excursion can be made up the *Forsæludalr*, a very beautiful valley abounding in falls, under the first of which salmon are occasionally caught. A walk up this valley for about three miles above this fall will be highly interesting to the geologist, for here he will see some of the most remarkable basaltic dykes in Iceland. Deep narrow rifts exist in the older rocky strata forming this part of the island, which have been filled up with molten basaltic lava. Where these intersect the valley, they jut out in high narrow walls of rock, weathered into gigantic pinnacles in many places.

THIRTY-FIRST DAY.—*Haukagil* to *Hjaltabakki*. The first part of the day's journey will be down the thickly-peopled *Vatnsdalr*. The best road is on the west side of the river; but any one geologically minded should ford the river and ride down on the east side, and see the vast slopes of débris under the mountains on that side of the valley. They should also examine the remarkable cones of upheaval on the *west* side of the river, north of the lake, between it and *Sveinstaðir* (Swain-stead). Many ages ago volcanic matters attempted to force an outlet here from a deeply seated channel, but the superincumbent rocky strata offered such great resistance, that the exertion of force necessary to fracture these undoubtedly forced an outlet elsewhere, for, although innumerable cones of upheaval were formed, no molten matter issued here, beyond cores of lava that welled up through outlets, in the centre of several of the cones. Many of the cones have weathered away, as also have the outer and more porous portions of the rocky cores, leaving immense blocks which, if it were not that there is abundant evidence of their formation in the manner stated around, would be taken for ice-borne boulders. Are any of the so-called ice-borne boulders (*blocs perchés*) found in Scotland and other parts of the British Isles, some of which it is asserted by geologists have been brought from Norway, masses of rock of similar formation in the days of the decline of volcanic activity in the northern part of our own isles? A few pounds of dynamite, and a little excavation, would soon show whether this is the case or not. As showing how deeply seated the reservoir of the volcanic force was, the author may mention that he gathered from the slopes of one cone specimens of seventeen varieties of rock, presumably fragments of the different strata lying above the channel containing the molten matter, which were brought to the surface by the eruption. The cones vary from 100 to 10 feet in height, and there is a vast number of them. It is said there are three things in Iceland that cannot be counted, and the tourist on this tour has now had an opportunity to see all three: they are the cones of upheaval here, the lakes on the *Arnarvatnsheiði*, and the islets of the *Breiðifjörðr*.

About three centuries since, during a shock of earthquake—some say a volcanic eruption on the spot, but if so it is not recorded—a vast slice of the mountain, east of *Hnoisar* farm, slid down into the valley and buried a homestead.

About one hour's ride after leaving the *Vatnsdalr*, a small river will be forded, this is a *Laxá* which in showery summers, when there is an abundance of water, is a very good one. Last summer, to the author's knowledge, a party of tourists during their halt at *Hjaltabakki* caught two salmon. The parsonage is rather less than an hour's ride from the ford; the pastor speaks English with tolerable fluency. Another hour's ride further on is the trading post of *Blönduós*, where there is a primitive inn and two excellent stores. Steamers do not call here, as the harbour is a very bad one. The trading post is prettily situated close to the mouth of the *Blanda*, a large river which dashes over a bar into the fjord; and the view northward over the *Húnafjörðr* is a charming coastal landscape. An excursion can be made either from here or *Hjaltabakki* to the *Laxárvatn* and *Svínavatn* (Swine-lake), wherein trout are said to be very plentiful, and whereon ducks innumerable disport. Rough accommodation at the farms. The trading post of *Skagaströnd* (Shaw-strand), where the Danish steamers call, is distant an easy day's ride from *Blönduós*. There is a *Laxá* about midway, but it is now a salmon river only in name; a brace of fish *might* be caught in the lower pools. There is also another *Laxá* at the extreme end of the peninsula, an easy day's ride from

Skagaströnd. It is the only salmon river in the north that the author has not visited; a quantity of salmon is brought from the farms near it to the merchants, but whether they are caught in the fjord or in the river, the author cannot say.

THIRTY-SECOND DAY.—*Hjaltabakki* or *Blönduós* to *Víðimýri* (Willow-muir). The *Blanda* should be forded about three miles from *Blönduós*, not ferried there, as in the middle is a 'dangerous quicksand, upon which the ponies will be sure to land, and from which the travellers will be fortunate if they induce them to take to the water again before one or two are fixed inextricably in the sand. After quitting the valley of the *Blanda*, the route lies up the valley of a tributary, the *Svartá* (Black-river—abounding in trout and char), and thence through the *Vatnskarð* (Water-pass) to the farm, not parsonage, at *Víðimýri*. Fair accommodation. From here the baggage ponies should be sent on to *Akureyri*, viâ *Silfrastaðir* (Silver-stead—an inn) and *Steinstaðr*, the usual post route; but the travellers themselves should make a detour northward to visit *Hólar* cathedral; whence they will travel on to *Akureyri* by one of the grandest mountain passes in Iceland.

A delightful and interesting three days' excursion can be made from *Víðimýri* northward; to *Reykir*, one day; thence by boat to *Drángey* (Lonely-isle), which was the retreat of the hero of the Grettur Saga when outlawed. It is said that one Christmas night his fire went out, and having no means of relighting it, nor boat in which to row to the mainland, he swam from *Drángey* to the farm of *Reykir* to obtain a light. The scenery on the *Skagafjörðr* (Shawfjord) is very fine; on the west side of the fjord tower the peaks of the *Tindastóll*, a remarkably steep range, intersected with deep water-worn gorges; while opposite, *Málmey* (Sand-stone-isle) juts seaward north of a bluff peninsula, with a low-lying isthmus, that also looks like an island; and in the midst of the fjord stands *Drángey*, an immense deeply-fissured precipitous mass of rock, with an outlier which, from a certain point of view, presents the appearance of a ship in full sail heeling over to the wind. Very obliging people indeed at *Reykir*, but the travellers will have to sleep in a large room used as a carpenter's shop.

THIRTY-THIRD DAY.—*Víðimýri* to *Hólar*. Ford the *Héraðsvötn* (District-waters) north-west of *Víðimýri*, where two channels form an island, *Borgarey* (Burg-isle), and thence the track is down the valley till about three miles beyond *Hofstaðir* (Temple-stead). From this point a path branches off to the *Hjaltadalr*, and about an hour's ride up this somewhat swampy valley will bring the travellers to the door of the farm near *Hólar* church—once a cathedral. A commodious house, and very hospitable farmer.

The sacred edifice is built of a peculiar red tuff; its ground-plan would be a right-angled parallelogram thirty paces in length by ten paces in breadth, were it not that about eighteen feet from the front of the building it becomes of less width by six feet or so on each side. It has a ridge roof of wood: seven good-sized rectangular windows in the north wall, and six on the south; one each side of the doorway in front, three above to light a loft under the roof, and a small one above these. Inscribed in a stone over the door is the date of rebuilding, A.D. 1762. Within, the height is about fourteen feet, and the ceiling is flat with a loft above. Quite one-third of the interior lies within an altar screen, gaudily painted. This is a stout balustrade above panels in which are painted allegorical figures, Faith, Hope, Charity, Plenty, etc. The altar, at the time of the author's visit, was covered with a very old leather altar-cloth, embossed in gold, with tapestry hangings. On the wall at the east end of the church, over the altar, is a richly-carved altar-piece in a case, whose doors when open form wings to the main subject—a Crucifixion, about five feet in height, with men on horses, women weeping, etc. The two thieves have their legs and arms broken in a most unmistakable manner. The wings formed by the doors contain figures of the Apostles, Virgin Mary and others; some with remarkably well-carved faces; and on the outsides are painted two scriptural pieces, one, Christ appearing to Mary Magdalene; the other, the martyrdom of St. Jude, who is bound to a tree and being shot at with arrows by two men in armour. Within the altar-screen on the north wall, between the font and the altar, hangs a life-size figure of Christ on the Cross, carved in wood; and close by is a large oil painting of the Lord's Supper. The floor is largely composed of flat grave tablets, beneath which repose a number of bishops; and about a dozen of their portraits in oil adorn the walls. There is also a needle-work portrait of one, framed and glazed. In the belfry, the upper part of the narrowed-in portion of the edifice in front, are four old bells, one a very large one, but broken. The floor of the loft was strewed with Bibles and old theological works, many of which were printed here in the latter part of the sixteenth century. It is a great pity that these rare old works should be left here to be destroyed by the damp. The first printing press brought to Iceland was established here early in the sixteenth century—1530, it is believed.

THIRTY-FOURTH DAY.—*Hólar* to *Vellir* (Fields). The route taken will be what is known as the *Heljardalr* way. An altitude of 4,500 feet will be attained at the highest point of the pass, a spur of the *Unadals Jökull*. The view from this point is a really grand Alpine landscape, and the valley on the east side of the mountains, to which the descent is very precipitous, appears to be in another world.

The author and his guide, without relay ponies, were ten hours between *Hólar* and *Vellir*. A local guide was engaged at the last farm on the west side of the mountains. At *Vellir* parsonage resides the greatest of native artists, the Icelandic Doré, a self-taught man, whose *forte* appears to be the painting of altar-pieces. He was busily engaged on a very handsome one for *Vellir* church at the time of the author's visit in 1880.

THIRTY-FIFTH DAY.—*Vellir to Akureyri*. About seven hours' easy ride, chiefly along the western shore of the *Eyjafjörðr* (Island-fjord). Immediately facing the valley in which *Vellir* stands is *Hrisey*, a large island which gives the fjord its name. Upon it a Norwegian company has established a flourishing post for prosecuting the herring fishery. Midway between *Vellir* and *Akureyri* will be noticed a fine large wooden building faced by a church. This is *Möðruvellir* Agricultural College. Its head master is the learned Herra Jón A. Hjaltalín, who was formerly one of the librarians at the Advocates' Library, Edinburgh. The building and church, both quite new, are well worth a visit.

Shortly after leaving *Möðruvellir*, the *Hörgá* (Howe-river) will be forded. This is, at times, a bad river; but there is a ferry near the ford. Good newly-made road hence for several miles, and then the shingle beach of the fjord is utilized as a road for some distance, until another piece of made road is fallen in with. This will bring the travellers to a low flat naze, *Oddeyri* (Angle-beach) projecting at right angles into the fjord; in crossing which the *Glerá* (Crystal-river), a nasty little torrent when in flood, will be forded. Between the two rivers will be seen *Glæsibær* church; which is chained fast that the Demon of the Storm may not make off with it. It is built in a very exposed position and has to withstand the full force of the terrific squalls that at times come sweeping down the *Hörgádalr*. On *Oddeyri* will be seen a number of buildings and a very large store. Most of these belong to an Icelandic-Danish trading company, which has its chief trading-post here, and two branch establishments in other parts of the island. Another mile up the fjord will bring the travellers into

AKUREYRI.—Jensen's hotel is very comfortable, though small,

and Jensen himself is one of the most obliging, honest hosts that it has ever been the author's fate to fall in with. If the four beds in the hotel part of his buildings are taken up, he will obtain sleeping accommodation for the travellers at a private house, and the meals will be taken at the hotel. There is a spacious billiard room here, and a fair billiard board for so far north. One great drawback to a lengthy stay at *Akureyri* is the unconscionable demand that will be made by the neighbouring farmers for pasturage for the ponies. The best plan is to insist upon the guide taking the ponies to a farm on the opposite side of the river at the head of the fjord, where the farmer is a reasonable being, and the pasturage better than on the moors at the back of the town. This should most certainly be done if the travellers intend to proceed eastward to 'The Fire Focus of the North,' as in calm weather it is far more pleasant to transport oneself and baggage to the east side of the fjord by boat, than to ride round the head of it and through half a dozen river channels—the ponies being ordered to meet one at the farm opposite *Akureyri*.

Two days will be allowed in *Akureyri*, before starting eastward. This town has a population of about 400, and is the residence of the 'Amtmaŏr,' or Lieutenant-Governor, of the northern half of the island, and several other officials ; also of a doctor and an apothecary. There are four stores and resident merchants, an excellent saddle-maker, and a baker—who, by-the-bye, is likewise a photographer. The town also boasts a hospital and a jail—in the former a hot bath is obtainable, and in the latter the public free library may be inspected. *Akureyri*, it will be seen, is ahead of many considerable towns in our own isles in one thing at least— a free library. . There are, moreover, two printing establishments, at each of which a newspaper is printed. There are three or four fine mountain-ash trees in the town, of which the 'Akureyriites' are very proud. There is a recently erected spacious wooden church, which is kept in excellent order, but everything about it is quite modern and of little interest.

The store and meat-preserving house at *Oddeyri* will well repay a visit : and a stroll to the *Glerá* will be well rewarded by a sight of the very pretty fall formed by the river about half a mile from the fjord. An excellent photograph of the fall is obtainable from the baker in *Akureyri*. Sea trout are sometimes to be caught— with worms only—in the pool beneath the foss.

The gloomy black building between *Akureyri* and *Oddeyri* is a shark oil factory ; the stench from which, when the wind is from the north, renders the enjoyment of one's meals in *Akureyri* an utter impossibility.

THIRTY-EIGHTH DAY.—*Akureyri* to *Ljósavatn* (Lake-of-light). Cross the fjord in a boat to the ponies. It is a stiff climb to the summit of the *Vaðlaheiði* (Wade-heath), the mountain ridge east of the fjord, and will take two hours; the altitude of the highest point of the road being about 2,300 feet. Directly this is attained, the descent will commence to the *Fnjóskádalr* (? Touch-wood-river-valley). The east side of the ridge is by no means so precipitous as on the west, and there is a made road in places. In the *Fnjóskádalr* flourishes quite a forest of birch, which in the early part of August usually holds a few coveys of grouse. Several of the birds that the author has shot here have run larger than the general run of grouse in Iceland, and, as stated in Chapter III., he is convinced they were identical with the willow-grouse of the Scandinavian peninsula. Do not halt at *Háls* (Hause) parsonage for coffee, or you may be kept waiting an unconscionable time, possibly over an hour, before it is ready. From *Háls* to *Ljósavatn* the path traverses a narrow valley, the *Ljósavatnsskarð* (Lake-of-light-pass), which is rather a remarkable watershed; a stream that leaps down through a gorge in the mountains on the south-west divides into two arms at the base, one of which courses eastward to the lake and the other westward into the *Fnjóská*. *Ljósavatn* is a largish sheet of water, well stocked with trout; and in the autumn ducks and geese frequently flock here in vast numbers. The farm lies some little distance south-east of the lake; the outlet from which, the *Djúpá* (Deep-river), will be forded before reaching it. There are a number of old craters and ash-heaps here, with traces of lava, through which the river has worn a channel.

The author has always found the people at *Ljósavatn* farm very obliging, and he has frequently stayed at the farm several days together for the grouse shooting, which is very good in August on the moors south-east of the lake, and later on, on the fjelds at the back of the house. The guest-room is gorgeously painted in vermilion, blue, and yellow. The interior of the chapel of ease attached to the farm, a most primitive sacred edifice, is likewise resplendent with the same colours. There is an old pulpit within, however, worth seeing—date A.D. 1796.

THIRTY-NINTH DAY.—*Ljósavatn* to *Múli* (Mull), or *Grenjaðarstaðir* (Green-edge-stead), visiting the *Goðafoss* en route. An hour's ride over level moorland will bring the travellers to the *Skjáfandafljót* in the vicinity of the God's-fall. This is a very pretty fall, but of no great height. Upon the brink of the precipice, over which the river leaps, is an islet of basalt, which divides the falling waters. What is somewhat remarkable, the western fall is some seven feet higher than the eastern one, which is about 25 feet. There is a cleft in the islet, and the tiny stream flowing through forms a central cascade. About half a mile from this fall the river forms another, the *Geitafoss* (Goat-fall), where the river leaps in one bound about 15 feet. About a quarter of a mile below the *Goðafoss*, a bridge is in course of construction. Width of river, between the stone buttresses that are to support the bridge, 29 'alen'=to about 65 feet. Should the bridge not be finished by this summer (1882), and the travellers ride down the west bank of the river to the ford, beware of a little tributary, for, though it appears shallow near its junction with the main river, there is a deep rift in its lava-bed, into which the author's guide drove two pack ponies last year and nearly killed them. About five miles below the *Goðafoss* is another fine fall, the *Ullarfoss* (Wool-fall). It lies north of an island, on which in olden times the local Þíng held its meetings. Salmon late in the year are sometimes caught below the *Ullarfoss*.

Immediately after crossing the *Skjálfandafljót*, another mountainous ridge will have to be crossed, but there is now a good made road the greater part of the way, ascending by a series of zigzags. Grouse very plentiful here in the middle of August. East of the ridge, the travellers will descend into a well-peopled valley, the *Aðalreykjadalr*, through which the track winds until just before reaching the *Vestmannsvatn* (Westmen's or Irishmen's-lake), when it passes along the face of a hill covered with a considerable growth of birch. Grouse are plentiful on the hill, and the lake is well stocked with trout. The good old Dean at *Múli*, having been grossly libelled in a recent English work on Iceland, does not now care to accommodate English travellers, but he will not refuse a night's lodging. At *Grenjaðarstaðir*, ten minutes' ride further on, accommodation is obtainable for a stay of a few days, the Dean residing there being very obliging and hospitable. Magnificent trout fishing under the falls of the *Laxá*, near *Grenjaðarstaðir*, and also in a tributary on the *Múli* estate. In the latter, salmon are occasionally caught, but seldom of late years under the falls in the main river.

FORTIETH DAY.—*Múli* to *Húsavík*. There are two routes open, and the one that the author recommends is that on the west side of the river past *Nes* (Naze) to *Garðr*. Just north of this farm, on the delta between the two rivers, the *Skjálfandafljót* and *Laxá*, are a number of very remarkable lava-pillars and cones, similar to the one near Þ*ingvellir*, to which, it will be remembered, was given the name of Tintron, and which was said by 'Umbra' to be 'the only one known to exist in the world.' This region here should be called 'Tintronia,' for a level plain some miles in extent is studded with Tintrons. Some will be seen having an opening at its base as well as at its summit, and more than one of these is utilized as a sheepfold. It will be necessary to ferry the *Laxá* at a farm between *Nes* and *Laxármýri* (Salmon-river-muir). In the waters belonging to the latter farm a salmon may occasionally be caught. This farm is the richest in all Iceland, and the newly erected farmhouse is wholly of wood in the Norwegian style. The farmer declines to receive travellers: and it will be as well, perhaps, to mention that Englishmen are not very well received in this district, thanks to a defaulting and bankrupt English sulphur mining company, whose resident agent quitted the country without settling the debts he had contracted with the people here. This feeling, it is to hoped, will wear away in a few years, when the soreness felt at having been 'done' is felt less keenly.

An hour's ride from *Laxármýri* will bring the travellers to *Húsavík*, where there is a small inn, with a very obliging and painstaking landlady. There is but one merchant here, Herra Guðjohnsson, of whom every one who has visited *Húsavík* speaks very favourably. The Danish steamers call at this trading post.

FORTY-FIRST DAY.—Excursion to the *Uxahver*, or Northern Geysir, and return to *Húsavík*. If this excursion is made in August, a good bag of grouse may be made, the *Hvammsheiði*, a moor south of *Laxármýri*, being one of the best-stocked grouse-moors in all Iceland. The author was one of a party who, in 1880, shot 167 head, besides other game and a falcon, between *Húsavík* and the *Uxahver*. This geysir lies about three hours' ride south-east of *Laxármýri*; at the base of a range of hills, the *Lambafjöll*. The following is a description of the Northern Geysir and its satellites, from the author's diary in 1878.

THE UXAHVER, or Ox-Spring—so named as an ox once fell into it, and was after a short interval forcibly ejected to some distance as boiled beef—is a geysir spouting from an oval basin, about thirty feet in circumference, a column of water some four feet in diameter, to a height of from six to ten feet. The spouts take place with great frequency and regularity, five to six minutes only elapsing between the displays, their duration being about half a minute.

After a spout the water in the basin is lowered from four to five feet, but in less than four minutes the basin is refilled, and the water is violently agitated for about two minutes, when a spout follows. North of the *Uxahver*, and distant therefrom 170 paces, is a bed of rock containing two hot springs, and these were visited first as we approached from the north. From a basin about eighteen feet in diameter, full to the brim with scalding hot water, a column, about a foot in diameter, was ejected to a height of a trifle over four feet at frequent intervals. The other spring in this bed of rock was a large well, quite distinct from the basin, in which the water was boiling furiously, but no spouts took place, and the overflow found an outlet through a hole in the encircling rock. From here we walked down to the *Uxahver*, and saw a half dozen spouts. Since that time I have seen the famous *Strokkr* in his wrath; but I would rather see the *Uxahver* toss its crystal-clear water upwards ten feet, with the widely scattered spray glistening in the sunlight like diamonds, than the irritable Southerner—whose ire has to be excited by drastic herbal treatment in the way of doses of turf—spout its bemuddied water to ten times the height.

The remaining springs of the *Uxhaver* group are collected together in a bed of rock distant 280 paces south of the chief, who, as becomes his rank, has a dwelling to himself. The largest here is very similar in every respect to the one seen spouting in the northernmost basin; and there are a number of smaller ones in holes in the rock, the smallest, quite a geysir *en miniature*, spouting about half a pint of water to the height of some three or four inches.

What is very remarkable, although separated by less than 300 yards of boggy land, the springs in each bed of rock appear to have a distinct source of supply, not being in any way affected by each other's spouting, nor do the spouts take place simultaneously. The *Uxahver* was so affected by an earthquake preceding the *Askja* eruption in 1875 that for a considerable period it ceased to spout; but it has now recovered itself, and a boy told my guide that it throws its water higher than it did previous to the earthquake.

Should the travellers feel in need of refreshment, and inclined to exclaim with 'Digwell':—

> 'What avails it that the geysirs spout their steaming columns high?
> Can a fountain of hot water hungry longings satisfy?'

they can obtain excellent pancakes and coffee at *Reykir* farm, close by the springs.

The ponies should be allowed a day's rest on the morrow. If—

it is very doubtful—the farmer at *Laxdrmýri* could be induced to accommodate the travellers for a night, it would be far better to halt there than return to *Húsavík*, as the time could be very pleasantly passed fishing in the *Laxá*. Should this be arranged, do not fail to try the pool below the *lower* falls, where the fresh water falls into the tidal reach of the river, it is the most likely place for a salmon. Fish up stream on the opposite (western) bank, till abreast of the farm where the travellers ferried the river after visiting Tintronia. There is usually a boat below the falls, in which the anglers can cross the river, and at this farm they will recross, and walk over the moors back to *Laxdrmýri*. A seal may occasionally be shot at the mouth of the river; and the farmer is very glad to hear of the death of one, as the phocæ injure his salmon fishery.

From *Húsavík*, a pleasant day's excursion may be made to *Hringsverhvylft* (? The Cleft-of-the-ring), where there are some remarkable beds of 'Surtarbrandr,' a variety of lignite, and beds of fossil shells. Just before reaching the lignite beds, a pretty little fall, the *Skeifarfoss*, will be seen. About midway from *Húsavík* the path passes along the brow of a cliff, below which is a noted 'seal ground,' and, if the animals have not been recently disturbed, the rocks below will be seen literally alive with seals. A shot must upon no account be fired within a mile of this part of the shore.

FORTY-THIRD DAY.—*Húsavík*, or *Laxdrmýri* to *A's*. About six hours' ride; decent road, after crossing the fells and a lava-filled hollow.

As the traveller on this day's journey traverses that part of the country lying due north of the range of volcanoes intersecting the island from *Krafla* and *Leirhnúkr* southward, he will notice that the basaltic lava strata, composing this part of the island, are deeply fissured in several places by rifts running from south to north. A few miles farther south, the whole face of the country for a distance of over twenty miles from north to south, by a width of from seven to eight miles, has been completely shattered by explosions causing violent shocks of earthquake. Many rifts have been thus torn open during the last two decades, and steam was seen to belch forth from the newly opened rifts at the time of their formation. Some of the rifts stretch southward for quite twenty miles, almost to the volcano *Leirhnúkr*. In 1872 the shocks of earthquake here were terribly violent, and several farmsteads were levelled with the ground. The shock of earthquake caused by the explosion in *Askja* on the 4th January, 1875, was felt in this district very severely. The author last year (1881) struck across the desert in a beeline from the

Dettifoss to *þeistareykir* (Testie-reeks) solfatara, and he counted forty-seven rifts, most of which were passable with the greatest difficulty over masses of the débris. In Chapter II., when treating of the geology of the island, it was mentioned there is abundant evidence that, in the early days of the island's history, a rift (charged at times with volcanic matters) in the deeper-seated rock formations of the earth's crust extended from the south coast as far north as *Krafla*, and, from the shattered state of the country from that volcano northward to the coast, there is reason to believe the rift either completely intersected the island, or that a channel of post-tertiary formation, connected with the central volcanic outlet, extends northward from *Krafla*. A geologist could pass a month very pleasantly and profitably in thoroughly exploring and mapping out the volcanoes, rifts, and lava-floods lying upon the line of the vast volcanic outlet nearly, or quite, intersecting the island between the 16° and 17° W. Long.

The travellers should make a halt at *Garðr* for coffee; and thence from two to three hours' ride will bring them to the

ÁSBYRGI (God's-retreat, or inclosure). A remarkable ⊃-shaped valley, which must be classed among the most wonderful of the physical features of Iceland. As stated in the introductory chapter, it is such a valley as would be formed were it possible to remove a gigantic ⊃-shaped mass of rock, with arms 300 feet in thickness, 500 yards in width, and a mile apart at their extremities, leaving a triangular impression with vertical declivities on either hand. There can hardly exist a doubt that it owes its formation to the subsidence of a vast mass of rock that at one time filled in the abyss, and connected with the surrounding country the triangular rocky buttress now standing insulated; and, to judge from the configuration of the valley, there is every reason to believe that the mass which subsided lay above two forks of a subterranean channel at the point where they branched off. The insulated triangular buttress is about a mile in width at its base, which faces seaward, and gradually increases in height from this towards its apex, where its cliffs are quite 300 feet in height, its summit maintaining the downward slope towards the sea of the surrounding country, on the opposite sides of the insulating valley. The faces of the cliffs are but little weathered, remaining as clean cut as if the subsidence had taken place but a century or so ago, but nevertheless it is prehistoric. The floor of the valley is tolerably level, save at its southern end; and a forest of miniature birch trees flourish within its sheltering walls. One's dog while passing through the valley, if allowed to range, will find a covey or two of grouse among the birch. Not the least interesting of the phenomena to be observed here, are the sections of subterranean channels, in which molten lava flowed prior to the convulsion which caused the subsidence, that are shown in the cliffs. A well-defined channel is accessible by scrambling up the débris at the base of the cliff on the south, about midway through the valley, and here the travellers may secure some specimens of the ropy scoriaceous surface of the core of lava that now remains congealed in this subterranean duct.

The ride through this weird and wonderful valley is very impressive: one seems to be shut completely out of the world by the immense cliffs on either hand, which permit but a glimpse of a strip of sky above one's head. The echo is remarkably good.

After quitting the eastern outlet of the valley, a short ride will bring the travellers to their quarters for the night at *Ás* farm. There are two homesteads, but both very poor ones; and as the westernmost alone boasts any other room than the Baðstofa in which one can sit down, it will be best to seek accommodation there. 'Garnet Wolseleys' or box-beds will enable the night to be passed in tolerable comfort. People obliging, and abundance of milk, coffee and pancakes procurable.

FORTY-FOURTH DAY.—*Ás* to *Reykjahlíð*, visiting *en route* the *Hljóðaklettar* (Sounding or Speaking-cliffs) and the *Dettifoss*. Make an early start, as the party will be ten hours in the saddle. The first part of the day's journey will lie up the valley of the *Jökulsá*, a river valley which for wildness of scenery and magnificent falls it would not be easy to find a compeer.

The HLJÓÐAKLETTAR are a group of craters and amorphous masses of rock standing isolated in the valley west of the river, which appear like the ruins of a vast castle; and so perfectly do they echo back sounds one can fancy them the home of Mocking Genii, or, as observed in the introductory chapter, that Echo changed into stone here and not on the banks of the Cephisus. These rocks with their surroundings form a landscape which, if faithfully transferred to canvas on a large scale, would make the fortune of the artist.

Half an hour's ride hence will bring the travellers to the only farm that will be seen in this day's journey, *Svínadalr* (Swine-dale). People obliging, and coffee, milk and pancakes are to be had while the ponies rest for an hour. Upon the way a fine fall, the *Vígabjargsfoss*, will be passed. A flat rock will be noticed on the opposite side of the foss, with a narrow approach on the east. Tradition sayeth that the famous outlaw, Grettir the Strong, was once attacked here, and that after valiantly defending himself for some time he made his escape from his assailants by leaping over the river close by the foss. The spot where the leap is said to have been made is known to this day as *Grettishlaup* (Grettir's-leap).

An hour's ride from the farm the *Jökulsá* forms another pretty fall, the *Hafragilsfoss* (Goat-gill's-fall); and here the river rushes through a fine gorge which is said to resemble, but not equal, the Danubian iron gates. An hour and a half's ride hence will bring the travellers abreast of the *Dettifoss*. The ponies will have to be left in charge of the guide, while a visit is paid to this the most famous of the Icelandic falls, as a boulder-strewn tract bordering the river must be crossed on foot.

THE DETTIFOSS.—There is a gloomy abyss in the bed of the river here, about 200 feet in depth, bordered on the east by a sheer wall of igneous rock and scoriæ, quite 400 feet in height, and on the west by a steep slope; down which it is possible to descend to the foot of the fall at some risk to one's limbs, and the certainty of a drenching. The precipice in the river-bed does not intersect it at right angles, it being at its junction with the western bank about 400 feet further south than on the opposite side of the river. The precipice is a deeply crevassed basaltic cliff, whose base is invisible in the depths of the abyss. The crevasse is shaped as though a huge slice of rock in the form of a scalene triangle, some 100 feet in width at its base, and penetrating up stream for a distance of 200 feet, had been removed. Over the walls of this wedge-shaped crevasse, and the precipitous cliff on each side, the impetuous, milky-white waters of this mighty river leap in one bound.

'. . . . Rapid as the light
The flashing mass foams, shaking the abyss;
The hell of waters! where they howl and hiss,
And boil in endless torture; while the sweat
Of their great agony, wrung out from this
Their Phlegethon, curls round the rocks of jet
That gird the gulf around in pitiless horror set.'

It will be confessed, when the *Dettifoss* is seen, that the above lines from 'Childe Harold' convey as good an impression of this magnificent cataract as it is possible for words to do. The *Dettifoss*, and the other Icelandic falls on glacier-fed rivers, are to be seen in their greatest perfection in the height of summer; unlike the cataracts of most other countries, which at that time are usually at their worst, owing to the lowness of the water in the rivers where they occur.

A few hundred yards upstream, the *Jökulsá* forms a very pretty preliminary fall well worthy of a visit, it being somewhat remarkable. The river is about 250 yards across at this spot, and the channel is intersected by a horse-shoe-shaped ridge of basalt about 20 feet in height. This is battlemented, and through the embrasures, which have been formed by the carrying away of blocks of basalt, the water leaps in a multitude of miniature cascades.

Upon leaving the *Dettifoss*, the travellers will strike across the pathless *Mývatns Öræfi* in a south-westerly direction for a pass in the volcanic range on the west of the desert. It will, in all probability, be necessary to dismount several times, and lead the ponies into and out of hollows where subsidences have taken place during volcanic eruptions; but there are no insurmountable difficulties to prevent any one crossing this desert region: the author has upon more than one occasion scoured it in all directions for several days together in search of reindeer. If the travellers wish to get a shot at one of these animals, they should, if here in the month of August, strike due west from the *Dettifoss* for a lake near a mountain named *Eilífr* (the Eternal). South-west of this lake is an abandoned ruinous farm-house, known as *Hlíðarhæli* (Ledge-hall), wherein the author has frequently passed a night, as it is right in the heart of the habitat of a herd of reindeer.

It will take about three hours to cross the *Öræfi* to the *Námaskarð* (Solfatara-pass), the defile in the volcanic range. At the base of the mountain south of the pass will be noticed a plain of light-coloured earth, from which clouds of steam ascend. This is the chief of the famous *Mývatn* solfatarar, and the clouds of steam ascend from a number of cauldrons of boiling mud. A halt should not be made to examine these now, as this can be more conveniently done on the morrow, which will be devoted to the exploration of the volcanic phenomena east of *Mývatn*.

The travellers will doubtless be struck with the great difference in the nature of the landscape on the west side of the range to that on the east, which is an arid fire-blasted wilderness of volcanic ash, lava and sand. Rounding a projecting spur of the mountain on the north side of the pass, the circumscribed view of an unusually gloomy defile, wherein but a few blades of coarse grass clothe the acclivities, changes as if by enchantment to one over a wide expanse of lake, environed on the south and east with volcanoes, and studded with volcanic isles—miniature quiescent Strombolis, whose weather-worn crater-cones rise from bases green with a prolific growth of angelica and grasses; their verdure presenting a pleasing contrast to the bristling lava-floods that fringe the lake on the east. *Myvatn* ranks next to *Þingvallavatn* in size; and is said to have an area of about thirty square miles, and to lie 900 feet above sea-level.

From the pass, less than an hour's ride, first through a solfatara differing but little from the one east of the range, save that there are no cauldrons of boiling mud, and subsequently across a lava-bed abounding in rifts and crannies, some of which form natural ferneries of great beauty, will bring the travellers and their tired steeds to the door of *Reykjahlið* farm. The people here are very obliging, and the author has always found them very reasonable indeed in their charges. There is a newly-erected stone church on the rise upon which stood the old church that was left standing uninjured when the farm was destroyed by an eruption of lava in A.D. 1729. Three days' sojourn should be made here, if the party do not propose to travel on to *Seyðisfjörðr*.

FORTY-FIFTH DAY.—The ponies should be allowed to rest, but the members of the party may pass the day pleasantly in making an excursion on foot to the solfatarar in the vicinity, and to the *Hverfjall* (Hot-spring-mountain), a large crater south-east of the lake, plainly visible from *Reykjahlið*. The solfatara on the east side of the range will be the first examined; it being the most interesting on account of the mud cauldrons, which are the largest in Iceland. They are situated in a plain of light-coloured mineral earths, resting upon a substratum of hot, white, viscid clay. The earths, where wind and sun-dried, form a crust, in places capable of bearing a man; but there are large patches where it is unsafe to go, the crust being but an inch or so in thickness. The plain is studded with a number of low, cone-shaped hillocks, from whose apices jets of steam ascend. These fumarolar mark where sulphur sublimation is taking place. The slopes and summit of the mountain south of the pass are also covered with fumarolar. The boiling mud cauldrons lie on the eastern side of the plain, about 500 yards from its northern end, in knolls of sun-dried mud raised a few feet above the level of the plain. These were, in 1881, partly surrounded by a pool of hot water. The cauldrons vary greatly at times in number and size; but there are generally three or four principal groups of about half a dozen. When the author was here in 1880, the basin in the knoll which held the chief group contained seven cauldrons, the largest about 30 feet in diameter, and the smallest about the size of an ordinary pitch-kettle; but last year (1881) the spot where these existed the year before was crusted over, and there were but two or three little holes showing the boiling mud below, while a group of large cauldrons had been formed a short distance off. The boiling mud is as black as ink and of the consistency of porridge, and is very suggestive of the food one can imagine is provided in the infernal regions; and it therefore may perhaps be termed with propriety 'Hell Broth.' It is kept in a constant state of ebullition, and large quantities of that in the largest of the cauldrons is at intervals ejected with considerable noise to a height of from six to eight feet. These boiling mud cauldrons are a very interesting, though certainly not a beautiful phenomenon, and being situated at the junction of extensive lava-beds with a solfatara at the base of a range of volcanic mountains, which show signs of activity in the form of innumerable fumarolar, they and their surroundings are very suggestive, as an American said of the Yellowstone region, 'of the Inferno very thinly crusted over.' Some lines by 'Umbra,' though not intended to do so, graphically describe the landscape here:—

> 'Wide ruin spread the element around,
> His havoc leagues on leagues may you descry;
> And still the smouldering flame lurks underground,
> And tosses boiling fountains to the sky!'

After examining the eastern solfatara and its cauldrons, the travellers will return through the pass, and walk southward to the *Hverfjall* through the eastern solfatara; which differs somewhat from the one on the east side of the range, there being more fumarolar and no mud cauldrons.

The *Hverfjall* is a large circular crater, with an encircling wall of volcanic cinders and ash, about 700 feet in height above the lake = 1,600 feet above sea-level. It is said to have erupted in 1728, but its formation is prehistoric. It is the largest crater in the vicinity of *Mývatn*, and a conspicuous feature in the landscape, but its circumference and depth are not known to the author.

Some ten miles south of the *Hverfjall* is another solfatara, the *Fremrindmar* (Farther-solfatara), and a large crater; but these are seldom visited, it being a most fatiguing day's journey for the ponies, and there being but little to interest any one who has seen the volcanic phenomena nearer *Mývatn*.

FORTY-SIXTH DAY.—An easy day's excursion to *Leirhnúkr*, *Krafla*, and the *Hrafntinnuhryggr* (Raven-peaks'-back); returning to *Reykjahlíð*. The former are two famous volcanoes, and the third is a ridge, just east of *Krafla*, partly formed of obsidian—hence its name from the resemblance of this jet-like volcanic product to the black glossy plumage of the raven. On the way will be seen, about two miles north of the *Námaskarð*, a flood of lava that has leaped down the mountain on the west like a cataract. Three hours' easy riding will bring the party to *Leirhnúkr*, which in itself is a very low uninteresting eminence, on which are several small solfatarar; but cross to its western side, and then will be seen a view that will never be forgotten! It is remarkably wild and Plutonic, and the craters there reminded the author of a photograph he once saw—and which, doubtless, most people have seen—of the volcanoes in the moon. They are quite as fantastically shaped, though, of course, not so large as we are told by astronomers those of our satellite are. The points of interest about *Krafla* are two large craters on its western slope at an altitude of about 1,700 feet above sea-level, now partly filled with water, and a cleft running far into the mountain on the south-west, once a crater rift. The largest of the craters is called *Víti* (Hell); and, on the 17th May, 1724, such an immense quantity of pumice and ashes was ejected from it that 'on the eastern shores of *Mývatn* the layer of ashes was over three feet deep.' *Leirhnúkr* erupted in A.D. 1725, 1727, 1728, and 1729. It was active at the time *Reykjahlíð's* farm was destroyed by a lava-flood, but it will be seen that it is impossible this could have flowed from *Leirhnúkr*, there being a mountain range between it and the site of the farm; so that previous writers err in stating that the farm was destroyed by lava from this volcano. Its destruction was by lava that issued from volcanic outlets in this intervening range, which are to be seen by following up the floods of igneous rock to their source.

FORTY-SEVENTH DAY.—Excursion to the 1875 Lava-flood in the *Mývatns Öræfi*; and return to *Reykjahlíð*. This excursion should not be made, if it is purposed to proceed eastward to *Seyðisfjörðr*, for in that case the lava can be seen *en route*. The scene of the eruption lies four hours' ride east of *Reykjahlíð*. It should be approached by the newly-constructed road over the *Öræfi*, and followed southward for about a mile and a half, and quitted by the old road. This is as much as can be examined in a day's excursion from *Reykjahlíð*. To thoroughly explore this immense lava-flood it would be necessary to camp out on the *Jökulsá*, distant about six miles further east, there being, it is believed, no water nearer than the river.

The lava at the northern end of the bed lies in a hollow formed by a subsidence,[1] during the eruption, of a tract three to four miles in length between two deep parallel rifts, which run northward for several miles ; and the lava stretches away southward farther than the eye can follow it, when one stands upon the level ground. The depth of the subsidence is greatest near the lava, from which the surface of the sunken tract slopes gradually up to the level of the Öræfi, the rifts decreasing in size as the depth of the subsidence becomes less. The lava now forms a bed trending from S.S.W. to N.N.E., varying greatly in breadth, and said to be over twenty miles in length. To judge from its appearance, a vast quantity, most intensely heated, must first have welled forth from a rift, in the rocky strata underlying the desert, running down the centre of the bed for nearly its whole length ; this, owing to the comparatively level nature of the ground, spread freely westward and eastward wherever slight depressions existed in the plain of the Öræfi. In places these arms cover tracts several square miles in extent. This first eruption of molten rock congealed into a rugged sheet, twelve to fifty feet in thickness, very clinker-like along its borders, which are fragments of the earlier cooled fringe of the molten flood that were borne onward by that behind. It is evident from the veritable chaos of huge masses of lava piled up in places down the centre of the bed, above the rift whence the lava issued, that eruption after eruption took place ; each lava-flow being congealed into a layer of rock, which, in its turn, was subsequently upheaved and shattered by a later outburst, in whose fiery embrace the huge jagged masses of the torn-up bed were borne along partly imbedded, and from which, now that the later of these molten floods are also solid rock, they project at all angles. These masses are also built up into several groups of rude cone-shaped craters having an altitude above the lava of from 100 to 200 feet. Owing to the erratic manner in which the lava has spread around and been piled up down the centre of the bed, it is not an easy matter to compute the cubic contents of the enormous mass of molten rock that here issued in 1875 ; but the author believes that he shall under- rather than over-estimate if he sets down its bulk at 31,000 of millions of cubic feet. The lava-

---

[1] It is said by the people living around Mývatn, who scour the Öræfi every autumn in search of strayed sheep, that a similar subsidence is to be seen at the southern end of the lava-bed. The author cannot say whether this is the case or not, having only ridden southward along the lava for a distance of eight miles. He was told in 1878 that the rifts seen on each side of the northern end of the lava extended the whole length of the bed, but last year he discovered that this is not the case.

flood from *Hekla* in 1845 has been computed to contain 14,400 millions of cubic feet (Danish); while those from Vesuvius in 1794 and 1855 have been computed at 730 and 570 millions of cubic feet respectively. These, it will be seen, are dwarfed into insignificance by the magnitude of the lava eruption in the *Mývatns Öræfi* in 1875.

Jón Pétursson, of *Reykjahlíð*, gave the author the following particulars of the eruption. Lava was first seen issuing in the *Öræfi* on the 18th February, forty-five days after the earthquake accompanying an explosion in *Askja* on the 4th January; but it is probable the fiery flood commenced to stream forth immediately after the earthquake, which doubtless opened the rift, no one having crossed from *Reykjahlíð* to the eastward or *vice versâ* during that period. For nearly four months the lava continued to stream forth more or less freely, and then ceased to flow until the 15th August, when a smart shock of earthquake was felt, and a slight eruption of ashes and volcanic bombs took place from the rift at its northernmost end, the lava-flow recommencing and continuing for several days.

FORTY-EIGHTH DAY.—*Reykjahlíð* to *Skútustaðir* (Skúti's-stead). A three hours' ride, chiefly through the lava-beds fringing the lake on the east; a wild tract of tremendously rugged lava, split into deep ravines, where the cliffs occasionally present more the appearance of man's than nature's handiwork—here assuming the form of a vast ruinous castellated building, overgrown with mosses and lichens; there the ruins of some old cloister, the lava being hollowed out into arches, almost perfectly Gothic in form. At the south end of the lake many isolated rugged masses of lava of fantastic form jut out of the water. One, when seen at a certain angle, appears like an ancient galley, with its solitary huge square-sail set to the breeze, and a man sitting in the stern steering; a thin slab of upheaved lava-crust forms the sail, and a smaller piece, right aft, the steersman. Shortly after this is seen, a shallow bay will be waded, and the travellers will land on a sparsely grass-covered hill, which is a vast heap of cinders. Here the lake will be quitted for a short distance, and, after fording a small stream abounding in trout, the party will wend their way amid a number of crater-cones, in one of which, not far distant from *Skútustaðir*, a pair of eagles had an eyrie for many years. Good accommodation at *Skútustaðir* parsonage; and excellent trout fishing is obtainable in the upper waters of the *Laxá*, especially about three miles from its outlet from *Mývatn*. Duck shooting not allowed on the lake, nor in the river north of the water belonging to *Hofsta𝑣ir* (Temple-stead) farm. At *Hofsta𝑣ir* the people are willing to accommodate sportsmen, and splendid trout fishing and good grouse and duck shooting are to be had.

FORTY-NINTH DAY.—*Skútusta𝑣ir* to *Svartárkot* (Black-river-cot). Six hours' ride, at first through an extensive marsh, and then over wild moorland wastes. Feathered game very plentiful. The *Króká* (Croak-river), a deepish sluggish stream, has to be forded. Obliging people at *Svartárkot*, but only one small room. The farmer, Einar, is an excellent guide.

FIFTIETH DAY.—A quiet day to rest the ponies for the journey across the *O'dd𝑣ahraun* on the morrow. Trout fishing to be had in the river flowing from the lake. If ponies can be borrowed from the farmer—do not on any account use your own—make an excursion to the

ELDEYJAFOSS (Fire-island-fall), the finest of all the falls on the *Skjálfandafljót*. At a spot a few miles west of *Svartárkot* the river, by some prehistoric volcanic convulsion, has been diverted from an earlier channel, through which water now only flows during the floods. This channel, and the island formed by it and the river, is one of the grandest pieces of natural rock-work that one can conceive; and innumerable 'giant-pots' of unusual depth are here to be seen. For the information of those who have never heard of or seen a giant-pot, it may be mentioned it is a well-like cavity bored down into the solid rock by the attrition caused by the continuous rotary motion of a stone, lodged in what is at first a small hollow, kept revolving by running water. The *Eldeyjafoss* is at the southern end of the island formed by the old and present channel of the river, and the whole body of water leaps at one bound into a deep basin.

FIFTY-FIRST DAY.—EXCURSION TO ASKJA. Sleep all day and set out about six in the evening, so as to travel through the night across the plain of the *O'dd𝑣ahraun*, and commence the ascent of the mountain with the return of the sun. The travellers will then have all day before them for the exploration of the volcano; the journey across the desert, ascent of the mountain, and descent into the crater taking from ten to eleven hours. It is four hours' hard work to cross the lava-covered floor of *Askja* on foot to the site of disturbance in 1875. Einar mùst be hired as guide: his charge is 20 *kroner* for himself and two ponies. Sacks of hay, proportionate to the number of mounts, will have to be taken on pack-ponies. Owing to the fodder having to be taken, the members of the party should dispense with a remount, as the ponies laden with hay on the outward journey may be ridden on the return. It is almost unnecessary to add that the strongest of the travellers' nags should be selected for this journey.

The first hour's ride from the cot is across level moorland, which in 1880 was alive with willow-grouse, when the *Súðrá* (? South-river) is struck. This river, which is tributary to the *Skjálfandafljót*, flows through an extensive sandy waste—not lava-desert as shown on Gunnlaugsson's map, and there named *Súdrárhraun*—bordering the *Oddáhraun* on the north-west. The course of the *Súðrá* is followed for about four miles, and the river is quitted at a spot where there is a very remarkable pool in which the water is in rotary motion, caused by a small hole at the bottom, through which it is descending to some underground channel. The source of the *Súðrá* is somewhat singular, consisting of numerous shallow pools in the sand, wherein frequently as many as half a dozen beautifully clear springs briskly bubble forth. In less than an hour after quitting the river the lava desert is entered.

THE ODÁÐAHRAUN lies at an altitude of about 1,500 feet, and consists chiefly of countless lava-floods, varying greatly in age, some being thousands of years old and clothed with lichen, while others are as black and new-looking as those which flowed from the volcanoes east of *Mývatn* a century and a half ago. The newer lava-floods in the vicinity of the *Dyngjufjöll* on the north have flowed from rifts which have opened time after time in *Askja's* encircling mountain wall, and at its base; while the south-west portion of the desert is stated by Mr. Watts to be covered with those which have flowed from the *Trölladyngja* (Trolls-bower), which lies about 15 miles distant from *Askja* in that direction. A large extent of the desert, especially in the north and north-east, is covered with lava that has welled forth from huge rifts in the sub-strata, in the same manner as a small lava-flood did north-east of *Hekla* in 1878, and the far larger one from *Askja* in 1875. The lava-floods which have issued in this manner are the newest looking and most rugged. The oldest superficial lava appears to be the last of veritable oceans of molten rock that at one time overspread the plain; its surface, congealed into innumerable dome-shaped bubbles, starred with deep fissures formed by the contraction of the mass when cooling, is passable on horseback, so evenly and freely has the lava flowed. As one's pony picks its way carefully over the flattened domes, the sound of its hoofs striking against the rock rings hollow, as if caverns were beneath, which is doubtless the

case. Extensive tracts of black and lighter-coloured pumiceous
sand are met with, where depressions between the newer lava-beds
have been filled in by pumice eruptions, and sand-drifts in stormy
weather.

From the above brief description of the Misdeed-lava-desert,
it will be evident that it is not very favourable ground to travel
over. The more rugged beds of lava will frequently compel a
detour for some distance, so that one perforce pursues a zigzag route,
heading as straight as possible for a gap which marks a defile in the
mountain encompassing *Askja*. For six weary hours, after leaving
the *Súörd*, will the party thus slowly wend their way through this
fire-blasted wilderness, ere they reach the base of the mountain.

ASKJA.—This vast crater lies within the chief of a group of
mountains named the *Dýngjufjöll* (Bower-mountains), *Askja* presumably being the bower. The ascent of the mountain begins quite
seven miles distant from the highest part of the defile through which
one can more easily than elsewhere descend into *Askja*. The slope
is a gentle upward gradient until an altitude of about 3,500 feet is
attained, when the ascent becomes more steep, and one is compelled
to dismount and drag his reluctant steed after him ; carefully picking
one's way over lava-flows that have found vent through rifts
in the defile, and later on over ice, which forms a steep, slippery
declivity between two mountain walls, whose jagged summits rise
on either hand to a height of close upon a thousand feet. The
direction of this pass—named *Jónsskar's* (John's-pass) in honour of
Jón of *Víðikær*, the first man to visit *Askja*—is from N.N.W. to
S.S.E., and its length, at a guess, slightly exceeds two miles. Upon
both occasions when the author visited the volcano the summers
have been unusually hot, and the ice in the pass was consequently
very rotten and dangerous. It was quite black in colour in places,
owing to the immense quantities of black volcanic ash imbedded in
it. The highest point of the pass is a short distance from its southern
end, where it terminates in a precipitous declivity of ice and ashes.
From the verge of the precipice, a splendid view over *Askja's* weird
amphitheatre is obtained. Lying several hundred feet below is the
lava-covered floor of this huge crater, whose circumference, as
before stated, is between 17 and 18 miles, and its area at least 23
square miles. The somewhat jagged mountain wall encircling it
rises above the floor of the crater to heights varying from 800 to
1,500 feet. The highest hollows are filled with ice, and the peaks
are snow-clad for ten months out of the twelve. East of the pass
there is a glacier exceeding four miles in length by one in width.

Upon both occasions the floor of *Askja*, notwithstanding it lies 3,700 feet above sea-level, has been free from snow at the time of the author's visit; owing, probably, to internal heat, as 20 miles south we have the glaciers of the *Vatna Jökull*, with a mean altitude of less than 5,000 feet, and in the north-west of Iceland, at an altitude of less than 3,000 feet, there are the icy wastes of the *Glámu* and *Drânga Jöklar*, neither of which tracts can possibly be more favourably formed for glacial deposit than *Askja*. The encircling mountain wall is highest on the south and north, and lowest on the north-east, where it does not rise more than 800 feet above the floor of *Askja* for over a mile. East of this there is a gap to the level of the lava-floods deposited in *Askja*, through which lava has coursed down the outer slope and spread over the *O'dá'ðahraun*. There is another gap in the mountain wall in the south-west, but the author cannot say whether lava has also streamed out there or not, he having never been in that part of the crater.

The whole surface of *Askja*, save in the south-east where there is a tepid lake five miles in circumference, and an extensive tract covered with pumice erupted in 1875, is a chaos of rugged lava-floods that have issued here at different periods. From those on the left, looking south across the crater from the pass, over an area exceeding a square mile, ascend innumerable small jets of steam. These do not mark the site of the 1875 eruptions, however, for these stufa are dwarfed into utter insignificance by enormous volumes of steam that belch forth on the farther side of the amphitheatre close under its encircling mountain wall in the south-east. These bursts of steam issue from rifts and vents opened by the 1875 eruptions.

The crossing of the lava-coloured floor of *Askja* from the foot of the pass, where one perforce leaves his pony, is most fatiguing work; each time that the author has crossed, it has taken him—a young and active man—four hours to proceed as many miles, most of the way by the aid of his hands, protected by thick woollen mittens that they might not be cut by the lava. He may also mention that it utterly ruins the pair of boots worn while crossing ; so that an old pair with good soles should be taken by any one who purposes in the future to visit this volcano. When within a mile of the northernmost of the large bursts of steam, one is able to walk upright, the lava being buried under a covering of pumice, which rapidly increases in depth as the site of the 1875 eruptions is approached. The pumice is of three colours, light silvery grey, black, and golden-brown, the latter very fibrous, and presenting the appearance of masses of the interior of the outer husks of gigantic coco-nuts. This substance is fast degrading into pumiceous sand.

In crossing the crater four times no lava anywhere so new-looking that it could possibly have issued as recently as 1875 was seen by the author, but among the pumice were huge blocks of obsidian and pitchstone that had undoubtedly been ejected at the same time as that substance.

The apex of the slope formed by the pumice is a cone-shaped crater, whose summit lies about 250 feet above the superficial lava beneath the pumice. When seen in 1878, tremendous blasts of steam were belching forth almost continuously with perfectly deafening roars, but two years later, to the author's great astonishment, all was perfectly still; and upon climbing to the summit he found that in the crater at a depth of 150 feet was a placid pool of apparently cold water. About 10 feet above the surface of the water were several inconsiderable stufa. The diameter of the mouth of the crater is between 450 and 500 feet, and the interior tapers down to a diameter of about 300 feet at the level of the water. Mr. E. Delmar Morgan, F.R.G.S., who visited *Askja* last summer (1881), says in a paper read before the Royal Geographical Society on the 30th January, 1882:—Hardly had we taken up a position on the edge of the crater, ' than with a loud roar a jet of mingled water and steam was thrown up to a great height, subsiding just as suddenly as it began. This proceeded apparently from a new outlet and not from a circular pool alongside, which was boiling and bubbling furiously.' Thus, it appears, there is now a geysir of considerable size within this crater; which is named the Pumice Crater, as from it the greater part of the pumice erupted in 1875 was doubtless ejected.

This crater on the south-west slopes abruptly down to the surface of the tepid lake lying some 600 feet below. The bed of the lake was formed by the disruption and subsidence bodily into an abyss beneath *Askja* of a huge mass of the lava deposits, oval in shape, of unknown thickness, and five miles in circumference. That this disruption and subsidence took place during the 1875 eruptions is proved by the fresh appearance of the face of the cliffs encircling the lake on the north, which show the strata underlying the present surface of *Askja en profile*.

South-east of the lake, stretching into *Askja's* encircling mountain wall for nearly 1,000 yards, is a deep gorge bordered on either hand with sheer precipices 600 feet in height at the very least. Herein are innumerable vents, from which immense volumes of steam, perhaps also hot water, belch forth with such violence that the rock trembles under one's feet when standing 600 feet above them.

In the introductory chapter, page 11, the 1875 eruption was briefly described; and it will be seen it was a very remarkable one in several respects. No lava was ejected from the volcano itself, this substance forcing its way through a subterranean channel for a distance of 30 miles ere it found a vent, coming to the surface in the *Mývatns Öræfi* at a lower altitude by 2,400 feet than the rift and crater in *Askja*, from which the pumice and ashes were ejected.

To return to the travellers, whom the author has conducted as far as the pass, and there left them while he briefly described the volcano and its doings in 1875. They will probably find themselves in *Askja* at the foot of the pass about 5 A.M. of the

FIFTY-SECOND DAY—and, if twelve hours is devoted to the exploration of this vast crater, they will have time to make their way through the pass on the return journey, and accomplish the greater part of the descent of the mountain, before the chilly night hours overtake them. About 4 A.M. of the

FIFTY-THIRD DAY will see them safely back at *Svartárkot*; and, should the party have been favoured with fine weather, the author feels certain they will be charmed with their excursion, and inclined to agree with Mr. Delmar Morgan that 'the traveller to Iceland should not omit a visit to *Askja*.' Of course, immediately upon reaching *Svartárkot*, the travellers will seek their beds, and there pass the remainder of the day.

FIFTY-FOURTH DAY.—If it is intended to return to *Akureyri*, *Svartárkot* to *Stóruvellir*. An easy day's journey. The *Skjálfandafljót* should be forded near *Lundarbrekka* church. If it is purposed to go eastward to *Seyðisfjörðr*, ride back to-day to *Skútustaðir*, and thence on the morrow proceed to *Reykjahlíð*.

FIFTY-FIFTH DAY.—*Stóruvellir* to *Akureyri*. Do not let your guide take you by the path over the mountains north-east of *Stóruvellir*; it is a little nearer, but terrible hard work for the ponies. Insist upon going *via Ljósavatn*.

To SEYÐISFJÖRÐR.

FIFTY-SIXTH DAY.—*Reykjahlíð* to *Grímstaðir* (Grímr's-stead). A man, and two ponies for his use, will have to be taken from *Reykjahlíð* to ferry the travellers over the *Jökulsá*. The fixed charge is 6 *kroner* for the man and ponies, 25 *öre* for each person and his saddle ferried over, and a like sum for each pack-saddle and its load. It takes five hours to cross the *Mývatns Öræfi* to the river; there is now an excellent made road for the greater part of the way. See the 1875 Lava-flood *en route*, described on pages 151–153. A short distance east of the lava there is a remarkable crater, the *Hrossaborg* (Horse-burg). It is but a few hundred yards south of the road, and will well repay an hour's examination. It is an hour's ride from the lava to the ferry over the river, and one and a half thence to *Grimstaðir*. This is one of the best farms in Iceland, and people obliging.

FIFTY-SEVENTH DAY.— *Grimstaðir* to *Möðrudalr* (Madders-dale). Between four and five hours' ride only. Several streams, tributary to the *Jökulsá*, will be forded on the way. *Möðrudalr* is another rich farm, and the accommodation is very good. This place is an excellent base for reindeer stalking excursions among the mountains to the south-east, where a herd of about 200 reindeer are frequently seen.

The travellers may from here proceed to *Eskifjörðr* (Ash-fjord), or to *Djúpivógr* (Deep-voe) on the *Berufjörðr* (Bear-fjord), instead of to *Seyðisfjörðr*, but neither of these routes are to be recommended, owing to the difficulty in crossing the Eastern *Jökulsá*. The travellers cross one at a time in a box running on two ropes, considerably the worse for years of exposure to the weather, and the ponies swim over. A recent traveller thus describes the passage of this river, one day in August: 'Crossed the (E.) *Jökulsá* in the cage. The horses were driven to the ford, 200 yards below. Only four of sixteen swam over at first trial, in 1 hour 33 minutes. The rest were driven farther down, and seven passed over in 1 hour 30 minutes to 2 hours 30 minutes. The last five were towed over with a rope. Occupied 4 hours.' The cage is marked on the maps as a bridge (*Brú*). The route to *Djúpivógr* is shown on the map attached to this work by a dotted red-line. From *Möðrudalr* to this trading-post is a three days' journey. The first night should be passed at *Valþjófstaðir* (Valthjolfr's-stead), near which is the *Hengifoss* (Hanging-fall), said to be 1,200 feet high. Less than an hour's ride distant are the ruins of *Skriðuklaustr* (Avalanche-cloister). The second night's quarters will be at *Berufjörðr* parsonage—a long day's journey. The next day will bring the party to *Djúpivógr* trading-post. *Eskifjörðr* is distant two days' ride from *Möðrudalr*. *Hallormstaðir* should be the goal of the first day's journey, fair accommodation.

FIFTY-EIGHTH DAY. — *Möðrudalr* to *Hofteigr* (Temple-close).

ROUTE III.—A SUMMER'S TOUR IN ICELAND. 161

Rough road for the first two hours, when, first fording a stream, the track passes over a level stretch of country overgrown with birch-brush, amongst which grouse are usually plentiful in August. About five hours after leaving *Möðrudalr*, the travellers will descend by a steep path to the valley of the Eastern *Jökulsá*, near *Arnórstaðir*; and thence two hours' ride down the valley will bring them to the door of *Hofteigr* parsonage. A good deal of pumice from the 1875 eruption will be seen during this day's journey.

FIFTY-NINTH DAY.—*Hofteigr* to *Seyðisfjörðr*. The *Jökulsá* will be crossed by a narrow wooden bridge, over which it is only possible to lead one pony at the time. This bridge is about an hour's ride from *Hofteigr*, down the valley; and the *Hvanná*, a small tributary stream with an unusually foul channel, full of boulders, will have to be forded. Between the valley of the *Jökulsá* and that of the *Lagarfljót* (? Log-flood) is an extensive heath, the *Fljótsdalsheiði* (Flood-dale-heath); and the geologist in crossing it will see evidence that this part of the island is of older formation than the *Mývatns Öræfi* and the *O'ddðahraun*, for it is said that '*roches moutonnées* are seen peeping out here, there, and everywhere, and there are also huge boulders (*blocs perchés*) left by the glacier in its line of retreat from the sea.' After crossing the heath, a descent is made into the valley of the *Lagarfljót*, which will be ferried at *Rángá* farm. This lake-like sheet of water is sometimes fordable. On the opposite side of the river is *Eyðar* farm and chapel of ease. Good accommodation here, and there is said to be first-class grouse shooting and trout fishing in the neighbourhood. Between here and the *Seyðisfjörðr* lies an elevated plateau studded with numerous lakelets, the *Vestdalsheiði* (West-dale-heath); the crossing of which and descent to the shore of the fjord will take five hours.

SEYÐISFJÖRÐR.—There are trading posts upon each side of the fjord, but the recently erected hotel is on the north shore. This place, to judge by its rate of increase during the past two years, bids fair to shortly rival *Ísafjörðr* in its claim to rank as the town next in importance to the capital. The Norwegians have established a cod and herring fishery here, and built several large stores and fish-curing houses. Excellent sea-fishing to be had from a boat a short distance down the fjord, halibut and cod of immense size are to be caught.

EXCURSION TO ESKIFJÖRÐR.—Should the party have to wait several days for the arrival of the steamer, this excursion should be made —it is but a day's ride. The baggage should be left at *Seyðisfjörðr* for shipment, as the travellers will embark at *Eskifjörðr*, where the steamer arrives a few hours after leaving the former place. In the vicinity of *Eskifjörðr* is the largest and finest deposit of Iceland spar in the island. The mine is now government property, and though unworked may be visited.

ROUTE IV.

A SIX WEEKS' EXCURSION UP THE WEST COAST.

STARTING FROM REYKJAVÍK AND RETURNING THERETO, OR PROCEEDING ON TO AKUREYRI. VISITING THE GLYMRFOSS; REYKHOLTSDALR; ELDBORG; THE NORTH-WEST PENINSULA AND THE GLÁMU AND DRÁNGA JÖKLAR; AND ÍSAFJÖRÐR AND THE LIGNITE BEDS IN ITS VICINITY.

FIRST DAY.—*Reykjavík* to *Reynivellir* (Rowan-fields). A six to eight hours' ride, depending on the state of the roads, or rather ruts. The *Ellíðaár;* the head of a shallow bay, the *Leirárvógr* (Lair-river-voe); and the *Laxá* near *Reynivellir* will be forded on this day's journey. A narrow mountain pass between *Esja* and the *Skálafell,* the *Svínaskarð* (Swine-pass), will be traversed before descending into the valley of the *Laxá*. The country here is very mountainous, and the scenery, consequently, has much of wild beauty in it.

If preferred, the travellers can send their ponies round to *Kjalarnes* (Keel-naze) under the charge of the guide, proceed there themselves by boat from *Reykjavík,* and thence ride round the coast to *Reynivellir*. The remains of a 'doom-ring,' which marks the site of a Hof or Pagan temple, will be seen on the way. The geologist would doubtless find it worth his while to make an ascent of *Esja,* its formation is said to differ considerably from that of the other mountains in the neighbourhood. The angler must not forget that the river at *Reynivellir* is a *Laxá*.

SECOND DAY.—*Reynivellir* to *Lundr,* visiting the *Glymrfoss* (Clashing-fall) *en route*. After crossing the hills north of *Reynivellir*, the *Fossá* (Fall-river) will be forded, and thence the travellers should quit the direct track to *Lundr* and skirt the head of the *Hvalfjörðr* (Whale-fjord) to the first farm in the *Botnsdalr*

(Bottom-valley). Here obtain a boy to show the way to the *Glymrfoss*. It is formed by a small stream, the *Botnsá*, which leaps into a chasm some 1,200 to 1,500 feet deep, and 'so narrow that daylight scarce reaches to the bottom; yet so sheer is the fall, so clean the split of the earth, that by long and attentive peering a tiny thread of silver may be seen winding along at the bottom of the cañon.' The bird's-eye view of the fjord from this spot is really charming. A hilly ride from the *Botnsdalr* to the head of the *Skorradalsvatn* (Magpie-dale-lake), the river feeding which will have to be forded. Another ridge has to be crossed between this valley and the valley of the *Grímsá*, in which lies *Lundr*, the halting-place for the night. Fair accommodation. Salmon fishing in the *Grímsá*, and it is said there is excellent trout fishing in several streams in the vicinity.

THIRD DAY.—*Lundr* to Þ*ingnes* (Thing-naze). An easy day after the fatiguing one yesterday. Three hours' ride down the *Grímsdrdalr*, and thence about an hour will bring the party to Þ*ingnes* farm. Fair accommodation; salmon fishing; and shooting in August.

AN EXCURSION TO THE SNÆFELL PENINSULA, taking fifteen days, may be made from here, rejoining the route at *Borðeyri* trading post. See Route III., *ante*, pages 125 to 132. Since that route was printed, the author's attention has been called to the fact that an attempt was made in 1872 by Lord Garvagh—well known as a reindeer stalker in Norway—to attain the summit of the *Snæfell Jökull*. His lordship thus describes his assault upon the icy giant. His starting-point was *Búðir*. He premises that 'never till to-day having attempted any glacier work, various causes of delay prevented me starting until noon.' He borrowed here a rope and a couple of primitive iron-headed poles, to serve as Alpenstocks, and his guide 'had a trowel, which he intended to use like an ice axe for cutting steps. At first there was a ride of two hours. . . . At two o'olock P.M. we left our horses in charge of some one; at four, after getting up some way and traversing a whole district of loose pumice stones, *gained the ice*.

'We pushed on. Pure and transparent as the atmosphere upon this glacier proverbially is, the deception of it led us on for a considerable time in full view of the summit, before we knew or had any idea how far the summit actually was. But as this annihilation of distance appeared to be somewhat supernatural, we did not believe it, and accordingly went straight on; the snow was in good order, and promised an easy ascent.

'Yawning fissures in the ice came frequently across the way, sometimes of great width, and compelling us to go right round; very beautiful to look into, but of a frightful depth, and lit up with a blue-green colour. Delighted by every prospect of accomplishing what the good people of Reykjavík had declared impossible, I strove to reach the summit before night. But the guide complaining of some sickness that he felt, and since the evening had already set in, I found it necessary to retrace the way—no easy matter upon ice—and find somewhere to pass the night on *terra firma*.

'That night was spent upon the mountain. With a stone and a piece of waterproof upon it for our pillow, this man and I slept in the open air. At daybreak, half-past two, we set to work again—by the light of a splendid sunrise, Oriental in beauty and grandeur. None of the vapour of England rose here to prevent our view of two seas (Breiðifjörðr and Faxafjörðr) at once; while the low coasts and harbours around each lay spread out underneath us like a map... At first the ice and snow work was a pretty piece of business, for it had all frozen over since last evening, and afforded scarcely any footing whatever, so, until the rising sun had somewhat thawed the surface, we were hardly able to make any head. However, by cutting a step here and there, we overcame the slopes of ice; and by seven o'clock, or somewhat about that time, in four hours after commencing the ice work, arrived within only a quarter (*sic*) of the highest point.' Here the guide, who had been showing signs of giving in for some time, 'at last sank right down upon the snow, utterly powerless to proceed another step, with blood from his ears and in his eyes... He was evidently unable to breathe atmosphere so rarified and thin; directly, therefore, he was able to move, we descended, having lost the grandest opportunity of doing what, in Iceland, would have made any man, native or foreigner, immortal.' In conclusion his lordship says, Having 'given some faint outlines for the benefit of travellers to come, I wish the evil genius who lives upon it—farewell; and hope the laurels which I did not win, may fall upon that man, who, more favoured by Fortune, shall first succeed in making the ascent. The earlier in the summer this glacier is attempted, the easier it will be; for the ice has not cracked and split into chasms like we now had to encounter, and the winter snow, still undissolved, remains in one steady slope the whole way up, making allowance for the possibility of places where one might sink in, if the chasms of last year have been only partly drifted over.' From

Lord Garvagh's experience it will, be seen that this virgin peak might, under favourable circumstances, be vanquished by men not new to mountain work in one day, by setting out from Buðir early in the morning, so as to reach the ice about nine or ten A.M., just as the heat of the sun has taken the glaze from the night's frost off the surface of the ice.

FOURTH DAY.—Excursion from Þingnes to the Geysirs in the *Reykholtsdalr*. An interesting and easy day's excursion, returning to Þingnes. For description of the thermal springs, see *ante*, pages 125 and 126. A week may be pleasantly spent in this part of the country by anglers, there being three salmon rivers within easy reach. See List of Salmon Rivers. Good shooting is also to be had in August.

FIFTH DAY.—Þingnes to *Staðarhraun*, or *Hvammr*. There are two routes from this place to the N.W. peninsula, but the one *viâ* Staðarhraun, although a day longer, is recommended, as *Eldborg*, the first volcano to erupt subsequently to the settlement of Iceland, will be seen, and the scenery is far superior to that on the other route. *Eldborg* is described *ante*, page 127. The *Hvítá* has to be ferried shortly after leaving Þingnes, and then the road to *Hvammr* lies up the valley of the *Norðrá*. From *Hvammr* a stiffish day's ride over an elevated plateau, the *Holtavörðuheiði* (Holt-cairn-heath), will bring the travellers to *Borðeyri* trading post. About midway in crossing the heath will be seen a mass of rock, known as the *Hæðarstein* (Height-stone), which is believed to have been a Pagan sacrificial altar. From *Hvammr*, those of a geological turn of mind may ascend *Baula* (the Cow), a cone of curious formation.

SIXTH DAY.—*Staðarhraun* to *Hjarðarholt* (Herd-holt). *Eldborg* will be seen shortly after setting out. Thence the travellers will ride up to the head of the *Hítárdalr*, and wend their way between the mountains at the base of the *Snæfell* peninsula, by a route not shown on the map, to the head of the *Hvammsfjörðr*. Grand scenery during this day's ride. Good quarters at *Hjarðarholt*. This neighbourhood is full of interest to those who have read the Njál and Laxdæla Sagas. *Hjarðarholt* was the home of Olave the Peacock, and *Höskuldstaðir*, on the opposite side of the river, the birth-place of Hallgerða, Gunnar's wife. There are salmon in the river here.

SEVENTH DAY.—*Hjarðarholt* to *Borðeyri*. An easy day's ride. The route lies up the *Laxárdalr*, and thence over the *Laxárdalsheiði* to the shore of the *Hrútafjörðr*. The merchant at *Borðeyri* receives travellers.

EIGHTH DAY.—At *Borðeyri*. The ponies will need a day's rest, and, probably, the travellers likewise. There are some hot springs on the east side of the fjord, to which a boating excursion may be made. The plover and curlew shooting here is excellent early in August. The Danish mail steamers do not call at this trading post, but the Camoens usually makes a voyage thereto in September. See Sailing Bill.

NINTH DAY.—*Borðeyri* to *Guðlaugsvik*. An easy day's journey, keeping close to the fjord the whole way. From this point, the route is mainly compiled from Shepherd's 'North-West Peninsula,' the author of which made a lengthy tour in this part of the island in 1862. At that day there lived at *Guðlaugsvik* a farmer speaking English, and he provided Shepherd's party with first-rate accommodation.

TENTH DAY.—*Guðlaugsvik* to *Berufjörðr* (Bear-fjord). Shepherd proceeded to *Fell*, but the track is a very mountainous one, hard upon the ponies, and it is better, therefore, to cross the isthmus to *Berufjörðr*, where there is very fair accommodation, and the scenery of the fjord, with its countless isles and the *Snæfell* peninsula beyond, is magnificent. Upon the way will be seen a picturesque fall, the *Gullfoss*. On the shores of the *Gilsfjörðr* (Gill-fjord) huge petrified trees have been disinterred. Good accommodation, it is said, at *Berufjörðr*.

ELEVENTH DAY.—*Berufjörðr* to *Kirkjubòl*. A long and hard day's journey over the Þorskafjarðarheiði (Cod-fjord-heath). If the ponies are not in good condition, it is better to cross the heath to *Staðr*, at the head of the *Steingrimsfjörðr*, to-day, and cross the Steingrimsfjarðarheiði to *Lagidalr* farm, north of *Kirkjubòl*, on the morrow. Shepherd's party were three days accomplishing the distance between *Fell* and *Staðr*, but the ponies were in a very exhausted condition.

TWELFTH DAY.—At *Kirkjubòl*. The ponies will need a day's rest, if the travellers cross to this place from *Berufjörðr* in one day. Ascertain here whether it is possible to ascend the *Glámu Jökull* from the farms at the head of the *Ísafjörðr*. Because, if so, it will save a long, doubtful boating excursion to *Kleifar* farm at the head of the *Skötufjörðr* (Skate-fjord). It will be best to make the ascent of the *Glámu Jökull*, if an assault is practicable from the head of the *Ísafjörðr*, before proceeding northward to the *Dránga Jökull*. *Lógidalr* (Log-dale) was the farm selected by Shepherd as a base from which to ascend the *Dránga Jökull*, but it is believed better quarters are obtainable at *Kirkjubòl*.

THE SCENERY OF THE ÍSAFJÖRÐR is thus described by Shepherd:

'There was something awfully grand in the scene. There were the dark blue mountains, snow-capped and precipitous, which lined the opposite shore, and towered, one above another, far inland—solemn and forbidding to look at. Heavy clouds lowered over the fjord, and clung to the mountains towards the sea. Huge masses of rock, torn off from the heights and hurled into the valley below, were lying all around us—awful witnesses of the fury of the Arctic winters in these wind-swept regions—while hundreds of dead sea-fowl floated on the surf, and the whitened bones of whales and ponies were scattered along the beach. At the point where we then were, the fjord was about three miles broad ; for we had come down a side valley, and had struck the fjord a considerable distance from its head.'

Allowing three days for an assault upon the *Gláma Jökull*, if practicable from the head of the *I'safjörðr*, the

SIXTEENTH DAY.—*Kirkjuból* to *Hamar* (Crag). Three hours' ride only ; an easy day to rest the ponies for the fatigues of to-morrow. Good road, says Shepherd, ' over a shingly beach, with good grass above it, and, occasionally, small woods of scrub, in which we shot a few ptarmigan.' At *Hamar* Shepherd's party were made very welcome, and the farmer provided a boat and men for excursions on the fjord. *Hamar* is the best farm to make head-quarters, as from here it is but two hours' ride to *Armuli*, at the foot of the *Dránga Jökull*, where a guide can be obtained. It is also but ten hours' row in calm weather to the town of *I'safjörðr*, which ranks next in importance to *Reykjavik*. It is about the same distance to *Kleifar* farm, at the head of the *Skötufjörðr*, whither the travellers will proceed to attack the *Gláma Jökull* if it is unassailable from the head of the *I'safjörðr*.

SEVENTEENTH DAY.—Ascent of the *Dránga Jökull*. Shepherd obtained his guide at a farm about two hours' ride from *Hamar*, in the *Skjaldfannárdalr*, a valley leading up into the *Jökull* south of *Armuli*. The ascent is up this valley, and is thus described by Shepherd: ' We left the farm at 1·30, and proceeded up the northern branch of the valley,' which narrowed in 'until it assumed the dimensions of a ravine, and the torrent was roaring beneath us between two walls of snow, two or three hundred feet deep. At 3·15 our guide declared the ponies could go no farther, and we gladly dismounted, leaving them in the charge of Olavur. The barometer which stood at 29° at the sea-level now marked 28° 27'. Our small barometer was left with Olavur, with instructions to move the pointer over the indicator exactly at 5 o'clock.

'We began to walk at 3·25, taking an easterly direction across a steep snow-slope, into which we sank deeply. On leaving the snow the walking was very bad and stony.

'Soon after, we descended again to cross the ravine which, by an unlucky bend, had come athwart our direction. The descent was not long, for a narrow snow-covered glacier, which ended abruptly in a precipice, filled up the ravine. It was about 100 yards across. The visible crevasses were very few.

'At 4·40 we changed our direction to north-by-west, and at five o'clock the barometer marked 27°. Nothing was now to be seen. We were enveloped in mist, and seemed to be the centre of an ever-advancing circle of about forty yards in diameter. Latterly, our route had been more level; and, at 6·30, all upward progression ceased.

'Our guide then declared that we were at the top. This was very pleasant news, as it was very cold; but we saw nothing. The barometer marked 26° 5'; thermometer 32°, and the wind was easterly. . . .

'Just as we were giving up all hopes of a view, the fog again broke up and gave us an extensive prospect. To the north we saw the Arctic Ocean, with a few, tiny white sails, probably French fishermen; but the North Cape Horn was still shrouded in mist. To the south our view extended far, far away over vast and apparently endless snow-fields, which in part composed our old friend Steingrímsfjarðarheiði. Some of the domes of the Glámu, too, showed their white heads above the mists that hung to the mountain sides; and on the southern shores of Ísafjörðr there were some wild and desert mountains, deep blue in colour. . . . The summit of the Dránga represents a round barrel of snow, and any cairn raised up on its back might be called the top. We were anxious to descend by the western side to examine the immense ice-fall which goes down into Kaldalón, but before we had proceeded far, heavy clouds of mist rolled over us from the east; and, as our guide was unwilling to accompany us, we relinquished our desire.

'We descended the mountain by the same track by which we had ascended.' The ponies were regained at 9·45 P.M., the explorers having been absent therefrom six hours and a half; and two hours later all were safely back at the guide's home. The altitude of the *Jökull* is given by Gunnlaugsson as 2,837 Danish feet=2,921 English.

EIGHTEENTH DAY.—At *Hamar*, a day's rest.

NINETEENTH DAY.—An excursion should be made to-day to the

head of the *Kaldalón* (Cold-inlet), to see the arm of the glacier here, which calves into the sea. It is about three hours' ride each way, with a good road along the beach for the best part of the distance. The stream from the *Skjaldfannárdalr* is a wicked one to ford, and must not be attempted without a resident to point out the right spot.

TWENTIETH DAY.—To *Ísafjörðr* by boat—about ten hours' row. After the fatigues of yesterday and the seventeenth day, the party will probably be inclined for a little town-life, especially if an assault upon the *Glámu Jökull* is contemplated from the head of the *Skötu-fjörðr*. Five days will therefore be allowed for an excursion to *Ísafjörðr*. On the way, the party should land at *Vigr* (Spear) and *Æðey* (Eider-isle), two islets famous for the vast number of eider-duck that breed there.

ÍSAFJÖRÐR town stands upon a demi-circular, low, flat headland—doubtless a moraine—jutting outward from the western shore of the *Skutilsfjörðr* (The Page's-fjord). The inn is somewhat primitive, but the people are obliging. There are a large number of stores, and the Danish steamers call here. The ponies and all dispensable baggage will, of course, be left at *Hamar* or *Kirkjubol*.

An excursion should be made by boat to *Ós* (Oyce), where large beds of 'Surtarbrandr,' a variety of lignite, are to be seen. It will occupy a day, and is only practicable in calm weather. Ponies can be hired, and an excursion made by land, if preferred, to other beds of Surtarbrandr on the *Súgandafjörðr*, a pleasant but mountainous day's excursion. Sir David Wedderburn, while on a trip round the coast in 1878, visited these remarkable strata during the stay of the Danish steamer at *Ísafjörðr*, and he says: 'The Surtarbrandr has been exposed by the action of a mountain torrent, about 400 feet above the sea. The lignite is in thin layers, mixed with slaty-rock; it is partly carbonised, partly in the condition of ordinary wood, with the bark still adhering, but infiltrated with a certain amount of mineral matter; over it lie enormous masses of basaltic rock.' 'There are no trees growing now in Iceland except dwarf birches and willows, but here are the almost uninjured remains of great forest-trees under mountains of superincumbent rock, which must have spread over them in a molten condition, when they were imbedded in mud beneath the sea-surface.'

TWENTY-SIXTH DAY.—*Ísafjörðr* to *Kleifar*, if an assault is to be made on the *Glámu Jökull*, and if not, to *Hamar*. In either case about ten hours by boat. If the party land at *Kleifar*, be sure to ascertain, before the boat is allowed to leave, whether another—and men to man it—is obtainable here to row the party to *Hamar*, and if not, retain the boat and men from *I'safjörðr* until after the ascent of the *Jökull*.

TWENTY-SEVENTH DAY.—Assault upon the *Glámu Jökull*. Shepherd's party did not make the ascent. Gunnlaugsson gives the altitude of the *Jökull* at 2,872 Danish feet = 2,957 English.

TWENTY-EIGHTH DAY.—*Kleifar* to *Hamar*. Ten hours by boat.

TWENTY-NINTH DAY.—*Hamar* to *Staðr*. A stiffish day's journey. The *Steingrimsfjarðarheiði*, the dreary mountain waste between the fjords east and west of the isthmus, will be crossed.

THIRTIETH DAY.—*Staðr* to *Kirkjuból*, on the *Steingrimsfjörðr*, or to *Berufjörðr*. The former route is, perhaps, to be preferred, being over fresh ground, but it is rough travelling, and if the ponies show signs of giving in, the party will do better to return the way they came, *viâ Kirkjuból*. Shepherd describes the travelling as very bad, whenever the beach is quitted. He says: 'We found short, deep valleys with perpendicular sides, rocks, stones, and slippery ways, intersected with bogs and miry places.' The summer that he was in Iceland, it must be observed, was an unusually wet one.

THIRTY-FIRST DAY.—*Kirkjuból* to *O'spakseyri*. Another day over difficult and broken ground. Shepherd describes the valley in which stands *Fell* church, and into which a descent has to be made, as a very break-neck place. The scenery is charming, however, though perhaps it will seem tame after that of the *Jöklar*.

THIRTY-SECOND DAY.—*O'spakseyri* to *Borðeyri*. An easy day's ride, the greater part of the way close to the fjord.

THIRTY-THIRD DAY.—At *Borðeyri*. A day's rest. From here the party can either return to *Reykjavik* in four to five days by the same route as they came, or proceed to *Akureyri*. If the latter course is resolved upon, send the ponies and guide round the head of the fjord to *Þóroddstaðir* (Thóroddr's-stead), a farm directly opposite *Borðeyri*, with instructions to await the travellers on the following day.

THIRTY-FOURTH DAY.—*Borðeyri* to *Borg* (Burg). Cross the fjord to the ponies in a boat; and thence ride over the *Hrútafjarðarheiði* to *Staðarbakki* (Stead-bank) in the *Miðfjarðardalr* (Midfjord-dale). A good many salmon are caught in nets in the lower part of the river flowing through this valley.

When the author was here in 1880, he heard that the osseous remains of a whale had recently been discovered on the summit of a mountain in the neighbourhood. A geologist, with a day to spare, could not better employ it than in visiting this object. Its presence confirms the author's view that sudden upheavals of immense masses of the older rock formations took place towards the close of the glacial epoch. See Chapter II.

The track—which skirts a large lake, the *Vestrahópsvatn*, for some distance—between *Midfjarðardalr* and the *Víðidalr* is not over-good, and the travellers will be six hours, probably, in accomplishing this part of the day's journey. *Borg* is in the lower part of the *Víðidalr*, and is the abode of an English-speaking farmer, Pétr Kristophersson, who is famous for his hospitality. The river is well-stocked with salmon, but they seem very reluctant to take the artificial fly. Three English anglers, beside the author, have tried this river without success. Good grouse and duck shooting here in August; and trout fishing to be had in the upper waters of the river, and also in a tributary from the *Vestrahópsvatn*.

A day should be spent here, and a visit paid to the Burg, a circular crater, more than once the refuge of outlaws. In the days anterior to gunpowder this natural fortress was quite impregnable in the nightless summer months, when held by a handful of resolute men, with abundance of provisions. A story is told how an outlaw once sought refuge here, taking with him several sheep belonging to the neighbouring farmers, who, when his provisions were running short, adopted a ruse to deceive his besiegers as to the state of his larder. Seeing that they were dining somewhat meagrely, he threw them his last sheep, ready dressed, and they, judging from this that there was but little chance of capitulation, abandoned the siege.

THIRTY-SIXTH DAY.—*Borg* to *Hjaltabakki* or *Blönduós*. Six hours' ride, good track the best part of the way. One short swampy piece, however, will be passed through after skirting the *Hóp* (Hope), a large land-locked salt-water inlet; and an appropriately named little stream, the *Gljúfrá* (Cliff-river), will be forded before reaching the *Vatnsdalr*, where a junction will be made with Route III. (See p. 134, 31st day. Do not fail to notice the cones of upheaval, amid which the track winds down to the *Vatnsdal*. Salmon fishing to be had at *Hjaltabakki*.

Hence on to *Akureyri*, see Route III., pages 136–138.

ROUTE V.

SEYÐISFJÖRÐR TO AKUREYRI.

A FORTNIGHT'S EXCURSION; VISITING 'THE FIRE FOCUS OF THE NORTH';
THE 1875 LAVA-FLOOD AND ASKJA; THE ELDEYJAFOSS, AND THE
GOÐAFOSS.

FIRST DAY.—*Seyðisfjörðr* to *Hofteigr*. See Route III., 59th day, p. 161.

SECOND DAY.—*Hofteigr* to *Möðrudalr*. See Route III., 58th day, p. 160. There is another and more direct route, *vid Fossvöllr* and *Hof*, to the *Mÿvatn* district, but for some reason unknown to the author it is seldom travelled.

THIRD DAY.—*Möðrudalr* to *Grimstaðir*. Between four and five hours' ride only, down the valley of the *Jökulsá*.

FOURTH DAY.—*Grimstaðir* to *Reykjahlíð*. See Route III., 56th day, p. 159. The ferryman will be obtained at *Nýbær* (Newby) farm. The fixed charge is 2 *kroner* for the man, 25 *öre* for each person and his saddle ferried over, and a like sum for each pack-saddle and its load.

THE 1875 LAVA-FLOOD will be seen on this day's journey. Described *ante*, pp. 151-153.

An excellent view will be obtained while crossing the *Mÿvatns Öræfi* of *Herðubreið* (Broad-shouldered), a mighty insulated buttress 5,290 Danish (= 5,477 English) feet in height, whose snow-clad summit is a virgin peak, notwithstanding some half-dozen assaults within the last decade. The author believes this mountain to be one of the fragments of the old basaltic plateau left standing on the site of Iceland after the disturbances of the glacial epoch. It is the only mountain not of recent—geologically speaking—volcanic origin for many miles around, and it projects through a plateau built up of sheets of igneous rock, the more superficial of which, at least, have been deposited in post-tertiary times.

FIFTH DAY.—'THE FIRE FOCUS OF THE NORTH.' Excursion to *Krafla* and *Leirhnúkr*, examining *en route* the Boiling Mud Cauldrons in the solfatara east of *Myvatn*. See *ante*, p. 144.

SIXTH DAY.—*Reykjahlið* to *Skútustaðir*. See Route III., 48th day, p. 153.
SEVENTH DAY.—*Skútustaðir* to *Svartárkot*. See Route III., 49th day, p. 154.
EIGHTH DAY.—EXCURSION TO THE ELDEYJAFOSS. *Ante*, p. 154.
NINTH AND TENTH DAYS.—EXCURSION TO ASKJA. *Ante*, pages 154 to 159.
ELEVENTH DAY.—A day's rest at *Svartárkot*.
TWELFTH DAY.—*Svartárkot* to *Stóruvellir*. Route III., 54th day, p. 159.
THIRTEENTH DAY.—*Storuvellir* to *Ljósavatn*, visiting the *Goðafoss* en route. *Ante*, pages 140, 141 and 159.
FOURTEENTH DAY.—*Ljósavatn* to *Akureyri*. *Ante*, pages 140 and 141.

ROUTE VI.

AKUREYRI TO REYKJAVÍK.

BY THE DIRECT POST ROUTE, SEVEN TO EIGHT DAYS' JOURNEY.

FIRST DAY.—*Akureyri* to *Steinstaðr* (Stone-stead). About four hours' ride. The first two hours of the way are close to the *Eyjafjörðr*, and then it branches off into the *Hörgárdalr*, up which it lies until a side valley, the *Öxnadalr* (Oxen-dale), is entered. The view up these two valleys is charming. The *Vindheima Jökull* (Wind-home Glacier) towers above the valleys on the east, and in summer time

'A thousand rills
Come leaping from the mountains, each a Fay,
 Sweet singing then:
O come with us out seaward, come away!'

Immediately opposite *Steinstaðr* is a remarkable peak, the *Drángjutindr* (Lonely-peak), like unto a huge church steeple.

SECOND DAY.—*Steinstaðr* to *Silfrastaðir*. A longish day's ride, with a very indifferent track, especially where it crosses the *Öxnadalsheiði*, and in the valley beyond. *Silfrastaðir* is, at the present day, the only licensed inn in Iceland out of sight of the sea. It is a very primitive one.

174   GUIDE TO ICELAND.

THIRD DAY.—*Silfrastaðir* to *Blönduós*. A longish day's ride, fording the *Blanda, Herqðsvötn*, and several smaller rivers.
FOURTH DAY.—*Blönduós* to *Haukagil*. Eight hours' ride, excellent path.
FIFTH DAY.—*Haukagil* to *Kalmanstúnga*. Long day's ride over the *Arnarvatnsheiði*. See the *Surtshellir* caves *en route;* described *ante*, p. 133.
SIXTH DAY.—*Kalmanstúnga* to *Þingnes*, easy day: or to *Þingvellir*, twelve to fourteen hours' bad road—unshown on map.
SEVENTH DAY.—*Þingnes* to *Reynivellir*. See *ante*, pp. 162-3, or *Þingvellir* to *Reykjavik*. See Route I., 1st day, pages 93 and 94.
EIGHTH DAY.—*Reynivellir* to *Reykjavik*. See Route IV., 1st day, p. 162.

DESERT ROUTES.

IN BRINGING this work to a close, a few words must be said with reference to crossing the desert interior of the island from south to north, or *vice versâ*, by the two routes known respectively as the *Sprengisandr* (Bursting-sand), and the *Vatnahjallavegr* (Lake-ledge way) routes. The author's advice to the traveller in Iceland is, have nothing whatever to do with either, unless it should happen that a volcanic eruption were taking place at the time of his visit, or had recently taken place, somewhere in the interior, which was to be reached by one of these seldom travelled routes. There is nothing whatever to recompense one for the fatigue and discomfort of crossing the island; the volcanoes, glacier-covered mountains, and other points of interest can be far more pleasantly and thoroughly explored by making an excursion into the desert in light marching order from some farm on its border, than by a hurried flight with a number of pack-ponies through a region where fodder for the ponies is scarce, and fuel to cook the traveller's food utterly wanting. Good ponies are indispensable, and tents of course will be necessary, likewise a spirit or paraffine cooking stove.

THE SPRENGISANDR ROUTE.—This is considered the most difficult and risky of the two routes mentioned. It has been crossed within the last six years, to the author's knowledge, by two parties: Dr. C. Le Neve Foster and two friends, in 1876, and by Mr. Cuthbert Peek, Mr. E. Delmar Morgan, and Mr. J. Coles, Curator of Maps at the R.G.S., in 1881. The former crossed from north to south, the latter from south to north; and their guides were respectively Páll Pálsson, Mr. Watts' companion over the *Vatna Jökull*, and Zœga's nephew, mentioned before in this work. Each party took a local guide from the last farm on the fringe of the desert; *Ishóll* (Ice-hill) on the north, and *Hagi* (Pasture), or *Hagaey* (Pasture-isle), on the south. It appears to be preferable to cross from north to south than in the opposite direction; as from *Akureyri*, the chief town in the north, the last farm before entering the desert, *I'shóll*, may be reached in one day's easy journey, with no large rivers to ford or ferry by the way, while from *Reykjavik* to *Hagi* is three days' stiffish ride, and the ponies have to swim at least two wide rivers and ford several others. Dr. Foster's party killed one of their ponies on this journey. They set out from *Húsavík;* and their halting-places were *Stóruvellir*, the first night; *I'shóll*, the second night. Left here 11·10 A.M., and arrived at *Ki'ðagil* (Kid-gill), the camping place for the night, at 4·50 P.M., poor pasturage. Set out at 6·15 A.M. of the fourth day, and at 6·10 P.M. reached the camping ground, near *Arnarfell* (Eagle-fell), 'a well-marked group of three sharp peaks surrounded by ice on three sides. Here there was good pasturage.' Left at 9 A.M. the fifth day, and 'at 6·10 P.M. we reached our quarters for the night, the good farm of *Hagi*.' From this place the party made a forced march to *Reykjavik* in two days, halting the first night at *Reykir*, south-west of Þingvallavatn. 'In all we had sixty streams to cross,' Dr. Foster says, 'all very rapid, and of course icy cold.' It must not be forgotten there are no well-known fords, and, as most of those streams drain glaciers, their beds deepen and change with the floods every summer. Dr. Foster adds: 'Quicksands abound not only between the streams, but sometimes in them; down your pony goes, floundering up to his middle, and off you must jump to give him a chance of recovering himself.'

Mr. Peek's party crossed by a slightly different route, passing fifteen miles to the east of the *Arnarfell*, and were five days between *Hagi* and *Mjófidalr*, a farm a short distance north-east of *I'shóll*. The first night's encampment was at a place known as *Knappölduhver*. The next day's journey was 'over a complete desert,' and the camp-ing place for the night on the right bank of the Þjórsá, at a small grassy oasis named *Sóleyjahöfði* (Sun-island-head). The next day's ride brought the party to *Eyvindarkofahver*, 'a place so remote from all the farms, that an outlaw named Eyvindr lived there unmolested for many years.' At this place, and also at *Knappölduhver*, there is probably a hot spring, to judge by the suffix 'hver.' Ten hours' ride on the fourth day brought the party to *Ki'ðagil*, and the next day's journey to *Mjófidalr*. Mr. Peek, in a paper describing the journey read at a meeting of the Royal Geographical Society on the

30th January, 1882, also makes mention of ' very large and dangerous quicksands' in this region, and says that 'it is mainly from this fact that so few persons ever cross it. In several places these quicksands extend over a space of several acres, and it is quite impossible to tell, except by practical experience, the position of the solid ground.'

THE VATNAHJALLAVEGR.—No English traveller, it is believed, has ever crossed the island by this route, though several have visited the *Hverarvellir* hot springs at the base of the *Hofs Jökull*. The Rev. F Metcalfe, in 'The Oxonian in Iceland,' gives an account of a journey over part of this route. The scenery in many parts of the interior traversed by this mid-island track is magnificent, especially the view of the grand group of ice-clad mountains, of which the *Láng Jökull* is the chief. The *Hvitárvatn* (White-river-lake) at the base of the *Jöklar*, the source of the southern *Hvitá*, is a grand Alpine lake, and is frequently floe-covered far into the summer. In light marching order the distance between farm and farm may be accomplished in three days, and the journey from *Reykjavik* to *Akureyri*, or *vice versâ*, in seven days: *Reykjavik* to Þingvellir the first day, thence to *Haukadalr* the second day. Thus far, see Route I. 1st and 3rd days, pages 93–101. A local guide must be obtained here. The first night's camping ground will be near *Bláfell* (Bluefell), and the second near the *Hverarvellir* (Hot-spring-fields). Pasturage very poor at both places. The next day's journey will bring the travellers to the head of the *Eyjafjarðardalr*, where there are several farms. *Akureyri* may be reached from here in six hours, good bridle-path down the valley.

There is another route from south to north, that over the *Stórisandr* (Great-sand). This is frequently travelled, as it is only necessary to camp out one night. Going south from *Akureyri*, Route VI. is followed as far as *Silfrastaðir*, whence one branches off to *Mælifell* (Measure-fell), four hours' ride only. Shortly after leaving here the Great-sand is entered, and the second day's journey will bring the travellers to *Kalmanstúnga*, whence to *Reykjavik*, see Routes IV. and VI., pages 162 to 165 and 174.

In conclusion, the author earnestly advises visitors to Iceland, especially the young and hardy, to strike out paths for themselves in the inhabited districts to places lying three to four days' ride off the routes given. There is many an interesting spot where an alien has never yet set foot, and trout stream and 'fish lake' whose waters have never laved an angler's line. Two promising fields may be mentioned; the north-eastern part of the country, and the N.W. peninsula north of the *Dránga Jökull*. In the district first named, doubtless

CONCLUSION—DESERT ROUTES.

a very pleasant excursion could be made to *Rifstángi*, the northern-most point of Iceland; and on the N.W. peninsula, Route IV. might be extended to Cape Horn. Besides these, an interesting excursion off Route I. may be made by those desirous to prolong their tour a couple of days, to *Rauðukambar* (Red-combes), a volcano that erupted in A.D. 1343. The base for this excursion would be *Hruni* (*ante*, pages 106, 108, 109). A tent can be borrowed here, for use on the night it will be necessary to camp out. The country around this volcano is said to be a fearfully wild region. Route I. can also be pleasantly prolonged another day, by paying the *Þurárhraun* (Dry-river-lava) a visit. This lava was erupted during the debate at the Alþíng as to the adoption of the Christian religion (see *ante*, p. 61). Apart from its historical interest, the scene of the eruption is in itself well worthy a visit. The lava burst forth on an 'upland plateau called *Hellisheiði* (=Hollow-heath, *i.e.* the cavernous heath; even to-day it sounds cavernous in certain places, as the traveller rides over it); it took an easterly current over the plateau, and issued finally through a pass on the eastern, somewhat precipitous, side of it into the lowland plains below' (Thoroddsen). *Eyrarbakki* will be the starting-point for this detour, and the halting-place for the night will probably be *Strandarkirkja*. *Ante*, pages, 112–13. Off Route II., also, a pleasant day's excursion, over unknown ground, may be made to the *Suðrnámur*, a solfatara, as its name implies, in the South. This spot has not, as far as is known to the author, been yet visited by an Englishman. It lies in the plain between the *Tungnaá* (Tongue-river) and the *Torfa Jökull*. *Ásar* or *Búland* should be made a base for the excursion. *Ante*, pages, 119–20.

INDEX.

A.

Aðalreykjadalr, 141.
Æðey, 169.
Áfall, 117, 123.
Agricultural College, 138.
Akranes, 9.
Akrey, 87.
Akureyri, 15, 19, 20 to 22, 33, 34, 84, 124, 132, 136, 138 to 140, 159, 162, 170 to 173, 175, 176.
Almannagjá, 2, 57, 59, 61, 64, 73, 94 to 96, 99.
Alþing, 2, 57, 59, 61, 64, 67, 73, 94, 96, 97.
Alþing, founded, 57, 59.
  ,,   abolished, 63.
  ,,   reestablished, 63.
  ,,   reconstituted, 64.
Alternating Geysir, 126.
Angling, 80 to 86, 112, 132, 134, 135, 141, 144, 153, 162, 163, 171.
Area, 38.
Arnarfell, 175.
Arnarstakksheiði, 76, 79, 83, 132, 135, 174.
Arnarvatn, 132, 133, 134.
Arnarvatnsheiði, 76, 79, 83, 132, 135, 174.
Arnórstaðir, 161.
Askja, 11, 12, 15, 20 to 22, 32, 41, 45, 46, 47, 109, 132, 143, 144, 153, 159, 173.
Askja, Author's Visits to, 41.
Auðkúla, 84.
Axarfjörðr, 76.

Á.

Álar, 117, 122.
Álftá, 82.
Álftanes, 91, 92.
Álftavatn, 112.
Árhver, 125.
Ármansfell, 97.
Ármúli, 167.
Árnesþing, 109.
Ás, 144, 146.
Ásbyrgi, 14, 48, 145, 146.
Ásar, 118 to 121, 177.

B.

Baðstofa, 51, 146.
Baggage, 5, 23, 24, 28.
Barð, 131.
Bárðardalr, 110.
Barkarstaðir, 117.
Baula, 165.
Bedding, 26.
Bergþórshvoll, 16, 66, 67, 72, 73, 123.
Berserkjahraun, 129.
Berufjörðr (E.), 60, 121, 160.
Berufjörðr (N.W.), 166, 170.
Borvik, 128.
Bessastaðir, 21, 91 to 93, 114.
Bjargtángar, 37.
Bjarnarflag, 12, 47.
Bláfell, 108, 176.
Bláfjall, 154.
Blanda, 84, 85, 135, 136, 173.
Blesi, 101, 105, 106.
Blönduós, 135, 136, 171, 173.

Blood Stone, 96, 130.
Boiling Mud Cauldrons, 14, 113, 114, 148 to 150.
Bones of a Whale, 170, 171.
Borðeyri, 20, 83, 84, 131, 165, 166, 170.
Borg, 78, 84, 170, 171.
Borgarey, 136.
Borgarfjörðr, 79, 82, 110.
Botnsá, 163.
Botnsdalr, 162, 163.
Boots, 30.
Boxes, 23, 24.
Box-bed, 26, 27, 132, 146.
Bræðratúnga, 108.
Breiðabólsstaðir, 116 to 118, 122, 131.
Breiðifjörðr, 16, 21, 37, 38, 83, 130, 131, 135, 164.
Brú, 160.
Brúará, 86, 100, 124.
Brunnar, 125.
Bryson's Tintron, 99.
Buðir, 97.
Buðir (W.), 128, 129, 163, 165.
Búland, 120, 177.
Búrfell, 125.
Burton, Capt., quoted, 10, 53, 97, 99, 102, 111, 127, 128, 130.
Buying Ponies, 9.

C.

Camoens, S.S., 1, 2, 9, 20, 21, 29, 83, 93.
Cape Horn, 168, 177.
Cathedral, 88, 89.

INDEX.

Climate, 52, 53.
Clothing, 30.
Coins, 7.
Commerell, Capt., quoted, 113.
Companionship, 5.
Cones of Upheaval, 134.
Conflicts, 60.
Cooking Stoves, 27.
Cost of Tours, 3, 7, 8, 15.
Culdee Anchorites, 53.
Culdee Relics, 54, 89.

D.

Dalfjall, 47.
Danish Steamers, 2, 29, 78, 83, 85, 121, 142, 161, 169.
Dasent, Dr., quoted, 53, 65.
Dettifoss, 14, 79, 107, 145 to 148.
Discovery of America, 60.
" Greenland, 60.
Divisions, 59.
Djúpá, 140.
Djúpivogr, 160.
Dogs, 32.
Doom Ring, 130, 162.
Drànga Jökull, 15, 22, 157, 162, 166 to 169.
Drángey, 136.
Drángjutindr, 173.
Dufferin, Lord, 1, 97.
Dwellings, 51.
Dyngjufjöll, 46, 156.
Dyrastaðir, 83.
Dyrhólar, 122.
Dyrhólarey, 37, 122.

E.

Earthquakes, 135, 143, 144.
Earthquake Rifts, 144, 145.
Eider-ducks, 90, 169.
Eilífr, 148.
Eiríka Jökull, 133.
Eldborg, 16, 21, 22, 127, 128, 131, 162, 165.

Eldey, 48, 115.
Eldeyjafoss, 14, 22, 154, 173.
Eldvötn, 120.
Elli Saðr, 80, 92, 93, 162.
Elli Savatn, 80.
Engey, 87, 90.
Enni, 128.
Eruptions, 11, 13, 48, 61, 96, 109, 110, 115, 119, 134, 143, 144, 151 to 153, 157, 158.
Esja, 93, 111, 162.
Eskifjörðr, 86, 121, 160 to 163.
Eyðar, 161.
Eyjafjalla Jökull, 112.
Eyjafjarðardalr, 176.
Eyjafjörðr, 86, 138, 173.
Eyrarbakki, 112, 123, 177.
Eyrbyggja Saga, 129, 130.
Eystri Rángá, 116.
Eyvindarkofahver, 175.
Eyvindr, 175.

F.

Faroes, 2.
Faxafjörðr, 37, 80, 87, 93, 128, 164.
Fell, 166, 170.
'Fire Focus of the North,' 12, 22, 148 to 154, 172.
Fishing Tackle, 31.
Fiskivötn (N.), 22, 76, 79, 82, 83, 132 to 134.
Fiskivötn (S.), 79, 111.
Flies, 31.
Fjallabaksvegr, 119.
Fljótsdalsheiði, 161.
Fljótsdalr, 117.
Fnjóská, 76, 86, 140.
Fnjóskárdalr, 140.
Food, 6.
Forest, 16, 121.
Forsæludalr, 134.
Fossá, 162.
Fossvöllr, 172.
Foster, Dr. C. Le Neve, quoted, 174, 175.
Fremrinámar, 46, 150.
Fúlilækr, 122.

G.

Gagnheiði, 97.
Game, 17, 18, 19, 29, 75 to 80, 83, 84, 94, 98, 132, 134, 140, 141, 142, 153, 154, 161, 163, 165, 171.
Garðr (N.), 78, 141.
Garðr (N.E.), 145.
'Garnet Wolseleys,' a sleeping sack, 6, 26, 117, 125, 132, 146.
Gautavik, 60.
Geitafoss, 141.
Geitlands Jökull, 15, 124, 126.
Geir Zoëga, 3, 4, 8, 9, 22, 29, 32, 88.
Geology, 32, 37, 40 to 49, 132, 134, 144, 145, 170, 172.
Gerpir, 37.
Geslravatn, 114.
Geysir, 1 to 9, 11, 15, 20, 21, 93, 95, 98 to 108, 116, 124, 125.
Giant Pots, 154.
Gilsfjörðr, 166.
Glámu Jökull, 15, 22, 39, 157, 162, 166 to 170.
Glæsibær, 138.
Glerá, 138, 139.
Gljúfrá, 171.
Glymrfoss, 162, 163.
Goðafoss, 14, 22, 140, 141.
Goðalands Jökull, 112, 116, 118.
Granton, 1.
Gravarvaug, 80.
Grenjaðarstaðir, 85, 140, 141.
Grettir, 133, 136, 146.
Grettishlaup, 147.
Grettur Saga, 133, 136.
Grimsá, 82, 83, 127, 163.
Grimsárdalr, 163.
Grimsey, 37.
Grimstaðir, 159, 160.
Grimstúngur, 134.
Grimsvötn, 121.
Gröf, 81.

INDEX. 181

Grouse, 76 to 78, 83, 140, 141, 155.
Grundafjörðr, 129.
Grundare, 129.
Guðlaugsvik, 166.
Guides, 3, 9, 32, 33.
Gullfoss (S.), 2, 15, 16, 21, 93, 106, 107, 116, 124.
Gullfoss (W.), 166.
Guns, 31.

H.

Haðarstein, 165.
Hafnarfjörðr, 21, 79, 91 to 93, 114.
Hafragilsfoss, 147.
Hafravatn, 94.
Hagaey, 174, 175.
Hagi, 174, 175.
Hallardalr, 85.
Hallbjarnareyri, 129.
Hallmundarhraun, 133.
Hallormstaðir, 160.
Háls (W.), 81.
Háls (N.), 140.
Hamar, 167 to 170.
Haukadalr, 4, 8, 9 9 to 101, 105, 107.
Haukadalsá, 86, 176.
Haukagil, 132, 134, 173.
Haukavörðugjá, 115.
Hedinn the Sorcerer, 16, 61, 122.
Heimaey, 38.
Hekla, 1 to 4, 7 to 9, 11, 15, 20, 21, 39, 47, 93, 106, 107, 109 to 112, 116, 124, 153, 155.
Helgafell, 21, 129 to 131.
Heljardalr, 138.
Hellishei ði, 177.
Hellisskarð, 124.
Hengifoss, 160.
Hengill, 97.
Héraðsvötn, 86, 136, 173.
Herðubreið, 172.
Hiring Ponies, 9, 20.
Historical Notice, 53 to 65.
Hit, 131.
Hitá, 82, 131.
Hitárdalr, 131, 132, 165.

Hjaltabakki, 84, 134 to 136, 171.
Hjaltalin, Hr., quoted, 53, 57, 63, 64.
Hjarðarholt, 131, 165.
Hjörleifshöfði, 122.
Hlíðarendi, 16, 66, 69, 70, 117.
Hlíðarhæli, 148.
Hlíðarnámar, 46, 149, 150.
Hlíðarvatn, 113.
Hljóðaklettar, 14, 146.
Hljóðufell, 111, 124.
Hnausar, 135.
Hobbles, 34, 35.
Hof, 172.
Hof, The, 56, 162.
Höfðabrekka, 121, 122.
Hofs Jökull, 38, 39, 176.
Hofstaðir (N.), 136, 154.
Hofteigr, 160, 161, 172.
Hólar, 15, 22, 89, 91, 124, 136 to 138.
Hólmi, 108.
Holt, 122.
Holtavörðuheiði, 165.
Hóp, 78, 171.
Hörgá, 86, 138, 173.
Hörgárdalr, 138, 173.
Höskuldstaðir, 66, 131, 165.
Hotels, 9, 88, 161.
Hot springs, 40, 97, 100, 102, 113, 114, 125, 126, 165, 166, 175, 176.
Hrafnabjörg, 97.
Hrafnágjá, 95, 98, 99.
Hrafntinnuhryggr, 12, 150, 151.
Hrafntinnudalr, 111.
Hreppholar, 106, 108, 109.
Hringsverhvylft, 144.
Hrisey, 138.
Hrossaborg, 160.
Hrossadalr, 12, 47.
Hrúni, 81, 106, 108, 109, 177.
Hrútafjörðr, 83, 131, 165, 170.
Hrútr, 66, 67.
Hrútshellir, 122.

Húnafjörðr, 84, 85, 135.
Húsavik, 20, 21, 33, 78, 81, 99, 141, 142, 144, 175.
Hvalfjörðr, 81, 162.
Hvammr, 83, 165.
Hvammsfjörðr, 66, 83, 86, 165.
Hvammsheiði, 78, 142.
Hvanná, 161.
Hverarvellir, 176.
Hverfisfljót, 120, 121.
Hverfjall, 149, 150.
Hvítá (S.), 2, 81, 83, 86, 102, 106 to 108, 112.
Hvítá (W.), 29, 82, 83, 86, 126, 127.
Hvítárvatn, 108, 176.
Hvítdrvellir, 82.

I.

Iceland Spar, 162.

Í.

Ingólfsfjall, 112.
Ingólfshöfði, 74, 122.
Isafjörðr, 16, 22, 161 to 163, 166 to 170.
Isafjörðr Town, 162, 167, 169, 170.
Ishóll, 174, 175.

J.

Jarlhettur, 108.
Jökulsá (N.), 14, 15, 20, 43, 76, 79, 146 to 148, 151, 159, 160, 161, 172.
Jökulsá (E.), 160, 161.
Jón of Víðiker, 156.
Jónsskarð, 156.
Jornkliff, 97.

K.

Kaldá, 127, 131.
Kaldalón, 168, 169.
Kálfafell, 120, 121.
Kálfholt, 112.
Kálfstindar, 99.
Kalmanstunga, 132, 173, 174, 176.

Káratjörn, 123.
Kerlingafjöll, 108.
Kerlingárdalr, 16, 61, 122.
KiSagil, 175.
Kirkjubær, 69, 120.
Kirkjuból, 166, 167, 169, 170.
Kjalarnes, 162.
Kleifar, 166, 167, 169, 170.
Kleifavatn, 114.
Knappölduhver, 175.
Kötlugjá, 13, 16, 17, 21, 33, 48, 112, 116, 119, 120.
Krafla, 12, 45 to 47, 79, 144, 145, 150, 151, 172.
Krúká, 154.
Krisuvík, 2, 21, 29, 40, 79, 93, 112 to 116.
Kross, 118, 122, 123.
Kverkfjöll, 47.
Kverkhnúkarani, 47.

L.

Ladies' Outfit, 28.
Lagarfljót, 76, 79, 86, 161.
Lagidalr, 166.
Lambafjöll, 142.
Lángá, 82.
Láng Jökull, 15, 38, 39, 97, 108, 111, 176.
Largest Tree, 118.
Laug, 10, 90.
Laugafjall, 101, 105, 106.
Laugarbrekka, 128, 129.
Laugardalr, 100.
Laugarvatn, 100.
Lava, 47, 92, 115, 116, 120, 124, 127, 132, 148, 150 to 158, 172.
Lava Deserts, 38.
Lava-flood in 1875, 11, 15, 22, 151 to 153, 172.
Law Courts, 58, 59.
Laxárdalr (N.), 99.
Laxárdalr (N.W.), 165.
LaxárdalsheiSi, 165.
Laxdrmýri, 85, 142, 144.
'Laxás,' 31, 66, 79, 80 to 86, 128, 135, 142, 162.

Laxdæla Saga, 165.
Leirárvogr, 81, 162.
Leirhnúkr, 12, 46, 47, 144, 150, 151, 172.
' Letters from High Latitudes,' 1.
Lignite, 22, 144, 162, 169.
Little Geysir, 106.
Little Strokkr, 106.
Ljósavatn, 76, 77, 140, 159, 178.
Ljósavatn Farm, 140, 159, 173.
LjósavatnsskarS, 140.
Lögberg, 66.
Lögmen, 58.
Lómagnúpr, 121.
Lón, 57, 110.
Lónsvík, 85.
Loptsalahellir, 122.
Loss of Independence, 62, 63.
Lundarbrekka, 159.
Lundr, 162, 163.
Lutheranism Intr., 63.

M.

Mackenzie, Sir G., quoted, 113.
Mælifell, 176.
Mælifellsandr, 119.
Map, 30.
Markarfljót, 111, 116, 118, 122.
MeistaSr, 83, 84.
Merkr Jökull, 112, 116, 118, 119.
MiSdalr, 100.
MiSfjarSard, 83, 84, 170.
MiSfjarSardalr, 170, 171.
MiSgarSr, 37.
Miklaholt, 83, 127, 128.
Miklakvisl, 121.
Minni Laxd, 81, 109.
Mjófidalr, 175.
MöSrudalr, 160, 161, 172.
MöSruvellir, 33, 138.
Monastic Ruins, 91, 160.
Money, 7.
Mosafell, 5.
MosfellsheiSi, 94.

Moorlands, 39.
Morgan,E.D.,Esq.,quoted, 158, 159.
Múli (N.), 140, 141.
Múli (S.), 99, 100.
Museum, 77, 88, 89.
Mýrareysla, 79.
Mýrdals Jökull, 13, 16, 21, 39, 116, 119 to 121.
Mýrdalssandr, 121.
Mývatn, 12, 13, 17, 20, 21, 31, 40, 76, 78, 79, 98, 148 to 154, 172.
Mývatns Öræfi, 11, 15, 48, 148, 151, 152, 153, 159, 161, 172.

N.

Næfrholt, 107, 109, 112.
NámaskarS, 148, 151.
Native Artist, 138.
Nes, 141, 142.
New Constitution, 63, 64.
' Njál Country,' 21, 65, 116 to 123.
Njál Saga, 16, 53, 58, 59, 60, 65 to 74.
NorSrd, 28, 83, 85, 127, 165.
Norse Discovery, 54.
,, Settlement, 54 to 56.
NúpstaSr, 121.
N.W. Peninsula, 22, 39, 162, 165 to 170, 177.
Nýbær, 172.

O.

Oddeyri, 20, 33, 138, 139.
Oddi, 123.
Old Bible, 89.
Olves, 110.
Ok, 124, 126.
Ordering Ponies, 8.
Outfit, 22 to 29.
Outline of Routes, 21, 22.

O'.

O'ddSahraun, 11, 12, 32, 38, 43, 45 to 47, 154 to 156, 161, 173.

INDEX.

Ólafsvík, 128, 129.
Ós, 169.
Óseyri, 112.
Ós Luxd, 85, 135, 136.
Óspakseyri, 170.

Ö.
Ölfus, 61.
Ölfusá, 111, 112.
Öræfa Jökull, 13, 14, 16, 21, 47, 111, 116, 121.
Öxará, 2, 95, 96, 99.
Öxnadalr, 173.
Öxnadalsheiði, 173.

P.
Packing, 35, 36.
Pack Saddles, 26.
Pagan Altar, 165.
„ Oath, 58.
Papafjörðr, 85.
Pastures, 39.
Peek, C., Esq., quoted, 175.
People, 49 to 51.
Piscatorial Rambles, 17.
Polar Ice, 52, 76.
Ponies, 3, 7, 33, 93.
Population, 51.
Portland, 37.
Pronunciation of Icelandic Words, 2.
Provisions, 29.

Þ.
Þeistareykir, 46, 145.
Þing, 56, 122, 125.
Þingey, 78.
Þingnes, 163, 165, 174.
Þingvallavatn, 29, 40, 57, 79, 86, 94, 99, 113, 114, 175.
Þingvellir, 2 to 9, 11, 15, 20, 21, 57, 61, 67, 73, 79, 81, 93 to 99, 116, 124, 142, 149, 174, 176.
Þjórsá, 29, 109, 111, 112, 116, 123, 175.
Þorskafjarðarheiði, 166.
Þoroddstaðir, 170.

Þórsmörk, 21, 116, 118, 119.
Þórsnes, 130, 131.
Þríhyrníngr, 70, 112, 116.
Þúrarhraun, 177.
Þverá (W.), 82, 86, 127.
Þverá (S.), 116, 117, 123.

Q.
Quarters, 4, 6, 29.

R.
Rángá, (E.), 161.
Rángá (W.), 67, 109, 110, 116.
Rauðukambar, 176, 177.
Reformation, 63.
Reindeer, 17, 18, 21, 29, 79, 148.
Reykholt, 15, 21, 124, 125 to 127, 132.
Reykholtsdalr, 21, 22, 83, 124 to 126, 132, 134, 162, 165.
Reykir (S.W.), 112, 175.
Reykir (N.), 84, 136.
Reykjahlíð, 78, 146, 149 to 153, 172.
Reykjanes, 48, 115.
Reykjavík, 2, 3, 8 to 10, 12, 15, 19, 20 to 22, 29, 32, 33; 63, 77, 78, 80, 82, 83, 87, 88, 90, 91, 93, 112 to 115, 121, 123, 132, 162, 167, 170, 173 to 176.
Reynivellir, 81, 82, 162, 174.
Rifles, 31.
Rifstángi, 37, 177.
Rivers, 40.
Routes, 93 to 176.
Routes, Outline of, 21, 22.
Ryper, 76 to 78, 83.

S.
Saddles, 35.
Salmon Fishing, 17, 80 to 86, 112, 132, 134, 135, 141, 142, 153, 162, 163, 165, 171.

Sandfell, 21, 121.
Sauðkrókr, 20, 34, 84.
Scenery, 10, 93, 94, 106, 108, 111, 118, 124, 127, 132, 133, 135, 136, 146, 148, 151, 153, 163, 164, 166, 167, 168, 176.
Sea-fishing, 161.
Seals, 79, 80, 144.
Seljadalr, 94.
Seljadalsfoss, 122.
Seljaland, 122.
Seljalandsfoss, 16, 121.
Selsund, 107, 109, 112.
Seltjarnarnes, 87, 92.
Senate House, 89.
Seyðisfjörðr, 19 to 22, 34, 42, 79, 86, 121, 124, 149, 151, 159, 160, 161, 172.
Shepherd, quoted, 126, 166 to 168.
Shooting, 17, 18, 19, 29, 75 to 80, 83, 84, 94, 98, 132, 134, 140, 141, 142, 153, 154, 161, 163, 165, 171.
Short Excursions, 90.
Silfrastaðir, 136, 173, 176.
Skagafjörðr, 85, 88, 136.
Skagaströnd, 85, 135, 136.
Skálafell, 162.
Skálholt, 89, 91, 106, 108, 109, 124.
Skaptá, 120.
Skaptár Jökull, 13, 16, 21, 39, 48, 79, 111, 115, 116, 119.
Skeiðarár Jökull, 38, 121.
Skeiðarársandr, 38, 121.
Skeifárfoss, 144.
Skjaldbreið, 59, 97, 111, 124, 125.
Skjaldbreiðar Jökull, 124.
Skjaldfannárdalr, 167, 168, 169.
Skjálfandafljót, 38, 43, 75, 78, 140 to 142, 154, 159.
Skjálfandi, 85.
Skógarfoss, 16, 122.
Skogasendr, 122.
Skerradalsvatn, 86, 163.
Skötufjörðr, 166, 167, 169.

Skriðuklaustr, 160.
Skútilsfjörðr, 169.
Skútustaðir, 153, 154, 159, 172, 173.
Snæfell (E.), 79.
Snæfells Jökull, 15, 37, 52, 83, 93, 126, 128, 131, 163.
Snæfell Peninsula, 15, 21, 45,126,127,163,165,166
Snorri's Bath, 125.
Sog, 86, 99, 112.
Sóleyjahöfði, 175.
Solfatarar, 40, 46, 47, 113, 114, 148 to 151.
Sport, 17, 18, 19, 29, 75 to 80, 83, 84, 94, 98, 132, 134, 140, 141, 142, 153, 154, 161, 163, 165, 171.
Sprengisandr, 9, 21, 38, 43, 174, 175.
Stærra Laxá, 81,108,109.
Staðarbakki, 84, 170.
Staðarhraun, 127, 132, 165.
Staðastaðir, 128.
Staðr (N.W.), 166, 170.
Staðr (S.W.), 115.
Stafholt, 126, 127, 132.
Stapi, 15, 83, 126, 128.
Steingrímsfjarðarheiði, 166, 168, 170.
Steingrímsfjörðr,166,170.
Steinstaðr, 136, 173.
Stóra Dímon, 116.
Stórísandr, 21, 38, 176.
Stóruvellir (N.), 159.
Stóruvellir (S.), 107, 109, 112, 116, 124, 173, 175.
Strandarkirkja, 113, 177.
Straumfjarðar Os, 83.
Strokkr, 101, 104 to 106, 125, 143.
Stykkishólmr, 31, 83, 131, 134.
Súðrndmur, 177.
Sulur, 97.
Summer in Iceland, 4, 14, 15, 124 to 162.
Surtarbrandr,22, 144, 169.

Surtshellir, 15, 21, 133, 174.
Svartá, 85, 86, 136.
Svartárkot, 78, 154, 159.
Svartdrvatn, 76, 86.
Sveinstaðir, 134.
Svínadalr, 146.
Svínafell, 121.
Svínaskarð, 162.
Svínavatn, 84, 135.
Súðrá, 155, 156.
Súðrdrhraun, 155.
Sýðrnes, 84.

T.

Temples, Pagan, 55, 56.
Temple Priests, 56, 57.
Tents, 3, 27.
Tepid Lake, 158.
Thangbrand, 16, 60, 61, 122.
Thoroddsen, quoted, 119, 120, 177.
Tíndaskagi, 97.
Tíndastóll, 136.
Tindfjalla Jökull, 112,117, 118.
Tintron, 99.
'Tintronia,' 99, 142.
Tjörn, 87.
Topogpaphy, 37 to 40.
Torfa Jökull, 116, 177.
Travelling Companions, 5.
Trout-streams, 86, 134, 141, 153, 154, 161.
Trölladýngja, 155.
Túnga, 70.
Túngnad, 177.
Túngufljót, 101, 107, 124.
Túnguhverir, 125.

U.

Ullarfoss, 141.
'Umbra,' quoted, 5, 129, 150.
Unadals Jökull, 138.
United to Denmark, 63.
Uxahver, 14, 46, 142, 143.
Utklíð, 124.
Útlandeyjar, 66, 117.

V.

Vaðlaheiði, 140.
Vakurhestar, 33.
Valþjófstaðir, 160.
Varmá, 120.
Varmárdalr, 120.
Vatnahjallavegr, 174, 176.
Vatna Jökull, 18, 21, 33, 38, 39, 43, 45, 47, 85, 116, 121, 157.
Vatnsdalr, 48, 78, 84, 134, 135, 171.
Vatnsdalsá, 84, 134.
Vellir, 137, 138.
Vestdalsheiði, 161.
Vestmannaeyjar, 37, 111.
Vestmannsvatn, 141.
Vestrahópsvatn, 84, 171.
Vestri Rángá, 67, 109,110, 116.
Víðey, 87, 90.
Víðidalr, 171.
Víðidalsá, 84.
Víðidalsfjall, 78.
Víðidalstúnguheiði, 134.
Víðimýri, 136.
Vigabjargafoss, 146.
Vigr, 169.
Villingaholt, 112.
Vincent, O. W., quoted, 113, 114.
Vík, 121, 122.
Vindheima Jökull, 173.
Víti, 12, 151.
Volcanic Islets, 21, 38, 130, 148, 149.
Volcanoes, 40.
Vopnafjörðr, 86.
'Voyage de la Recherche,' quoted, 133.

W.

Waterproofs, 30.
Watts, Mr. W. L., 41, 155, 174.
Waller, Mr. S. E., quoted, 23, 65, 98, 117, 118.
Wedderburn, Sir D., quoted, 169.

www.ingramcontent.com/pod-product-compliance
Lightning Source LLC
Chambersburg PA
CBHW020738230426
43665CB00009B/482